Research Methods for Social Workers

Also available from Oxford University Press

Doing Research: The Hows and Whys of Applied Research, Third Edition
By Nel Verhoeven

Human Behavior for Social Work Practice: A Developmental-Ecological Framework, Second Edition
By Wendy L. Haight and Edward H. Taylor

Policy, Politics, and Ethics: A Critical Approach, Third Edition
By Thomas M. Meenaghan, Keith M. Kilty, Dennis D. Long, and John G. McNutt

Navigating Human Service Organizations, Third Edition
By Rich Furman and Margaret Gibelman

The Recovery Philosophy and Direct Social Work Practice
By Joseph Walsh

Best Practices in Community Mental Health: A Pocket Guide
Edited by Vikki L. Vandiver

Child and Family Practice: A Relational Approach
By Shelly Cohen Konrad

Social Work and Social Development: Perspectives from India and the United States
Edited by Shweta Singh

Social Service Workplace Bullying: A Betrayal of Good Intentions
By Kathryn Brohl

Social Work Practice with Families: A Resiliency-Based Approach, Second Edition
By Mary Patricia Van Hook

Getting Your MSW: How to Survive and Thrive in a Social Work Program
By Karen M. Sowers and Bruce A. Thyer

Social Work with HIV and AIDS: A Case-Based Guide
By Diana Rowan and Contributors

Research Methods for Social Workers

A PRACTICE-BASED APPROACH

Second Edition

SAMUEL S. FAULKNER
CYNTHIA A. FAULKNER
Morehead State University

OXFORD
UNIVERSITY PRESS

Oxford University Press is a department of the University of Oxford. It furthers the University's
objective of excellence in research, scholarship, and education by publishing worldwide.
Oxford is a registered trade mark of Oxford University Press in the UK and
certain other countries.

Published in the United States of America by Oxford University Press
198 Madison Avenue, New York, NY 10016, United States of America.

© Oxford University Press 2016

Library of Congress Cataloging-in-Publication Data
Faulkner, Cynthia A.
Research methods for social workers : a practice-based approach / Samuel S. Faulkner, Cynthia A.
Faulkner, Morehead State University.—Second edition.
pages   cm
Revised edition of: Research methods for social workers : a practice-based approach / Cynthia A.
Faulkner and Samuel S. Faulkner, published in 2009.
Includes bibliographical references and index.
ISBN 978-0-190615-38-3 (pbk. : alk. paper)
1. Social service—Research—Methodology.   I. Faulkner, Samuel S.   II. Title.
HV11.F37   2014
361.0072—dc23
2013008342

Cover image © Photopal604 | Dreamstime.com

7 9 8 6

Printed in Canada

Contents

Preface

Welcome to the second edition of *Research Methods for Social Workers: A Practice-Based Approach*. When we set out to write the first edition (now almost ten years ago) we had two major goals in mind: to create a research text that students would be able to understand and a book that they would actually read. Now, after having taught from the first edition since its publication in 2009, the feedback from students has been gratifying and rewarding. Students tell us over and over again that they appreciate this text because it makes research accessible to them—they actually read it and understand it.

At the same time, having garnered candid and appreciated feedback from other faculty who use the text, we have made some important additions and changes to the original text (while staying true to the readable and understandable style of the first edition). Also, we have included some much-needed information to meet the changing and evolving standards of social work education.

In this edition we have included the **CSWE Core Competencies** at the beginning of each chapter. You will also find a chart at the front of the book that outlines which competencies are addressed and in which chapter they occur. We hope this will aid in your own curriculum development and help in addressing the Educational Policy and Accreditation Standards.

We have also included a new chapter, "Survey Research." Survey research fits with classroom assignments and works well with the included example research proposal in chapter 13. This new chapter will help students better understand how to develop and conduct a survey instrument. This chapter also addresses the topics of defining survey research, appropriate survey topics, developing a survey, administering surveys and expected rates of return, and advantages and disadvantages of survey research. At the end of each chapter we have included a **practice exam**. In addition, in chapter 13 we have added an **example research proposal** and an **example research report** to demonstrate how to report findings. Every chapter has a **case scenario** with associated **critical-thinking questions** based on the scenarios. We have also added **examples** throughout the text that relate to social work practice. In addition to the updated (and expanded) new text, we have also included a new (and improved) instructor's manual complete with test questions, vocabulary, and chapter summaries.

In short, we feel that this new edition will be even more valuable in helping you teach research methods to your students. As you use this book, we invite your comments, feedback, suggestions, and other responses to help us know how we might improve future editions (and what you like or don't like about this current edition). As fellow educators, we want to be as responsive and helpful as possible.

Thanks,
Sam and Cindy Faulkner

Acknowledgments

As with most writings, there are many people who contributed their time and expertise to this text. A special thank you goes to our colleagues and friends Lisa Shannon and Lynn Geurin, assistant professors of social work at Morehead State University, Kentucky, who have given us valuable feedback and support. We also want to thank our research students at Morehead State University who provided feedback for this second edition. Our love and gratitude go to our children (Wayne, Shay, Christina, Alisa, McKennzie, and Ezra) for inspiring us to be lifelong learners, and to our fourteen (so far) grandchildren for helping us stay young. "I can do everything through God who gives me strength" (Philippians 4:13).

CSWE Competencies

CHAPTER	1	2	3	4	5	6	7	8	9	10	11	12	13
EPAS 2.1.2		X											X
EPAS 2.1.3	X		X		X	X	X	X	X	X	X	X	X
EPAS 2.1.6	X	X	X	X	X	X	X	X	X	X	X	X	X
EPAS 2.1.9	X	X	X	X	X	X	X	X	X	X	X	X	X
EPAS 2.1.10(b)	X	X	X	X	X	X	X	X	X	X	X	X	X
EPAS 2.1.10(d)									X	X			X

Note: EPAS stands for Educational Policy and Accreditation Standards.

What Is Research?

CSWE Core Competencies

IN THIS CHAPTER, you will find the following Council on Social Work Education (CSWE) core competencies:

Educational Policy 2.1.3—Apply critical thinking to inform and communicate professional judgments

Educational Policy 2.1.6—Engage in research-informed practice and practice-informed research

Educational Policy 2.1.9—Respond to contexts that shape practice

Educational Policy 2.1.10(b)—Assessment

Research has become an increasingly valuable tool for social work practitioners and scholars. **Research** is a systematic and methodological approach to creating knowledge. In social work, research is instrumental in the development of effective practice outcomes, or the outcomes of professional activities that are designed to improve or change the well-being of an individual, agency, or other system. For instance, we can research an issue concerning practice accountability, such as whether an intervention is effective, or we can measure an issue related to the characteristics of an agency population, such as changes in the ages of substance abuse admissions over time. Measuring practice accountability and monitoring agency populations both provide information that can be used to create evidence-based practices. **Evidence-based practices** are practices whose efficacy is supported by evidence. In this chapter, we discuss why research is important in social work practice and what research entails, critically examine ways of knowing, define two fields of research, and provide an overview of four methods of research.

Importance of Social Work Research

Perhaps you are thinking something along the lines of "Why should I have to take a class in research? After all, I am interested in working with people. I couldn't care less about research methods." The reality is that research is gaining an increasingly important place in the practice of social work. For instance, managed-care companies, insurance companies, and consumers themselves are demanding that social workers be able to demonstrate not only that the techniques, methods, and practices that they employ are useful and effective but also that these practices can be used effectively in other settings and with other populations. Gone are the days when a social worker could rely on personal intuition and undocumented outcomes as proof that his or her practices were effective. In fact, the Code of Ethics of the National Association of Social Workers (see appendix) has an entire section on evaluation and research. Section 5.02 stresses that "social workers should monitor and evaluate policies, the implementation of programs, and practice interventions." In addition, "social workers should promote and facilitate evaluation and research to contribute to the development of knowledge" (National Association of Social Workers, 2008).

There are other reasons researchers are compelled to adopt more rigorous ways of measuring the effectiveness of social work practice. In difficult economic times, as programs are experiencing a decrease in funding, it is becoming increasingly important to utilize evidence-based practices to demonstrate accountability. An increasing number of both government and private grant-funding sources are requiring that evaluation components be incorporated into grant proposals. In this age of shrinking dollars, foundations and governmental funding agencies want assurances that money is spent in the most effective way possible. Program evaluation can help agencies obtain or retain grants and other such funding by demonstrating program success. When writing proposals and developing new programs, social workers need to have at least a basic understanding of how to carry out a program evaluation.

In addition, by researching specific social problems, social workers can become agents of macro change. Social workers can devise social policies and large-scale interventions to alter inequality and injustice in their agencies and communities. For instance, a social service agency identifies a significant amount of no-shows for job-skills training appointments. The agency conducts a telephone survey to identify barriers that prevent clients from keeping appointments and discovers that lack of access to transportation is the most significant barrier and lack of child care the second most significant barrier. In response to these findings, an agency policy is developed to provide taxi tokens and child-care vouchers to consumers with financial need.

Defining Research

With that in mind, we turn to the question, What is research? Chances are, you are already a researcher and do not know it. We often use research methods without actually labeling what we are doing "research." For example, think back to the last time you were going to see a movie. If you have ever solicited a review from a friend or read a review in a paper or magazine and then based your decision to see the film on the reviewer's opinion, you were utilizing research methodology. Similarly, if you have ever consulted a newspaper or a local television station for information about the weather so that you could decide how to dress for the day, you are utilizing research methods.

Research is, in its simplest form, the assimilation of knowledge and the gathering of data in a logical manner in order to become informed about something. We often consult with others whose opinions we value (e.g., friends, experts) and then make a decision based on our informed judgment. The process of conducting research is essentially the same, but much more thorough.

Ways of Knowing

The Code of Ethics of the National Association of Social Workers (2008) states: "Social workers should promote and facilitate evaluation and research to contribute to the development of knowledge" [section 5.02(b)]. Have you ever wondered how we gain knowledge (how we know what we know)? Here we discuss four ways in which knowledge can be gained.

First, we can use our own experiences to gain knowledge. Simply by trial and error we can gradually make decisions about a problem and eventually develop enough knowledge to solve a problem. For instance, you require a certain amount of sleep at night to feel rested the next day. A pattern of sleep experiences over time provides you with enough information to determine the specific amount of sleep you require. However, in social work practice, personal experiences can be misleading, because our experiences and the experiences of our consumers may be different, just as others may need more or less sleep than you do.

Second, we can rely on the knowledge of others. Agency supervisors and other coworkers who have years of practice experience can be important sources of knowledge. Many have developed tried-and-true practices that have over time become evidence-based practices. For instance, a supervisor explains that a particular judge prefers for documentation on a case to be presented in a certain way and that this practice increases the possibility of a positive outcome in court. In addition, consulting an expert or some authority in a field outside our own expertise can help us make better practice decisions.

However, if we rely on faulty information, we may be taking misperceptions as truth. For instance, many self-help books are available on how to intervene with an active alcoholic. While many of these books are reliable resources, authors without evidence-based practice experiences may be offering advice that is based on just one person's experience. Therefore, you must look at the qualifications of the person who is offering advice and ensure that their advice has been shown to be reliable and valid through repeated positive outcomes.

Third, we can rely on traditions. Tradition provides us with knowledge that is passed down over time. Many new social work practitioners are indoctrinated into agency practice through the established practices of those who have worked there over time. For instance, agency traditions may include weekly team meetings to staff cases, debriefings with a supervisor after a difficult assessment, and identification of caseload counts to ensure equitable distribution. These practices have proved to increase accountability, reduce turnover rates, and help monitor workloads, all of which are beneficial. However, there are traditions that are not best practices. For instance, taking consumer files home to work on, giving consumers our home or cell phone numbers, and standardized group notes are practices that can bring up issues of confidentiality, boundaries, and lack of individualized documentation. We have to be careful relying on tradition, however. Just because a practice or tradition is "how it has always been done" does not make it a best practice. In some ways, tradition is the least reliable source for gaining knowledge.

The fourth way to gain knowledge is by using scientific methods to answer our questions. By researching our questions, we can increase our knowledge about a particular issue or population. It should be noted that one misconception about research is that studies are large experiments that are able to solve whole problems. The truth is that the research process involves small incremental steps. Each study adds a small piece of information to the whole. The process is much like painting a picture. Each brush-stroke, each dab of paint, adds a small amount of detail until eventually a coherent picture emerges. Each stroke or dab of paint, standing alone, may not represent much, but when all the dabs of paint are viewed together as a whole, we see a picture. Research studies, by themselves, may explain only a small part of the whole, but when linked together with other studies, they begin to help us see a larger picture or describe an occurrence. For example, there is a plethora of child maltreatment research. Some studies may examine characteristics of the abusers, others the abused children, and still others the family dynamics of families in which child abuse is occurring. Each study is a small part of the overall understanding of a phenomenon that, in this case, contributes to our understanding of child maltreatment.

Therefore, one study is not sufficient to apply to everyone. Different studies may have different, and sometimes opposite, findings because of the specific characteristics of the populations being researched. For instance, a child protection agency in a large urban city may report a high percentage of parents using street drugs, whereas a small rural community may report a high percentage of parents using prescription drugs. As you can see, the findings of the larger urban study do not apply to the rural study because the characteristics of the populations are different.

In summary, it is important to explore all possible ways of knowing about social work practice. The Code of Ethics of the National Association of Social Workers (2008) emphasizes that "social workers should critically examine and keep current with emerging knowledge relevant to social work and fully use evaluation and research evidence in their professional practice" [section 5.02(c)]. Critical examination of personal experiences, the experiences of others, traditions, and research methods can contribute to evidence-based practices in social work. The ability to use critical thinking to determine the reliability of information is an important skill for all social work practitioners. Incompatible findings are the result of different decisions made by researchers, and this book will teach you to determine which studies are relatively better.

Qualitative, Quantitative, and Mixed-Method Research

There are two overarching ways of gathering data, or fields of research. These are qualitative research methods and quantitative research methods. **Qualitative research** is concerned with developing knowledge where little or none exists, and it uses words, observations, and descriptions to develop this knowledge. **Quantitative research** is concerned with expanding knowledge that already exists and using numerical data to report the findings from the research. But perhaps you want to use both qualitative and quantitative methods, or a **mixed-method design**, in your research. Mixed-method designs allow researchers to design a study using both qualitative and quantitative methods by using numerical and textual data.

Qualitative Research

Social work is a profession that owes a large debt of gratitude to many other disciplines. Anthropology, psychology, sociology, and medicine have all contributed to the development of our profession. One of the areas in which this becomes exceedingly clear is the field of qualitative research. Qualitative research has deep roots in the fields of anthropology and sociology, where the development of rigorous and exact methods for fieldwork has long been fostered.

The use of qualitative research methods is debated among social work practitioners, faculty, researchers, and other professionals. It is generally agreed, though, that qualitative research is employed when little or nothing is known about a subject, or when the researcher wants to gain an in-depth understanding of a person's experience. Some may argue that qualitative methods are better suited for studies on complicated topics such as a person's comfort level with death, how it feels to be unemployed, or how a child views the drinking habits of an alcoholic parent. Qualitative research primarily relies on information generated from observations of the researcher and discussions and interviews with study participants. However, researchers engaged in qualitative research might also gather some descriptive information, such as the demographics of participants and their settings in order to place their experiences within a context. In their simplest form, qualitative research methods are used to help us understand the characteristics of a phenomenon. Often this type of research uncovers these characteristics by focusing on the ideas of the people involved.

As an example, let us imagine for a moment that you are a case manager in a community health agency and the year is 1982. You have noticed that a large number of your consumers who report being intravenous drug users are also suffering from a strange new illness that seems to impair their immune system. You are aware that AIDS is a relatively unknown disease and that scientists were just beginning to understand the causes of its transmission. As a case manager, you may want to design a qualitative study that will help you explore the experiences of those who are suffering from this disease by interviewing people living with AIDS (recording their own words). You may also want to collect some demographic information such as sex, age, race, and length of illness to describe their experiences in the context of the research population.

Quantitative Research

Advocates of quantitative research argue that it is only through the use of methods that report numerical representation that the social sciences can become truly valid. Quantitative research seeks to explain relationships between two or more factors. The aim of quantitative research is to determine how one thing (a variable) affects another in a population. A **variable** is any attribute or characteristic that changes or assumes different values. Variables can represent subject characteristics (e.g., age, race, sex) or the things you are really interested in (e.g., agency performance; rate of relapse in addiction treatment; physiological, psychological, or sociological causes of child maltreatment). Variables can also represent the effect of any intervention that subjects receive, such as a cultural sensitivity training.

Mixed-Method Research

Mixed-method research uses both qualitative and quantitative research designs. Using more than one research method while collecting and analyzing data in a study is called concurrent mixed-method research. When data collected through the use of one type of research design provide a basis for the collection of data using the other type, this is called sequential mixed-method research. There are several reasons to use a mixed-method design. Among these are that it can test the consistency of findings obtained through different forms of data collection. This is referred to as triangulation, which means that the findings from the methods used are consistent and support one another. Or a researcher might use a mixed-method design because it allows him or her to use qualitative methods to add richness and detail to the results obtained from the use of quantitative methods. Researchers may also choose a mixed-method design so they can use results from one method to shape subsequent methods or steps in the research process. This is frequently seen when a qualitative study is used to shape a quantitative study. In addition, mixed-method research can be used as a means to develop new research questions or to use one method to challenge results obtained through another method.

Developing Your Research Questions

You may be asking yourself at this point, "Where do research questions originate?" Research questions may arise from your personal experience.

Thus, a person who was adopted may feel compelled to study the factors that make adoptions work well for children. Research questions may develop out of research articles or theories you are studying. A **theory** is a statement or set of statements that is designed to explain a phenomenon on the basis of observations and experiments and is often agreed upon by most experts in a particular field. For example, you may want to test the credibility of the claims put forth by a developmental theory on aging that you learned about in one of your human behavior classes. Research questions may arise out of your own practice experience. Regardless of the source, most questions are born of the researcher's personal interest in a subject.

To illustrate this process, we may begin with an observation ("This person smiles at me and goes out of her way to help me"), then we have an idea ("This person would make a good friend"), and then we develop a question ("Does this person like me?"). We can examine this question by drawing from our past experiences, by consulting others, or by asking the person directly.

When you are developing research questions, there are some issues to keep in mind. The first thing to consider is whether the question is empirical. This means that the researcher must decide whether the question can be quantified. For example, a question such as "What is the best religion?" is both value laden and subjective ("the best"). As a researcher, you need to be careful to remember that we can study values in order to understand what others think, but we cannot conduct research on values in order to evaluate them. Therefore, we can approach value-laden issues through qualitative methods that are meant to deal with the subjective questions we would have—this would eliminate any objectivity from the research. "How many people cheat on their partner?" and "Has having an abortion prevented further unwanted pregnancies?" are both examples of questions that attempt to quantify issues of moral worth and can be measured through quantitative methods.

What Is a Hypothesis?

A **hypothesis** is a research statement about relationships between variables that is testable and that can be accepted or rejected on the basis of the evidence. Therefore, you can only develop hypotheses that are quantifiable. To design a study to test your hypothesis, you use quantitative research methods. Hypotheses are divided into two categories: research hypotheses and null hypotheses. The research hypothesis asserts that there is a relationship between the variables, and the null hypothesis claims that the relationship between the variables can be rejected. In other words, the null hypothesis is what the researcher is attempting to reject. For example, we may have a null hypothesis that no difference exists between a treatment group and a non-treatment group after intervention. If this is rejected, then the research hypothesis that the treatment group will be different from the non-treatment group after intervention (e.g., less sick, more educated) is supported. Hypotheses are typically abbreviated as H_o (null hypothesis), H_1 (research hypothesis), and H_1, H_2, H_3 (a number is used when there is more than one research hypothesis).

Imagine that you are working at an emergency shelter with a consumer named Joe. Joe has been living on the streets for the past two years and is in need of permanent housing. While you are collecting assessment history with Joe, he discloses that he has a long history of drug abuse. One initial hypothesis may be this: "A history of substance abuse is related to not having stable housing." In further discussions with Joe, you explore this hypothesis with him, and he confirms that his substance abuse has interfered with his ability to seek and keep a job—a strong factor in his being homeless. You then decide to design a research study to determine whether this relationship between substance abuse and homelessness exists beyond your client. You can also test a second hypothesis that looks at the relationship between substance abuse and unemployment.

Research Designs

There are different designs that researchers can choose from to collect data in conducting qualitative, quantitative, and mixed-method research. Exploratory designs are exclusively grounded in qualitative research, and explanatory designs are exclusively grounded in quantitative research. Descriptive designs, evaluative designs, and single-subject designs can draw from either or both types of research.

Exploratory Research Designs

An **exploratory design** is a type of research design that allows us to use our powers of observation, inquiry, and assessment to form tentative theories about what we are seeing and experiencing. This design is generally used to explore understudied topics. In essence, we need to find out about a phenomenon. By asking an **open-ended question** (i.e., a question that is worded in a way that allows the respondent to answer in his or her own words as opposed to merely soliciting a yes or no response) and observing the environment, we can begin to identify common themes from the information we gather. For instance, imagine you are a crisis call worker shortly after the 9/11 terrorist attacks. You are receiving a high volume of calls from rescue workers involved in the recovery of human remains. You have little or no knowledge about this experience; therefore, you explore the callers' experiences with them by asking questions such as "What is it like for you?" After listening to several workers, you might discover evidence of a common theme, for example, that the callers have been experiencing periods of tearfulness. On the basis of this evidence, you can then tell other callers that this experience appears to be common among rescue workers.

Explanatory Research Designs

An **explanatory design** is a type of research design that focuses on examining the relationships between two or more factors and attempting to determine whether they are related, and if so, in what ways and how strongly. For example, you may believe there is a relationship between the amount of time students spend studying for their research methods class and their final course grade in that class. Your hypothesis might be this: "The more students study research methods, the better their grades in that course will be." In fact, you would be able to find studies that have provided evidence that a relationship exists. If you were so inclined, it would be possible to design a study to examine just how strong the relationship is between hours spent studying and final course grades.

Descriptive Designs

In a sense, all research is descriptive by nature, as it describes how and/or why a phenomenon occurs. Qualitative research methods do this using words, and quantitative research methods by using numbers. A **descriptive design** is a method that can be used to seek information that uses numerical language (e.g., how many, how much) to describe a population or phenomenon. This can be used in both qualitative and quantitative methods of research. For example, if you were conducting a quantitative study of victims of domestic violence, you might want to collect information on certain characteristics, such as their average age, what percentage of them have children, and the type of abuse and how frequently it occurs. You might also ask them to interpret the severity of the last abuse episode, using a scale from 1 to 5. It is important to note here that although this type of research looks at patterns such as how often an event occurs or ways that the answers develop in relation to each other, it does not try to address why the patterns exist.

Descriptive information is also collected during qualitative studies to help put the experiences into context with the population reporting them. For example, while conducting interviews with 9/11 rescue workers, you might also collect information on how many of these individuals are firefighters, police officers, health professionals, volunteer civilians, and so forth. By using this mixed-method design, you may also be reporting how frequently the rescue workers reported similar textual information—for example, "Six out of ten volunteers stated they would volunteer again, regardless of the difficulties they are experiencing now."

Evaluative Designs

Evaluative designs can also draw from both fields of research. An evaluative design draws from qualitative research methods when statements made in interviews and focus groups and written comments are used to describe outcomes. For instance, positive comments from a survey may be included in a program evaluation to demonstrate consumer satisfaction. Evaluative designs can also draw from the quantitative field of research. For instance, an evaluative design might examine how many and what type of residents an agency serviced over the previous month.

Single-Subject Designs

Finally, a **single-subject design** uses systematic methodology to measure an individual's progress over time and whether a relationship exists between an intervention and a specific outcome. These designs can also draw from either or both methods of research. In a study using qualitative methods, the consumer's own statement that he or she is suicidal might be used to justify an extension for mental health treatment from an insurance company.

Strengths and Limitations of Research

A major strength of research is that it can help us gain an understanding of many social problems. Through research, we can gain knowledge of issues such as child maltreatment, domestic violence, and substance abuse. Another benefit is that research has led to the development of new agency policies, greater practice accountability, evidence-based treatment strategies, and new knowledge.

Research also has inherent limitations. First, research is conducted in small steps that are often repeated to build evidence. Each new study adds to the overall body of knowledge, which is considered a strength. However, knowledge is built slowly over time—not in quantum leaps. A second limitation of research is that the knowledge that it yields is confined to the questions that are asked. Only by asking enough relevant questions can we obtain useful answers. Finally, research is subject to bias. **Bias** is the unknown or unacknowledged error created during the design of the research method, in the choice of problem to be studied, over the course of the study itself, or during the interpretation of findings. This is not to say that the research is necessarily flawed—only limited. For example, if your study examines parents' use of corporal punishment with their children but all your research participants are white, your findings are racially biased. Therefore, bias can be unintentional and sometimes unavoidable, but it must always be identified as a limitation.

Case Scenario

You are a case manager working in a homeless shelter in a large metropolitan city. Assigned to your caseload is a family of four—the father, Art; the mother, Janice; and twin boys (age seven), Matt and Justin. The mother and father are both hearing impaired. The twin sons do not have a hearing impairment, but they use American Sign Language (ASL) to communicate with their parents. Art and Janice communicate with each other using American Sign Language and communicate with you (and other hearing people) using a combination of lipreading and written notes. Both the parents were employed at a local manufacturing plant until about six months ago, when they were laid off. They moved in with relatives until the relatives were no longer able to afford having an additional four people living with them. The family is now homeless and living on the street. As a case manager, you wish to learn more about them, their challenges living with a disability (hearing impairment), and the customs and culture of the deaf community.

Critical-Thinking Questions

Using the information in this chapter, answer the following questions:

1. Which research method, qualitative (exploratory) or quantitative (explanatory), would be most appropriate with your clients? Give reasons for your choice of this method.

2. What are three questions that you might ask your clients that would help you to better understand them, their world, and their culture?

3. What would be at least one limitation of your findings?

Key Points

- Research is the process of systematically gaining information.

- Research is becoming increasingly important as funding agencies demand evidence that programs and practices are effective.

- We gain knowledge from our own experiences, others' experiences, tradition, and the use of scientific methods.

- There are two types of research methods: qualitative and quantitative. When both research methods are used, this is called a mixed-method design.

- Research questions may arise from personal experience, out of research articles or theories under study, or from practice experience, and they are born of the researcher's personal interest in a subject.

- Hypotheses are research statements about relationships between variables that are testable and that can be accepted or rejected on the basis of the findings from a study.

- Exploratory research designs allow researchers to use their powers of observation, inquiry, and assessment to form tentative theories about what they are seeing and experiencing.

- Descriptive research designs use descriptive language to provide information about a phenomenon.

- Explanatory research designs attempt to explain the relationship between two or more factors.

- Evaluative research designs attempt to examine the effectiveness of programs and services.

- Single-subject designs are used to measure a person's progress over time.

Practice Exam

True or False

1. There are four types of research. These are qualitative, inferential, descriptive, and informative.

2. Quantitative research is usually characterized by the fact that results are reported in numerical terms (in numbers and figures).

3. The Social Work Code of Ethics promotes social workers' conducting of research.

Multiple Choice

4. Knowledge is transferred in four ways. These four ways are the following:

    a. Tradition, others' experience, our experience, our best guess

    b. Others' experience, our experience, scientific inquiry, expert opinion

    c. Our experience, others' experience or knowledge, tradition, and the scientific method

    d. Others' experience, our knowledge, tradition, and the Internet

5. Quantitative research is most often associated with:

    a. Explanatory research

    b. Research that determines why a phenomenon exists

    c. Research that is generalizable to a large population

    d. Exploratory research

    e. None of the above

Fill in the Blank

6. The NASW _____ of _____ recommends that social workers conduct research.

7. Hypotheses are divided into two categories: _____ hypotheses and _____ hypotheses.

8. Single-subject designs measure a _____ progress over time.

CHAPTER TWO

Ethical Considerations

CSWE Core Competencies

IN THIS CHAPTER, you will find the following Council on Social Work Education (CSWE) core competencies:

Educational Policy 2.1.2—Apply social work ethical principles to guide professional practice

Educational Policy 2.1.6—Engage in research-informed practice and practice-informed research

Educational Policy 2.1.9—Respond to contexts that shape practice

Educational Policy 2.1.10(b)—Assessment

Just as ethics is an important part of our interactions with consumers and colleagues, and in carrying out social work practice on a daily basis, ethics is also important when we are conducting research. Research, like all parts of the social work profession, has ethics at its core. This chapter introduces you to some ethical principles and applications used in research, including the protection of the rights of research participants.

Historical Overview

Today, most countries have laws in effect that require human subjects to be treated with dignity and respect during the conduction of research. The United States has regulations in place providing guidance and structure for the researcher. What is the history behind these regulations? It may surprise you to know that the impetus for these regulations and the implementation of oversight committees was research done during World War II.

In 1946, an American military tribunal opened a criminal trial in Nuremberg, Germany, against twenty-three Nazi physicians. The physicians were accused of conducting horrific medical experiments on prisoners at various concentration camps. After 140 days of proceedings during which eighty-five witnesses testified and 1,500 documents were entered as evidence, sixteen doctors were found guilty, and seven were sentenced to death. From this trial came the Nuremberg Code (Nuremberg Tribunals, 1949), ten principles for permissible medical experiments:

1. The voluntary consent of the human subject is absolutely essential.

2. The experiment should be such as to yield fruitful results for the good of society, unprocurable by other methods or means of study, and not random or unnecessary in nature.

3. The experiment should be so designed and based on the results of animal experimentation and knowledge of the natural history of the disease or other problem under study, that the anticipated results will justify the performance of the experiment.

4. The experiment should be so conducted as to avoid all unnecessary physical and mental suffering and injury.

5. No experiment should be conducted where there is an a priori reason to believe that death or disabling injury will occur; except, perhaps, in those experiments where the experimental physicians also serve as subjects.

6. The degree of risk to be taken should never exceed that determined by the humanitarian importance of the problem to be solved by the experiment.

7. Proper preparations should be made and adequate facilities provided to protect the experimental subjects against even remote possibilities of injury, disability, or death.

8. The experiment should be conducted only by scientifically qualified persons. The highest degree of skill and care should be required through all stages of the experiment of those who conduct or engage in the experiment.

9. During the course of the experiment, the human subject should be at liberty to bring the experiment to an end, if he has reached the physical or mental state where continuation of the experiment seemed to him to be impossible.

10. During the course of the experiment, the scientist in charge must be prepared to terminate the experiment at any stage, if he has probable cause to believe, in the exercise of the good faith, superior skill, and careful judgment required of him, that a continuation of the experiment is likely to result in injury, disability, or death to the experimental subject.

At this point you may be thinking, "How does this apply to *me*?" In this chapter, we will examine three ethical principles that social workers can use to protect human subjects in research.

Public Law 93-348, called the National Research Act, was signed into law on July 12, 1974, and addresses the protection of human subjects in research. It recognizes that research and practice may occur together and that any element of research should undergo review for the protection of human subjects. The Belmont Report, published in 1979, summarizes the law as proposing three basic ethical principles: respect for individuals, beneficence, and justice (National Commission for the Protection of Human Subjects of Biomedical and Behavioral Research, 1979).

Respect for Individuals

Respect for individuals involves acknowledging the autonomy of individuals and protecting those with diminished autonomy. Section 5.02(m) of the Code of Ethics of the National Association of Social Workers (2008) states that "social workers who report evaluation and research results should protect participants' confidentiality by omitting identifying information unless proper consent has been obtained authorizing disclosure." With this in mind, we first discuss the concepts of anonymity, confidentiality, and informed consent. We then discuss how to protect those whose capacity to make autonomous decisions is limited.

Anonymity

Anonymity is often confused with confidentiality. In research, anonymity means that the researcher will not collect any identifying information on the subjects participating in the research study. For instance, you design an exploratory study in which you will collect information on how consumers feel about the services in your agency. One way to do this is to have a comment box in the lobby or waiting room; consumers can write comments on a blank piece of paper and put them the box. This allows individuals to remain anonymous. However, you notice that only consumers with complaints are making use of the comment box. You then decide to do a descriptive study for which you develop a form that allows consumers to rate their satisfaction with various services on a scale from 1 to 4. To maintain the anonymity of the participants, you do not ask for any information that can be used to identify them, such as name, age, or occupation. Everyone checking into your agency is handed the form and asked to complete it before they leave and place it in the comment box. These are examples of a study that uses both qualitative and quantitative methods that protect the anonymity of participants.

Confidentiality

Confidentiality is the assurance that a researcher provides to subjects that all information about them, and all answers they provide, will remain in the hands of the investigator and that no person outside the research process will have access to that information. Subjects have a basic right to know that their information is kept confidential; this also ensures that they feel protected from potential repercussions for answering honestly. The researcher, however, may have the ability to identify the responses of a particular individual. You may be wondering, "How, then, do researchers publish their findings if all information remains confidential?" The answer is that all information is reported in the aggregate (i.e., the findings are combined). The researcher compiles the data and presents them in such a way that no individual can be identified.

Let's say that you are conducting a six-week smoking cessation workshop. You want to follow up with your participants in six months to see how many remain free of cigarettes, how many times they relapsed, and how many returned to smoking on a regular basis. In addition to this descriptive (quantitative) data, you will ask participants for written comments (qualitative data) on what worked for them, what did not work for them, what was helpful about the workshop, and what was not helpful. You will include the quantitative and qualitative data you collect in a grant proposal to fund additional workshops. In your summary, you would not state that John Smith relapsed twice and found that cinnamon gum helped curb cravings. But you might write, "One participant relapsed twice and found that cinnamon gum helped curb cravings."

Confidentiality can also become an issue in subtler ways, especially in small communities where the disclosure of too much information can result in the identification of an individual. For instance, you are reporting treatment outcomes of sex offenders to city council members. During your presentation you describe an offender by stating, "A recently released male sex offender with a history of child molestation has recently reoffended. He has been in treatment for only three months, and our statistics show that those in treatment for more than six months have a better chance of not reoffending." The audience may be able to identify this individual through news articles or even common knowledge about his recent release or arrest. One way you could have reported your research findings anonymously would have been to report the data in aggregate. In this example, you could report percentages: "100 percent of participants in treatment less than six months have reoffended, while only 54 percent of participants in treatment for more than six months have reoffended." Section 5.02(m) of the Code of Ethics of the National Association of Social Workers (2008) states: "Social workers who report evaluation and research results should protect participants' confidentiality by omitting identifying information unless proper consent has been obtained authorizing disclosure."

Informed Consent

Informed consent is the process of educating potential research participants about the basic purpose of a study, informing them that their participation is voluntary, and obtaining their written consent to participate in the study. Informed consent involves the researcher helping potential participants to understand exactly what is being asked of them and what their participation will entail. On the one hand, Ingelfinger (1972) argues that informed consent can never be entirely complete. On the other hand, Gorovitz (1985) believes that the individual has dominion over his or her own body and is responsible for what happens to him or her. In some ways, both are correct. As a researcher, it is your responsibility to provide as much information as possible to potential participants so that they can decide whether they wish to participate. The ethical researcher will take care to sit down with the participant and explain in detail what will be required of him or her and what will happen during the study.

The practice of informed consent is an important part of any study. One small part of the informed consent process is asking a research participant to sign a statement that outlines the information provided in the informed consent process (see example 2.1). It is important to note that informed consent must be obtained before any data are collected. In addition, if you are offering an incentive for participation (e.g., a gift certificate at a fast-food restaurant) in your study, then the subject will receive the incentive regardless whether or not he or she completes the study. The Code of Ethics of the National Association of Social Workers (2008) states that: "social workers engaged in evaluation or research should ensure the anonymity or confidentiality of participants and of the data obtained from them. Social workers should inform participants of any limits of confidentiality, the measures that will be taken to ensure confidentiality, and when any records containing research data will be destroyed" [section 5.02(l)]. In addition, section 5.02(h) states: "Social workers should inform participants of their right to withdraw from evaluation and research at any time without penalty." The informed consent form must provide the following information:

- The researcher's identity and the nature and aim of the research
- The subject's role in the project and the expected duration of the subject's participation
- A description of experimental procedures and any possible risks to the subject's physical, psychological, or emotional well-being
- Any benefits to the subject that may reasonably be expected from the research
- Contact information that subjects can use to obtain answers to questions about the research and research subjects' rights, and information on whom to contact in the event of a research-related injury or if counseling is needed as a result of the sensitive nature of the questions

In addition, the informed consent form must do the following:

- Explain to prospective subjects that they are free to refuse to participate or to refuse to answer any question or to withdraw from the study at any time and that refusal to participate or withdrawal from the project will involve no penalty or loss of benefits to which the subjects are otherwise entitled
- Describe how the confidentiality of the information will be maintained (e.g., surveys, audiotapes, or videotapes will be kept in a locked file cabinet) and the anonymity of the participants will be protected
- Explain that participants must be eighteen years of age or older, or parental and/or guardian consent must be obtained
- Provide verification statement and signature line for participants ("By signing below, I verify that I have been informed of and understand the nature and purpose of the project, freely consent to participate, and am at least eighteen years of age") (see example 2.1).

Social workers have a long-standing tradition of being the voice (i.e., advocate) of the person who has the least amount of power in a situation. This should be the guiding principle when you are designing your research

EXAMPLE 2.1: INFORMED CONSENT FORM

Dear Participant:

My name is _____. I am requesting your help with a research project I am conducting on the effects of challenge courses. Let me emphasize that you do not have to take part in anything that makes you uncomfortable. If you do not wish to take part in this project (or any of the exercises), you do not have to participate. This is true, also, for the attached questionnaire. You are free to refuse to answer any and all of the questions. The survey is voluntary (up to you), and you can withdraw from the study at any time.

If you agree to participate in the challenge course experience, you will be asked to participate in activities that require you to work with others as a group to solve problems and perform tasks. The facilitator and/or trainer will explain each activity before you begin.

Challenge courses are supervised by trained facilitators who are experienced and able to keep participants safe. The potential benefits for those who participate in the challenge course are increased communication and trust with group members.

This study has been reviewed to determine that participants' rights are safeguarded, and there appears to be minimal risk or discomfort associated with completion of this study. The answers you provide in the study will be kept strictly confidential, and all your responses (completed surveys) will be stored in a locked file cabinet accessible only to the researcher. This means that no one will be able to find out how you answered any of the questions. The results of this study may be presented at a conference or published as a research article in a journal. These records will be kept in Jones Hall, 100 University Drive, Anytown, Anystate, 10011. Please feel free to ask for help if something does not make sense to you or if you have any questions. If you experience any discomfort, you may contact Jane Smith, Caring Hands Help Agency, 101-000-1234.

If you decide to volunteer, please be sure to PRINT your name on the form and SIGN it to indicate your willingness to participate. That will be indication that you understand the purpose of the survey and that you are willing to help.

Name (Print): _____

Signature: _____

Date Signed: _____

study with any person or population who is considered to have diminished autonomy. These populations include individuals who have diminished rights or capacities, including minors; individuals with diminished capacity as a result of illness or mental disability; and people with severely restricted liberties, such as individuals who are incarcerated. There is a debate as to whether or not children and prisoners can truly give their informed consent (or whether there is an element of coercion that is subtly implied). Although no one has the ultimate answer to this question, it is important to keep in mind.

The legal guardians of minors and individuals with diminished capacity can weigh the risks and benefits of the research and then decide either with or for them whether or not they will participate in a research study. Section 5.02(f) of the Code of Ethics states: "When evaluation or research participants are incapable of giving informed consent, social workers should provide an appropriate explanation to the participants, obtain the participants' assent to the extent they are able, and obtain written consent from an appropriate proxy." In example 2.2, the signature lines were modified for the addition of consent of a parent or guardian (or power of attorney).

Informed consent is much more complicated for individuals with restricted liberties because the authorities in charge of their liberties may pressure them to volunteer. Volunteerism is an element of informed consent that requires the person to be free of coercion and undue influence. However, the individual may *want* to be involved in the research, and

---

EXAMPLE 2.2: MODIFIED SIGNATURE LINES FOR CONSENT OF A LEGAL GUARDIAN

If you decide to volunteer, please be sure to PRINT your name on the form and SIGN it to indicate your willingness to participate. That will be indication that you understand the purpose of the survey and that you are willing to help.

Name (print): _____

Signature: _____

Name of legal guardian (print): _____

Signature of legal guardian: _____

Date signed: _____

denying him or her that opportunity can also be viewed as a restriction of the individual's rights. While there is no easy answer to the dilemma posed by such situations, one should examine whether the benefits of participating outweigh the risks. For instance, let's say you are researching the effectiveness of a six-week anger management group. The possible benefits of participating in the treatment may outweigh the risk that the individual may feel obligated to participate. But if you are researching homophobia among men, the risk of harm is much greater, and the benefits nonexistent (with the exception that you, the researcher, may become more aware of your own attitudes and possible homophobia; however, here we are discussing benefits to the research subject).

Beneficence

The term **beneficence** refers to being charitable or acting with kindness. In research it is an obligation to do no harm and to maximize any **benefits** (i.e., positive values related to health or well-being) while minimizing possible harm. The issue of beneficence relates to determining whether the benefits (which can be direct or indirect and can seem large or small to a participant) outweigh the risks for the participants of the study. To minimize harm, we must identify the risks of the research on human participants.

Section 5.02(j) of the Code of Ethics of the National Association of Social Workers (2008) states: "Social workers engaged in evaluation or research should protect participants from unwarranted physical or mental distress, harm, danger, or deprivation." Participants need to be protected from the risks of participating in research. **Risk** refers to the possibility that psychological, physical, legal, social, or economic harm may occur. Risk is sometimes expressed in levels, such as "no risk," "little risk," "moderate risk," and "high risk." Much has been learned from past research studies that have involved a level of risk to the individual participants. One of these studies has come to be known as the Tuskegee syphilis experiment (1932–1972), a study conducted by the U.S. Public Health Service on a group of mostly poor African American men with syphilis living in the rural South. They were not told that they had syphilis so that the researchers could examine the etiology (progression) of the disease (Jones, 1981). Even after a cure in the form of penicillin became available, the men were not offered treatment, which caused long-term health issues for them and their families. This high level of physical risk would be considered unethical today.

In 1961, psychologist Stanley Milgram conducted an infamous study of how authority figures could abuse their power. Milgram designed a series of experiments in which subjects were instructed to administer a series of electric shocks to another subject. Unbeknownst to those administering the shocks, the individuals who were supposedly being shocked were actually working with the researcher. A disturbing number of subjects were willing to administer dangerously high levels of voltage even though the people they thought they were shocking were pleading for them to stop. Several subjects said that they did not feel comfortable continuing with the experiment but continued, regardless, when told to do so by the researcher (Milgram, 1963). To some people this research was a worthwhile endeavor, as it provides evidence of the strong influence that those in authority can have over others. One would only have to point to such tragedies as the atrocities carried out under the Nazis as justification for Milgram's study. However, others might argue that the potential trauma this study could cause the participants outweighs the benefit of the information it could provide. (Accounts of follow-up studies with research participants in the study who said they were not permanently harmed by the research have been published.)

Another study that has become somewhat infamous in research circles is a study conducted by a professor of psychology at Stanford University. Philip Zimbardo converted part of a basement in one of the buildings at Stanford into a makeshift prison and recruited students for the study. The students were randomly assigned to be either prisoners or guards. Within a few days, the subjects overidentified with the roles they were playing. Subjects who had been assigned the roles of guards became sadistic and mistreated the individuals assigned to be prisoners. The subjects playing the roles of prisoners soon began to identify as prisoners and worked to plot against the guards (Haney, Banks, & Zimbardo, 1973). The risk for psychological, physical, and legal harm was so great that the study, which was originally intended to last two weeks, was abandoned after a few days.

A debate still rages today (Haney, Banks, & Zimbardo, 2004) as to whether the information that was gained from these studies (benefits) outweighed the potential harm (risks) to participants. Our point is not to enter into this debate but to illustrate that the regulations governing research were established to ensure the safety and rights of those participating in research.

Debriefing is the process of fully informing subjects of the nature of the research when some form of deception has been employed or when some of the information is not disclosed. Rarely is it necessary for a researcher to deceive subjects. However, there may be times when fully disclosing the exact nature of the research will cause the subjects to act in a way that will skew (alter) the results. For instance, in medication research, participants are frequently placed into three groups. One group gets the new drug, one group gets a drug that is already on the market, and one group gets a placebo. It is not until after the experiment has concluded that research participates are debriefed as to which group they participated in. Section 5.02(i) of the Code of Ethics of the National Association of Social Workers (2008) states: "Social workers should take appropriate steps to ensure that participants in evaluation and research have access to appropriate supportive services."

When debriefing participants, the researcher must describe the nature and aim of the project, explain why participants were misled or provide the missing information, and provide the name and phone number of the person to contact in case participants have questions regarding the project. In addition, it is strongly suggested that the researcher have subjects sign a statement (or other form of documentation) indicating that the subjects have been debriefed and that all of their questions about the project have been answered.

Justice

The principle of justice finds its application in the moral requirement that fair procedures and outcomes be used in the selection of research subjects. Justice is the fairness of distribution of benefits and risks among all individuals. This principle can be formulated in four ways: to each person an equal share, to each person according to individual need, to each person according to individual effort, and to each person according to merit. Often in research, vulnerable populations such as the homeless, people of color, institutionalized individuals, and those living in poverty bear the burden of risky research endeavors, whereas those with more influence, wealth, and power are selected for research that has potential benefits.

The Tuskegee syphilis experiment is a good example of researchers imposing potential risks on an unknowing, vulnerable population. In an agency-based setting, the convenience of already having a population to research can create opportunities for beneficial interventions, such as new programs. For example, an agency offering and using research to evaluate an evening recovery program for residents of a homeless shelter has benefits for participants. When this recovery program is opened to the public, those benefits will be available to everyone.

This becomes problematic when the population is burdened with risky interventions, such as "holding" therapy techniques. Therapeutic holding is a commonly used intervention in residential facilities for the containment of aggressive behavior in children. Therapeutic holding involves a set of minimally invasive techniques that teach staff how to intervene in aggressive behavior that keeps children safe from harming themselves or others. Although often effective, the intervention has inherent physical and emotional safety risks.

Other Ethical Considerations

Section 5.02(n) of the Code of Ethics of the National Association of Social Workers (2008) states: "Social workers should report evaluation and research findings accurately. They should not fabricate or falsify results and should take steps to correct any errors later found in published data using standard publication methods." This code addresses two ethical issues: reporting findings accurately and not falsifying data. In research this is called laundering data and faking data.

Sometimes data from real-world sources are erroneous, incomplete, or inconsistent. For instance, on a survey a research participant might select "highly unsatisfied," thinking that he or she is selecting "highly satisfied." Data are incomplete when one of the ten questions asked on a survey is left unanswered. Data are inconsistent when one out of one hundred surveys has responses that are so different from the others that the answers are considered abnormal in the findings. To deal with erroneous, incomplete, and inconsistent data, researchers sometimes clean up the data, which is called laundering data. **Laundering data** is a way of statistically manipulating the data collected to reduce errors and make the findings more accurate. One way that a researcher can achieve this is by removing the abnormal responses from the data. However, most applications for laundering data require more complicated statistical techniques, such as grouping the data into blocks, reorganizing the data into tables, and then regrouping it into blocks after adjustments are made. The opportunity to manipulate the statistics to support a hypothesis or desired outcome can be tempting. The problem arises in how the manipulation is constructed; this can pose ethical problems if the results do not accurately reflect the findings.

Unfortunately, falsifying or faking data, though not often easily identified, can and does occur. **Faking data** is making up desired data or eliminating undesired data in research findings. One example of faking data would be to duplicate or multiply the answers collected in a research study in order to increase the number of responses. If only five people responded, the researcher might repeat their answers ten times and then have fifty responses. The findings are more convincing with a larger sample and can allow for more rigorous statistical analyses (discussed in chapters 10 and 11). Another example is to simply not include responses that do not support the hypothesis. For instance, researchers have collected data on how satisfied clients are with the services at their agency. They throw out some negative responses and keep all the positive responses to increase the percentage of clients reporting satisfaction. Perhaps the most devious type of faking is simply making up findings without conducting the research. This can occur when a person mimics another research study but changes the characteristics and findings.

There are as many reasons for faking data as there are examples: manipulating or changing findings to support a hypothesis, changing information to increase the chances of publication, providing evidence needed to apply for or continue a funded grant, or even meeting requirements of a class project are all examples of how data can be manipulated to fit a desired outcome. However, the ethical researcher needs to be on guard against unethical behavior.

One final ethical issue encountered in research that is often overlooked (especially by students) is plagiarism. Section 4.08 of the Code of Ethics of the National Association of Social Workers states: "Social workers should take responsibility and credit, including authorship credit, only for work they have actually performed and to which they have contributed" and "Social workers should honestly acknowledge the work of and the contributions made by others." Being ethical as a social worker means not only conducting research in a humane manner but also giving credit to others' work. The research process depends on an assumption that people are being honest and forthcoming when they write papers and report findings. If researchers, instructors, and students fail to be honest in their work, the entire process loses credibility and the research process becomes suspect. The issue of plagiarism has become an increasing concern among educators in the past few years. With access to the Internet, it has become increasingly easy for students to take advantage of others' work without assigning proper credit to the true authors.

In its simplest form, **plagiarism** means taking credit for work that is not one's own, either in whole or in part. This can take many forms, including copying or repeating research without giving proper credit. Individuals who plagiarize are not always intentionally being deceitful; many simply do not understand that when you use someone else's ideas, words, or work, you need to give proper credit. This means citing other people's work in the body of your paper and on the reference page. The same is true when a person paraphrases someone else's thoughts. The rule of thumb is that if you utilize another person's work, you need to give him or her credit. If you quote that person, then you need to enclose his or her words in quotation marks and give proper citation. If you utilize the person's thoughts or main ideas but paraphrase what he or she wrote, then you need to cite the person. Providing proper citations is more than a matter of ethical integrity in research—it is a form of courtesy shown to other authors and researchers.

An **institutional review board** (IRB) is a committee mandated by the federal government to oversee the protection of human and animal subjects in research. Any institution of higher learning that receives federal money (including financial aid for students) has an IRB committee that oversees research with human subjects and animals and ensures that all research is conducted in a safe, ethical, and humane manner. Hospitals and other facilities that conduct research with humans or animals also have committees to ensure that research is carried out in a humane manner. A review board can be beneficial to researchers by ensuring compliance with ethical practices and standards that protect the rights of research participants. In fact, section 5.02(d) of the Code of Ethics of the National Association of Social Workers (2008) states: "Social workers engaged in evaluation or research should carefully consider possible consequences and should follow guidelines developed for the protection of evaluation and research participants. Appropriate institutional review boards should be consulted."

Federal regulations stipulate that research that is conducted for the purposes of publication or presentation or to contribute to knowledge must gain IRB approval. If you plan to present your research in a journal or at a conference, plan to submit your research to the IRB at your institution. In addition, some universities require students to submit a research protocol and meet the board's requirements when conducting research as part of a class project. It is a good idea to keep in mind the principles established by these boards and to incorporate them into your own research. The first and foremost issue to consider is the safety of your subjects. It is imperative that as a researcher you always consider the issue of what might go wrong. It is a good idea to keep in mind Murphy's law (if something can go wrong, it probably will).

Case Scenario

You have been hired as a student research assistant to work with a faculty member at your university. The faculty member has a contract with a local nonprofit agency to conduct an outcome evaluation of a grant that has been funded by the federal government. Your job is to take information that is supplied by the agency (and your faculty member) and enter it into the computer. When entering some of the data, you notice that information has been changed from what the intake worker entered to what is reflected in the data that are being submitted. This change helps the agency to have a more favorable outcome for the grant funding. When you mention what you have found to the faculty member whom you are working with, he tells you, "Don't worry about it, the data are being altered slightly, but it is not a big difference, and the improved outcome will help this agency to gain continued funding which will help a great many people who depend on this grant money."

Critical-Thinking Questions

1. Based on the information in this chapter, and what you have learned so far, do you believe that as a research assistant you are being asked to contribute to unethical behavior? Why or why not?

2. Do you agree with the faculty member's argument that submitting data that have been altered will serve a greater good by continuing to secure funding for a much-needed program? Why or why not?

3. Given the information provided, what would you suggest as the best course of action for the student?

Key Points

- The three guiding principles for protecting human rights in research are respect for individuals, beneficence, and justice.

- Three methods for protecting human rights in research are confidentiality, anonymity, and informed consent.

- Confidentiality is the assurance that a researcher provides to subjects that all information about them, and all answers they provide, will remain in the hands of the investigator and that no other person outside the research process will have access to that information.

- Anonymity is the practice of not collecting any information that will identify the subject.

- Informed consent is letting potential subjects know what the basic purpose of the study will be and that their participation is voluntary, and obtaining their written permission to participate in the study.

- Debriefing is the process of fully informing subjects of the nature of the research when some form of deception has been employed.

- Plagiarism is the unauthorized use of another person's work and failure to give him or her credit.

- Institutional review boards oversee the rights of human subjects involved in research.

Practice Exam

Multiple Choice

1. The Nuremberg Trials were:

    a. An investigation into Germany's treatment of prisoners during World War II

    b. A study conducted on athletes during the 1936 Olympics in Nuremberg, Germany

    c. A jury trial that considered the legality of the Geneva Convention

    d. None of the above

2. Some people believe that one of the ethical issues with conducting research on children and prisoners is that:

    a. They may not be reliable test subjects

    b. They may not be in a position to fully consent to being a subject

    c. They may skew the results of the experiment

    d. All of the above

    e. None of the above; there are no ethical dilemmas with conducting research with children and prisoners

True or False

3. Institutional review boards (known as IRBs) grew out of the Nazis' unethical experimentation on prisoners.

4. The NASW Code of Ethics does not specifically mention ethics.

5. Plagiarism is considered unethical behavior.

6. Failing to acknowledge another person's work is a form of plagiarism.

7. Debriefing is the process of discussing with a subject what they thought about the experiment after it is over.

8. Governmental agencies are not immune from unethical practices.

CHAPTER THREE

Literature Review

CSWE Core Competencies

IN THIS CHAPTER, you will find the following Council on Social Work Education (CSWE) core competencies:

Educational Policy 2.1.3—Apply critical thinking to inform and communicate professional judgments

Educational Policy 2.1.6—Engage in research-informed practice and practice-informed research

Educational Policy 2.1.9—Respond to contexts that shape practice

Educational Policy 2.1.10(b)—Assessment

This chapter will introduce you to the concept of the literature review. It explains what a literature review is and how it is used to help the research process, the basic terminology found in research articles, and a six-step process for conducting a literature review. This chapter also explores the role of the literature review in shaping the overall type of research you choose to conduct and how a review of the existing literature can guide your development of a research question or hypothesis.

What Is a Literature Review?

Let us begin our exploration of a literature review with a definition of the term. A **literature review** is simply a search of published research that allows you to synthesize what is known about the topic you are studying. To clarify, when we say "published research," we are talking about rigorous forms of research, such as studies that appear in academic journals such as *Social Work and Research* and *Journal of Poverty*, as opposed to articles found in nonacademic magazines such as *People* and *Time*.

Literature reviews are used to explore past research findings to direct and improve future research. Taking the time to search through articles and published research can be a tremendous time-saver in the long run. It prevents you from reinventing a study that has already been conducted. A literature review can also provide a list of important variables, or the things you're measuring or collecting data on, to guide your study. By researching what is known and what is not known, you can design a study to build on the knowledge and experience of others or to explore or expand knowledge about which there is little or no research.

A literature review can also help situate a study within a theoretical perspective. A **theoretical perspective** might best be viewed as a model that makes assumptions about something, attempts to integrate various kinds of information, gives meaning to what we see and experience, focuses on relationships and connections, and has inherent benefits and consequences.

Previous research can assist researchers in numerous ways. First, earlier studies can be used to develop a list of variables to use in a study. Moreover, by reviewing these articles, you can tell whether a variable has been studied often and whether those studies agree on the importance of the variable. This way you will know if you are addressing a neglected topic or trying to solve a long-running debate about the effects of a specific variable. Second, reading published articles can help students define tricky concepts, learn how to develop surveys, and see which groups of people have been overlooked in research.

A question that often arises is "How do I know when I have enough articles?" The answer is that there is no real way to know. There is always the possibility that another new study will be published in some obscure journal of which you are unaware. However, as you become more familiar with the literature, you will begin to recognize authors who have written on and researched a topic extensively. After conducting a thorough search of a subject, you will intuitively have a feel for the literature and a sense of having a grasp of what is available. You do not have to read all the published works on a subject, as your intent is simply to gain an understanding of what is known, but it is possible to not review enough articles. Nobody would take a study on a well-researched topic seriously if it only had five to ten citations.

Exactly how large a literature review needs to be for a quantitative study is a matter for discussion. One has to use judgment in deciding whether there is enough research to support a quantitative study. It is not so much an issue of the number of articles; it is more an issue of considering which research designs were employed and what knowledge was created as a result of the studies. The important thing to remember is that a literature review is not a onetime event. It is conducted several times throughout a study. During a qualitative study the literature review would be conducted initially (to determine what has been published on a particular phenomenon) and again at the end of the study to help make sense of what has been found. In a quantitative study, the literature review is conducted initially to determine what is known and to guide the design of the research; it can be added to during data collection. The literature review is conducted again at the end of the study to help interpret results and to determine whether any new literature has been published since the initial literature review.

Step 1: Conducting Your Search for Research Articles

Keywords

Begin by going to your campus library or an Internet browser to access databases. We will say more about relevant databases later in this chapter. Before beginning, you need to select some terms to narrow your search. These are known as **keywords**. Keywords are words selected as search terms in any database search. These words may be found in the abstract of the article and again as identifiers for the article.

Let us assume that you are a case manager working at a group home for children, and you notice that a significant number of the children in the group home are displaying high levels of aggression toward other children. You want to design a study that will help you discover any common factors among the children that may be related to their aggression. For your search on children and aggressive behavior, you make a list of keywords that includes "childhood aggression," "physical aggression," and "aggressive behavior." These terms will define and narrow your search.

When conducting a search of the literature, you may conduct an initial search by entering keywords in a database such as Social Work Abstracts and find few or no published articles on a subject. You then conduct a second search in another database such as PsycINFO because each discipline has a database that maintains descriptions of studies in its subfields. However, this search may reveal similar results. This would indicate, at least initially, the need to begin conceptualizing a qualitative study. However, if the same search reveals several studies, then clearly a quantitative study is in order.

Searching for Sources

The next step in the process is to decide where to search. A literature search is somewhat like a treasure hunt. When one reference has been found, this can lead to others, and so on, in an ever-expanding quest. For example, you may begin your search at your university or college library. By accessing the library database and typing in the words "childhood aggression," you may find that the library contains more than ten thousand articles, books, monographs, and other items containing that exact term. While browsing through the list, you find a book titled *Trajectories of Physical Aggression from Toddlerhood to Middle Childhood: Predictors, Correlates, and Outcomes*, which may be worth an initial investigation. The next step would be to review the book's bibliography or list of references. This list would then lead you to similar journal articles and studies that have been conducted on childhood aggression. This list, in addition to your original list, could guide you in your search for journal articles.

To list all the social service–related databases that exist would be impossible (new ones are created and old ones deleted regularly). A reference librarian at your campus library should be happy to help you review the databases available at your campus. Many social work students limit their searches to social work databases such as Social Work Abstracts. This database is an excellent resource; however, we caution you to not limit your search to those databases that are specifically related to social work. There are many other useful databases, such as PsycINFO, CINAHL (a nursing database), Sociological Abstracts, and Dissertation Abstracts International (a database that publishes graduate students' research for a cost). Any database for social sciences might be helpful. Spending some time in your campus library will help you gain familiarity with these and other databases.

Library databases state whether an article is available online, and if not, whether the article is located at your library. You can retrieve full-text articles when available by selecting the link provided. Then you can save or print the article, if desired. Most university libraries provide an interlibrary loan service. This service is usually free or of minimal cost to students; it allows you to obtain articles and books for a short period of time. This service greatly expands the resources of the library. If an article is not available, you can order it through an interlibrary loan service. A copy of the article is either e-mailed to you or sent to your library for you to pick up.

Step 2: Choosing Your Articles

As you begin to compile a list of literature to review, it is important to have some general guidelines when you are deciding whether to use an article. Choose articles that are as closely related as possible to your subject. This will save you time, and by choosing articles that are specific to what you are examining, you will be able to focus your search. Choose articles (whenever possible) that are no more than ten years old. There may be times when you need to cite a work that is more than ten years old. For example, you may want to cite an article that is considered a landmark study, which will be evidenced by the number of other people who have referenced the work. Or it may be that some topics were thoroughly investigated during an earlier time period and have not been studied much in the previous decade. Although it is acceptable to use older articles for these reasons, do not rely solely on dated studies. Your credibility could be jeopardized, because it will look like your knowledge of the subject is not up to date.

Choose articles from reputable peer-reviewed journals (a research librarian, instructors, and colleagues can help you if you are uncertain which journals have a better reputation than others). A peer-reviewed journal is one that sends article submissions to experts in the field before accepting them for publication. These experts read the articles and evaluate them for content, accuracy, and methodological concerns. The reviewers are not provided with any information on the authors, which helps eliminate bias. This is referred to as a blind review. The blind review process is unique because the decision to publish a study does not fall on a single editor. Instead, the editors of the journal send out articles for reviewers to read so that they can make comments. Based on those comments, a determination is made as to whether to print the article as it is, ask for revisions, or reject the article.

Part of the reviewer's job is to consider the methodology employed and to look for flaws in the research. **Methodology** describes the research methods, procedures, and techniques used to collect and analyze information. However, the fact that a study has been subjected to a **peer review** and has made its way into print does not mean that it is stellar research. You, as a consumer, have to learn to discern between good research that has inherent limitations and just plain bad research. You can do this by becoming educated, learning to think critically about what you are reading, and questioning for yourself whether the methodology makes sense.

There is no doubt that the Internet is a technological boon to society. Today, we have more information available to us instantaneously than at any time in our past. Many journals and authors now post their articles on the World Wide Web. Some are free, and some require a subscription. However, the Internet needs to be viewed with some caution—especially when it is used for research. The fact that something is posted on the

Internet does not mean that it is factual information. Misinformation often makes its way online. Because of this, we recommend that you use websites that host peer-reviewed journals. In addition, most authors who post their research cite which journal has published the article.

Step 3: Reviewing Your Articles

To find relevant information in a research article, you need to understand the sections of an article and some terminology used in research. There are generally six main sections to an article: the abstract, introduction, literature review, description of methods used, results and/or findings, and discussion (see figure 3.1). You can also use this outline as a guide as you write your own research proposal.

Main Parts of an Article

ABSTRACT

The **abstract** is a brief summary of the article. In general, an abstract is no more than 250 words; it tells readers the purpose of the study (questions or hypothesis) and provides a brief description of the research method and design.

INTRODUCTION

The introduction of an article explains the question, problem statement, or hypothesis that motivated the study. Moreover, the introduction should tell the reader the main topic of the study, when the study was conducted, and why the topic is important. In chapter 1 we discussed how you start out with a basic research question. For instance, you might be wondering about your agency's services ("I wonder what my clients think about the services at this agency") or a new treatment ("I wonder if this intervention will work with my clients") or people's opinions ("I wonder if college students are more open minded than adults who have not attended college about gay, lesbian, bisexual, and transgender issues"). Remember that in a qualitative study, a researcher is looking for new information or more in-depth information. In a quantitative study, a researcher is looking to add to, confirm, or disprove existing knowledge.

Depending on the type of study, the researcher might use a **problem statement**. This is an open-ended statement that tells you what the study is intended to do, but it does not predict what the results might be—even if the researcher has an idea of what to expect. A problem statement might

FIGURE 3.1: FORMAT OF A RESEARCH ARTICLE

Abstract

Purpose of the study (questions or hypotheses)
Brief description of the research method and design (e.g., sampling, intervention, analyses)
No more than 250 words

Introduction

What is the problem statement?
What is the hypothesis?
What are the independent and dependent variables?

Review of Literature

Briefly state what the literature has said about this issue.

Methods

Describe the sample and/or subjects. Who are they? What are their characteristics? Where are they from? How many are there?
Was an intervention—such as a treatment, education, or service—used?
How did the researchers collect data? Did they use standardized (questionnaire, survey, records) or nonstandardized methods (observation, interviews, comments)?

Findings or Results

What were the results or findings of the study?
Did the results answer the questions or problem statement of the study?
Did the results accept or reject the hypotheses?

Discussion

What were the authors' conclusions?

---

be "This study will determine the effects of progressive muscle relaxation, as opposed to guided imagery, on body temperature."

In contrast, the hypothesis predicts the relationship between variables. A hypothesis can predict no outcome, a positive outcome, a negative outcome, or more than one outcome. As an example, a hypothesis might look like the following: "Being sexually abused during childhood will not affect the promiscuity of adults" (no outcome), "People who are sexually abused during childhood will be more promiscuous as adults" (positive outcome), "People who are sexually abused during childhood will be less promiscuous as adults" (negative outcome), or "Girls who are sexually abused during childhood will be more promiscuous as adults, whereas boys who are sexually abused during childhood will be less promiscuous as adults" (bidirectional outcome). This speculation would be based on the various ways of knowing—that is, on the researcher's own experience, the expertise of others, history of the issue, and a review of the literature on related research.

Social workers study an endless amount of variables. Some examples of commonly used ones are sex, age, education, income, self-esteem, drug use, and domestic violence. When we are attempting to understand the relationship between variables, it is important to label variables. Variables are commonly labeled "independent variables" and "dependent variables." An **independent variable** (IV) is the factor (stimulus) that supplies the intervention or is said to be manipulated by the researcher. A **dependent variable** (DV) is predicted by or depends on other variables (usually independent variables). In social work practice, the dependent variable is often called the outcome. For instance, consider the question "Did the smoking cessation classes help people quit smoking?" For this research question, the smoking cessation class is the intervention being introduced (IV) and the participants' smoking behavior is what is being measured (DV).

While every explanatory study needs at least one independent variable, all researchers should assume that reality is governed by a combination of different independent variables. For instance, a person's attitude toward homeless people can be governed by his or her race, gender, income, and perceptions of job opportunities; whether he or she lives in a rural or urban community; and his or her personal experience with poverty. These are all independent variables that may predict attitudes toward homeless people. There are other types of variables used in the data analysis that are discussed later in this text. For now, you are looking for how the information the researchers want to collect is being defined so that it can be measured.

LITERATURE REVIEW

The literature review is a discussion of what information the authors located or did not locate in relation to the research questions before they started the study. In essence, this is the result of their own literature review, which is presented in a narrative form following the abstract and introduction. Was there a wealth of information? Was there limited information? What was missing in the literature? Was there research that contradicted other studies?

METHODS

The methods section describes the sample, any intervention that was used, and how the data were collected. The sample of the study is basically the participants who provided the evidence. Sometimes an entire population is researched, as when all the clients in an agency have provided information on the services they received. However, most of the time we usually can't study everyone in our target population for practical reasons of time and cost, so we are faced with drawing a smaller sample for our study and then generalizing, or projecting, the sample results with some degree of confidence back to the target population at large.

There is an entire chapter on various types of sampling and how to conduct sampling located later in this text. For now, we will focus on collecting only the characteristics of the sample: who, what, where, and how. For instance, who are the participants? Are they college students, substance abuse clients, exotic dancers, residents in a shelter, or mothers of twins? What are their characteristics? In other words, what are their ages, sex, marital status, sexual orientation, and other identifying characteristics? Where are they from? Are they from a rural university, from an inpatient treatment facility, from several cities across the Midwest, from one homeless shelter, or from a large city? Finally, how many people were in the sample study?

If an intervention was used, what was it? For instance, was it a relaxation method, a parent education class, or a service (e.g., transportation, child care, house cleaning)?

Data collection refers to how the data were retrieved from the participants. Did the researchers use methods such as videotaping or audiotaping or keep journals or other field notes, in which the researcher records experiences, perceptions, feelings, statements from participants, and other information? Or did they use methods such as surveys or other questionnaires? Did they look at existing information such as records? Were there multiple methods of data collection, such as a survey and a follow-up interview?

RESULTS OR FINDINGS

In the results or findings section you will find an analysis or compilation of the findings of the research. Did the study address the problem statement or hypothesis stated in the introduction? A qualitative study might look at themes or at new information that was found. If applicable, did the study reject (disprove) or accept (support) the stated hypothesis? The finding for the hypothesis "Clients using progressive muscle relaxation will have a significant increase in body temperature over clients using guided imagery" might be "There was an average difference in body temperature of five degrees between clients using progressive muscle relaxation and those using guided imagery for the fifty sample subjects who participated in the interventions. This difference is statistically significant." The related conclusion might be "Therefore, it can be concluded that clients using pro-gressive muscle relaxation will have a greater increase in average body temperature than clients using guided imagery." The results support the hypothesis!

DISCUSSION

In the discussion section, you will find a discussion of what the authors think are the pieces of knowledge learned from the research study. The findings will be tied back into what the literature already informs us about the issue studied and what this new knowledge adds to, confirms, or rejects about that knowledge. Did the research inform us about a practice or a policy? Does the author think that more research is needed, and why?

Critique of the Article

Once you have collected all the information from the article, it is impor-tant to critique what is presented. By critiquing the articles you review, you are building a foundation for your own research. For instance, does the article leave out any important variables? Do you agree or disagree with the way the variables are defined and measured? Why? Was the sam-ple large enough to reflect the practices of people outside the study? What were the strengths and weaknesses of the study?

Step 4: Organizing Your Search Results

After getting copies of numerous studies, you will quickly discover that researchers do not always agree on the most important elements of an event or phenomenon. For instance, some studies may say that a person's sex predicts anorexia, whereas other studies argue that socialization, such as parenting, media, or peers, has a greater impact on people's eating behaviors. Your job is to organize these competing claims into a coherent list of different variables that may affect your research topic.

Index Cards

There is no single way to decide how to evaluate the amount of articles, books, and notes you will accumulate. One method that is time honored and has proved effective is to use a stack of blank index cards. Begin by writing some basic information for each article or book on each card. This should include the author's name, the title, date of publication, publisher (or journal), and page numbers. This information will be invaluable later when you compile your reference list and will be helpful should you need to find particular items again. On the other side of the card, record your notes about the publication. Notes about sample size, methodology, and strengths or weaknesses of the research design can help you decide later on which articles to focus on and which to ignore. This method allows you to save on the cost of printing the articles and to organize the information for when you write the literature review summary without creating a table or spreadsheet. In addition, you can alphabetize the authors' last names by sorting your cards.

Computer Software

Another approach to organizing your information is to use your computer. This requires you to save and/or print out your articles as you select them. Then you can enter the information into a table in a word processor (like Microsoft Word) or a spreadsheet (like Microsoft Excel), or you can use software such as EndNote that stores and organizes bibliographies. These methods allow you to sort entries alphabetically and to cut and paste or import the information.

Groupings

You may wish to use your printed articles or your note cards to organize them into categories of studies with similar findings and then construct a table that will display the patterns you find. This should assist you in identifying the variables that have been repeatedly studied and those that have been relatively ignored. Likewise, these groups will show whether the impact of a variable is confirmed by other studies or whether there are conflicting findings or incomplete conclusions about the impact of a variable.

Table 3.1 is an example of a table that might be produced for our literature review on childhood aggression. Notice that the last names of the authors dictate the order in which the studies are listed. Alphabetizing publications by authors' last name is a common practice. The example is not meant to be a complete table or to be exhaustive. It is simply a demonstration of how you may choose to organize data. Feel free to set up your tables in a way that make sense to you. Note that some of the studies in

TABLE 3.1: ORGANIZING REFERENCE INFORMATION

AUTHOR	DATE	WHAT WAS EXAMINED	RESULTS
Arsenio	2004	Presentations concerned with childhood aggression	Long-term patterns of childhood aggression are as stable as patterns of intelligence.
Bandura, Ross, & Ross	1961	Children's imitations of aggressive behavior	Children who witnessed adults hitting a doll were also aggressive toward the doll.
Brook & Whiteman	1992	Is childhood aggression related to adolescent delinquency and drug use?	Anger and/or aggression in childhood may be a predictor of drug use and delinquency in adolescence.
Brown & Parsons	1998	Are there subtypes of aggression?	Reactive (normal) and proactive (problematic) aggression are two types of aggression.
Eron & Huesmann	1984	Does gender role predict aggressive behavior?	Boys were found to be more aggressive than girls.
Evans, Heriot, & Friedman	2002	Are there temperamental characteristics that contribute to a pattern of hostility in children?	A pattern of irritability and negativity can account for hostile behavior in children.
Fuller, Chemack, Cruise, Kirsch, Fitzgerald, & Zucker	2003	Does intergenerational aggression and alcohol use predict aggression in children?	Aggression in grandparents predicted aggression and alcoholism in parents, which predicted aggression in children (third generation).
Geen & Thomas	1986	The relationship between media images and violence	A significant relationship between violence in media and aggression was found.

TABLE 3.1: (CONTINUED)

AUTHOR'S NAME	DATE	WHAT WAS EXAMINED	RESULTS
Greenburg	1983	The effects of aggression over time	Aggression in childhood is a predictor of adult aggressive behavior.
Herrenkohl & Russo	2001	What is the relationship between child maltreatment and early-childhood aggressive behavior?	The results suggested a relationship between severe physical discipline and childhood aggression.
Nangle, Erdley, Carpenter, & Newman	2002	Research on social-skills training for childhood aggression	Six major developmental areas were identified: age, gender, race, social cognition, peer-group influence, and interventions.
Rubin	1998	What causes childhood aggression?	Rejection and violence by parents were traits linked to aggression in children; watching violence on television was also linked to increased violence in children.
Wood, Wong, & Chacher	1991	Is violence in the media related to childhood aggression?	Viewing aggression on television and other media sources extended into aggression in other areas of the child's life.

the table (see the articles by Arsenio and Nangle, Erdley, Carpenter, and Newman) are not research studies but are essays that discuss, compile, or analyze research done by others. Also, one study dated 1961 (by Bandura, Ross, and Ross) is included because it is a landmark study that led the way as researchers worked to understand the effect of adult modeling on children's behavior.

Example 3.1 is a sample literature review based on the information in table 3.1. Notice how the sample summarizes what is known rather than

EXAMPLE 3.1: LITERATURE REVIEW

A review of the literature suggests that there are correlations between variables that account for childhood aggression. Some authors found that aggression in children can be a sign of several maladaptive factors within the family, such as drug use (Brook & Whiteman, 1992; Fuller, Chemack, Cruise, Kirsch, Fitzgerald, & Zucker, 2003) and violence (Bandura, Ross, & Ross, 1961; Fuller et al., 2003; Herrenkohl & Russo, 2001; Rubin, 1998). Other studies assert a relationship between children viewing violent television programs and aggressive behavior (Geen & Thomas, 1986; Rubin, 1998; Wood, Wong, & Chachere, 1991). Still others found that aggressive behavior is a gender issue (Nangle, Erdley, Carpenter, & Newman, 2002) and is more prevalent in male children (Eron & Huesmann, 1984). Finally, studies have suggested that individual or situational characteristics, such as a long-term pattern of aggressive behaviors (Arsenio, 2004), whether the aggression is reactive (normal) or proactive (problematic) (Brown & Parsons, 1998), and a pattern of irritability and negativity in the child (Evans, Heriot, & Friedman, 2002) may be related to acts of childhood aggression.

Given the findings of the studies mentioned here, children who spend time watching violent television programs and playing violent video games may demonstrate a higher level of aggression than other children. One theoretical model that emerges is the theory that children imitate what they see, which is known as social learning theory (Bandura et al., 1961).

discussing each study individually; each citation can contain multiple studies. A **citation** gives credit to the authors for what you are reporting; these are reported by last name, then date. Also, notice that when we are citing a study with more than two authors for the second time, we use the phrase "et al.," which is Latin for "and others."

Step 5: Developing a Problem Statement or Hypothesis

The last step is to use the literature to begin to develop some type of a problem statement or a testable hypothesis. But first you must decide whether you will be conducting a qualitative or quantitative study. Your literature review can help you to determine whether you will be conducting a qualitative study or a quantitative study. The role of the literature review largely depends on what type of study is being conducted. Conversely, the type of study that will be conducted is dependent on the literature review. Let us explore this seemingly circular logic. Knowledge emerges from qualitative research as an end product. Researchers first collect the data and begin to make tentative descriptions and develop common themes out of the information. Then, we go back to the literature and begin to search for similar information that will help us to make sense of our findings. With quantitative research, in contrast, we utilize existing knowledge and theoretical perspectives to guide the development of our research question or hypothesis. In some cases theories emerge from or are revised following the quantitative process.

Developing a Problem Statement

As we discussed earlier, problem statements are open-ended inquiries that do not predict what the results of the research study might be. Let us imagine for a moment that in the fall of 2001 you were a case manager working with the mentally ill in an outpatient clinic. You noticed that many of the consumers on your caseload suddenly began to miss appointments after the terrorist attacks of September 11, 2001. As a practitioner, you wanted to understand this relationship but were unsure what to do. A search of the literature revealed that there were virtually no articles dealing with the effects of terrorist attacks on the mentally ill. You decided to conduct an exploratory study in which you would interview three or four of your consumers to gain an in-depth understanding of what they were experiencing. Your research question was "What effect did the 9/11 terrorist attack have on mentally ill clients?" You then created the following problem statement: "Little is known about the effects of the 9/11 terrorist attack on mentally ill clients."

Developing a Hypothesis

As discussed in chapter 1, a hypothesis is generally considered a testable statement. This means that we can confirm or reject our hypothesis. After looking at the studies reviewed in table 3.1, perhaps you can develop a research hypothesis that will begin to guide and form your study. On the basis of what you have read in the sample literature, you learned that several things may be related to children's aggression: the child's sex, amount of violent television that the child views, family dynamics, and the child's individual characteristics or a situational event he or she is experiencing. Drawing from these findings, you might develop a research hypothesis. You develop a research hypothesis that states: "Male children demonstrate more aggressive behavior than female children after watching violent television programs." You can develop a study from this hypothesis.

Your goal is to develop a testable hypothesis, that is, one for which there are variables on which you can gather empirical data. There are two basic problems to watch for when you are developing a hypothesis. First, a researcher can accidentally leave out a basis for comparison. Suppose, for instance, that you formulate the following hypothesis: "Children watching violent television programs demonstrate more aggression." This statement begs the question "More aggression than whom?" Another form of nontestable hypothesis is one that is really more of the researcher's value judgment, or his or her opinion, such as "Children should not be allowed to view violent television programs because they may become violent." This is a value statement and is not testable.

We hope that at this point you are beginning to see the connection between the literature review and conducting research. Consulting the existing knowledge (conducting a literature review) early in the process will allow you to save time and energy by helping you gain an understanding of what is already known about a topic.

Step 6: Compiling Your Reference List

The last part of your literature review involves making a reference list. The **reference list** is the alphabetical list of studies that you chose to include in your review and is formatted according to the writing style you are using. For instance, most social work journals require articles to be submitted in American Psychological Association (APA) style. There are books and style guides published on the various writing styles, for instance, APA, Chicago, and MLA. Example 3.2 shows the reference list for the literature review in example 3.1 and is formatted in APA style. As a note of caution, be aware that APA and other writing styles change over time. Therefore, remember always to consult the current style guide.

Case Scenario

You are a social work student who is completing a practicum in a nursing home. You have been assigned to work with a social worker who wants to conduct a study on the effects of having residents interact with pets (dogs who are specially trained for this type of work) to see if it will help alleviate their depression. The social worker has the following research question in mind: "Will residents who interact with specially trained therapy dogs

EXAMPLE 3.2: REFERENCE PAGE

Arsenio, W. (2004). The stability of young children's physical aggression: Relations with child care, gender, and aggression subtypes. *Monographs of the Society for Research in Child Development, 69*(4), 130–144.

Bandura, A., Ross, R., & Ross, S. (1961). Transmission of aggression through imitation of aggressive models. *Journal of Abnormal and Social Psychology, 63*, 575–582.

Brook, J., & Whiteman, M. (1992). Childhood aggression, adolescent delinquency, and drug abuse: A longitudinal study. *Journal of Genetic Psychology, 153*(4), 369–384.

Brown, K., & Parsons, R. (1998). Accurate identification of childhood aggression: A key to successful intervention. *Professional School Counseling, 2*(2), 135–141.

Eron, L., & Huesmann, L. (1984). The control of aggressive behavior by changes in attitudes, and conditions of learning. In R. Blanchard & D. Blanchard (Eds.), *Advances in the study of aggression* (Vol. 1, pp. 139–171). Orlando, FL: Academic Press.

Evans, I., Heriot, S., & Friedman, A. (2002). A behavioral pattern of irritability, hostility and inhibited empathy in children. *Clinical Child Psychology and Psychiatry, 7*(2), 211–225.

Fuller, B., Chemack, S., Cruise, K., Kirsch, E., Fitzgerald, H., & Zucker, R. (2003). Predictors of aggression across three generations among sons of alcoholics: Relationships involving grandparental and parental alcoholism, child aggression, marital aggression, and parenting practices. *Journal of Studies on Alcohol, 64*(4), 472–484.

Geen, R., & Thomas, S. (1986). The immediate effects of media violence on behavior. *Journal of Social Issues, 42*(3), 7–27.

Greenburg, J. (1983). Parental behavior, TV habits, IQ predict aggression. *Science News, 124*(10), 148–151.

Herrenkohl, R., & Russo, J. (2001). Abusive early child rearing and early childhood aggression. *Child Maltreatment, 6*(1), 3–17.

Nangle, D., Erdley, C., Carpenter, E., & Newman, J. (2002). Social skills training as a treatment for aggressive children and adolescents: A developmental-clinical integration. *Aggression and Violent Behavior, 7*(2), 169–200.

Rubin, D. (1998). What makes a child violent? *Parenting, 12*(6), 96–102.

Wood, W., Wong, F., & Chachere, J. (1991). Effects of media violence on viewers' aggression in unconstrained social interaction. *Psychological Bulletin, 109*, 379–383.

show a greater decrease in their depression than those who don't interact with the dogs?" The social worker has a plan to select a depression inventory and measure the residents' depression before interacting with the therapy dog and then have the residents interact with the dog for one hour a week over an eight-week period, and then measure their depression again using the same scale. She will measure another group's depression, and participants in that group will not interact with the dog. The social worker has asked you to develop a literature review to help her formulate her research.

Critical-Thinking Questions

On the basis of the case scenario, answer the following questions:

1. Which search terms would you use to conduct your literature review? Give reasons for choosing those particular terms.

2. Which databases would you search?

3. On the basis of your initial search, do you believe that this research falls into the quantitative or the qualitative category? Give reasons for your selection.

4. Do you see any ethical issues that might be presented as a result of this study? If yes, how would you resolve them?

Key Points

· A literature review is a search of published research that allows you to review what is known about the topic you are studying.

· A literature review helps shape a research design by giving the researcher an overview of previous studies on a topic.

· To conduct a search of the literature, you must identify keywords to enter into a search database, such as Social Work Abstracts or PsycINFO.

Practice Exam

Multiple Choice

1. Keywords are words that are
    a. Key components in a study
    b. Words used to define search terms in any data search

    c. Words that define the independent variable

    d. Words that define the dependent variable

    e. None of the above

2. Social work uses which style manual:

    a. American Medical Association (AMA)

    b. Turabian

    c. MLA

    d. American Psychological Association (APA)

    e. None of the above

3. A hypothesis is:

    a. A chance for the researcher to demonstrate knowledge of a subject

    b. A testable statement

    c. A question about what might be found

    d. An attempt to see whether a study is qualitative or quantitative

    e. None of the above

4. CINAHL is:

    a. A medical method used to treat hypothermia

    b. A database for law students to help them identify laws

    c. A term that is used in literature reviews

    d. A qualitative inquiry method

    e. None of the above

True or False

5. Literature reviews are used to explore past research findings to direct and improve future research.

6. Problem statements are open-ended statements that tell you what a study is intended to do but do not predict what the results might be.

7. Variables are commonly labeled "independent variables" and "dependent variables."

8. The methods section of a research article describes the sample, any intervention that was used, and how the data were collected.

CHAPTER FOUR

Variables and Measures

CSWE Core Competencies

IN THIS CHAPTER you will find the following Council on Social Work Education (CSWE) competencies:

Educational Policy 2.1.6—Engage in research-informed practice and practice-informed research
Educational Policy 2.1.9—Respond to contexts that shape practice
Educational Policy 2.1.10(b)—Assessment

This chapter discusses how to develop your variables, how to conceptualize and operationalize your variables, and how to measure your variables. We first discuss how to operationalize concepts so that they can be measured for evidence. Measurements are discussed, including how to measure variables using four levels of measure. This chapter also introduces two new terms: reliability and validity.

Variables in Research Design

Variables are fluid and sometimes difficult to define and measure. For example, researchers may come up with many different ways of defining verbal abuse, such as yelling, cursing, and belittling. How you choose to specifically define particular variables is called conceptualizing variables, and how you measure a concept (variable) is called operationalizing variables. How you define and measure your variables depends on what it is you want to know or, more specifically, what your research problem statement, question, or hypothesis is.

Conceptualizing a variable refers to how we translate an idea or abstract theory into a variable that can be used to test a hypothesis or make sense of observations. Therefore, conceptualizing a variable is another way of saying how experts are defining a concept. For example, most literature defines child maltreatment as abuse or neglect. Then these broad categories are further defined into more descriptive categories. The category of abuse can be divided into physical abuse, sexual abuse, and emotional abuse. The category of neglect can be further divided into medical neglect, physical neglect, and emotional neglect. By using more descriptive categories, we are able to capture more specific information about the type of abuse an individual has encountered.

In research, it boils down to how we measure our variables or choose to operationalize them. How you operationalize a variable may depend on the information you want to collect and how you collect it. Do you only want to know if an individual has experienced childhood maltreatment, or do you want more precise information such as what kinds of maltreatment? We come back to this later in this chapter when we discuss measurements.

Viewing and Using Variables

It is important to keep in mind that variables are fluid and that the meaning attached to a variable can differ from person to person. In other words, variables evolve in how people view them and use them. The following two examples illustrate cases in which different people may view the variables of gender and race differently.

In some studies, gender is identified as either female or male, and gender is identified as either masculine or feminine. Sex is usually associated with a person's biology (chromosomes and hormones), and gender is a culturally constructed concept of what is female and what is male. Jack was born in 1957. Jack married his wife, Elaine, at age nineteen and had a son at the age of twenty. Now, at the age of fifty, Jack has officially changed his name to Jane. Jane has had a sex-change operation, wears dresses and a wig, and receives hormone shots. Jane is still married to Elaine and now considers their relationship a lesbian one. According to Jane's official birth certificate and marriage license, Jane is still a male, whereas physically and socially Jane is a female. How would you as a researcher record Jane's sex? Would this be different from how you would record her gender?

Race and ethnicity can also create similar concerns. Race is commonly used as a measure for biologically based human characteristics, known as phenotypes. Categories used for race are sometimes based on skin color (e.g., white, black) or other characteristics, such as Hispanic and Asian, whereas ethnicity is a culturally constructed concept connected with the history, culture, and national origin that form group identities, such as Irish, Jewish, or African American. What if someone has black parents but has ben raised in a white family? What if you can trace your family back to Ireland but do not know anything about that culture? A pressing issue is how to claim race when your father is black and your mother is Asian, as is the case for the famous golfer Tiger Woods. A person who is biracial is two nonspecified races, but what if your father is biracial (black and white) and your mother is Native American? Does that mean you are triracial?

Types of Variables

Variables can be placed into three general groups: independent variables, dependent variables, and control variables. As stated in chapter 3, the independent variable (identified as IV) is often thought of as the variable that is controlled or manipulated by the researcher. At other times, it is described as the variable that may have an impact on a change in the dependent variable. The dependent variable (identified as DV) is the variable that is changed by another variable, or is said to depend on the independent variables. For example, if we know how many alcoholic drinks a person consumes in an hour (the independent variable), we can predict his or her blood-alcohol level (the dependent variable). In social work practice, the dependent variable is the variable that is being measured to determine whether change has occurred. For instance, look at the question "Did the smoking cessation classes help people quit smoking?" For this research question, the smoking cessation classes (independent variable) are the intervention being introduced, and the participants' smoking behavior (dependent variable) is what is being measured.

A predictive variable is a type of independent variable, and a criterion variable is a type of dependent variable. Prediction is a special kind of relationship where one thing precedes the other and we use information about the first to forecast or predict the second. In predictive studies, variables are sequenced or are arranged in a distinct timeline. In predictive studies the predictor is the first variable (the one we have information about and are using) and the criterion is the second variable (the one being predicted). Also, you could have more than one predictor and/or criterion variable. This depends on your research question or problem statement. Let's look at some predictors of child maltreatment:

- Age (IV) is a predictor of abuse (DV)—younger boys are abused more than older boys, and older girls are abused more than younger girls.
- Income (IV) is a predictor of child maltreatment (DV).
- Stress (IV) is a predictor of child maltreatment (DV).
- Social isolation (IV) is a predictor of child maltreatment (DV).

A **control variable** is a variable that researchers control for in a research study. When researchers **control for** a variable, this means that they subtract the effect of that variable on the dependent variable by holding the variable constant. Researchers often use control variables as a type of theoretical insurance. That is, they may not think that the control variable will influence the dependent variables, but they include the variable just to be safe. Many control variables are demographics. **Demographics** are the physical characteristics of a population, such as age, sex, marital status, family size, education, geographic location, and occupation. For example, assume for a moment that, on the basis of the literature, you believe that a person's sex affects his or her self-esteem. Your support group for parents without partners has both male and female members. Therefore, you want to control for gender when you conduct your study of the support group by including sex in your study. In other words, you want to ensure that the support group helps consumers regardless of their gender.

By including gender, you can use statistical methods to look at the response differences between males and females or to subtract the influence of sex from the data (depending on what type of analysis you use). Another way to control for sex in your study on the support group would be to assign males to one group and females to another group. You could then compare their scores.

Going back to the child maltreatment literature, you can see from the following list that marital status (IV) and race (IV) were not found to be predictors of child maltreatment (DV) when income was controlled for. Similarly, the parent's sex (IV) was not found to be a predictor of abuse (DV) when time spent with the child was controlled for:

- Single parents (IV) seem to be more abusive (DV); however, the effect disappears when income is controlled for.
- African Americans (IV) are believed to abuse (DV) more often than whites; however, this effect disappears when income is controlled for.

- Mothers (IV) abuse (DV) children more often (60 percent) than fathers; however, this effect disappears when time spent with children is controlled for.

As you can see, the effect of a predictor can sometimes be explained by another variable. For instance, both race and marital status no longer appear to be predictors for abuse when income is controlled for. This illustrates the problem of omitting key variables in your study, which can distort the findings.

A **confounding variable** is a type of control variable that obscures the effect of another variable. In such cases, the effects of a variable's impact cannot be determined because of other influences confounding the relationship. For example, a relationship between traditional male gender-role expectations and wife abuse may be confounded by a history of paternal abuse. That is, the power of traditional gender-role expectations may be stronger for people who have been abused by their fathers. Several studies that look at the effect of a person's race on his or her comfort with homosexuality find that African Americans are more homophobic than whites. However, this association is misleading. When the studies add access to higher education as a variable, the impact of race disappears. That is, African Americans have attitudes about homosexuality that are similar to those of whites when they have similar educational levels.

As a result of the effect confounding variables can have on a study, researchers need to include many types of variables in their studies. A broad list of variables should include independent variables and control variables that are relevant to the study. To include all possibilities, the researcher consults the literature to identify what has already been studied. Let us examine the variables used in two separate studies. These studies used substantiated child maltreatment case files to look at the differences between families with twin children and families without twin children (DV). The variables used in the first study were as follows:

- type of maltreatment
- number of children in the home
- annual income
- use of fertility drugs to conceive
- whether or not the children were born prematurely
- whether or not children were born with birth defects
- number of adults in the home
- age of children in the home
- square footage of the residence

- parental psychological problems
- social supports available

The variables used in the second study were as follows:

- type of maltreatment
- number of children in the home
- annual income

Which study would you use? What makes your choice the better option?

What Is a Measure?

A **measure** is a tool or instrument that is used to gather data. For instance, a measurement tool could be a survey (e.g., population survey), a test (e.g., IQ test), a scale that has several questions (e.g., depression scale), or a poll (e.g., opinion poll). A measure has two parts—the item (stimulus) and the response. The item is generally a statement, question, or observation that requires some type of measurable response. A measurement tool is sometimes trying to measure a concept, such as alcoholism, depression, self-esteem, and marital satisfaction. Because a concept can have multiple definitions, it must be operationalized for the measure.

Defining and Operationalizing Measures

Now let us begin looking at how we develop the items of the measure. For this, it is important to discuss how concepts are defined and operationalized. Remember, the term *operationalize* refers to how we define a concept so that it can be measured. Let us look at some examples. Alcoholism is defined as excessive or compulsive use of alcohol in many standard dictionaries. How do we know excessive use or compulsive use when we observe drinking behavior? Whose standard do we use? If you did research on the prevalence of alcoholism at your university or college, you might find multiple conflicting statistics, depending on how you have operationalized the concept. For example, in one study you may operationalize alcoholism using criteria established in the American Psychiatric Association's *Diagnostic and Statistical Manual of Mental Disorders* (5th ed., 2013). In another study you may simply ask whether individuals believe they are alcoholic, and for still another study, you might investigate how many individuals have been diagnosed with alcoholism by a mental health professional. As you can guess, each of these studies would lead to different findings on the prevalence of alcoholism at your university or college.

An example of an instrument for measuring alcoholism that is commonly used is the Michigan Alcoholism Screening Test (MAST). The MAST was developed by Melvin L. Seltzer (1971) to detect alcoholism. This particular scale has twenty-four questions (on concepts defining alcoholism) with scores assigned for each response option (how concepts are operationalized). The total of all twenty-four scores can indicate nonalcoholism (score of 3 or less), suggestion of alcoholism (score of 4), or alcoholism (score of 5 or more). Question 8 of the instrument asks, "Have you ever attended a meeting of Alcoholics Anonymous?" If the response is yes, it is assigned five points and indicates alcoholism, according to this instrument's definition. Therefore, individuals who attended an Alcoholics Anonymous meeting for reasons other than their own alcohol use, such as to support a friend, would meet the criteria for alcoholism on the basis of how this measure was operationalized.

With this in mind, you can easily see how research can be corrupted by how a concept is operationalized. We can manipulate how we operationalize concepts such as abuse, poverty, crime, and homosexuality to fit our desired outcome or mislead readers. For example, city law enforcement might operationalize incidents of crime as all arrests or every conviction, including misdemeanors such as shoplifting. The findings might be used to support the need for more resources or to justify current resources. In another study, the travel and tourism office of the same city might operationalize incidence of crime as only felony crimes against individuals. This might be used to establish a lower rate of crime for the city in an effort to attract more tourists.

Poverty provides a good example of the difficulty that can arise when we try to operationalize a concept. The battle over how to define poverty has raged for years. The issue comes down to concerns over "relative" versus "absolute" poverty. Measures of relative poverty focus on deprivation from a subjective and comparative point of view—"How poor do I feel?" or "How poor am I compared to others around me?"—whereas measures of absolute poverty focus on the amount of income an individual or family has to purchase the goods that sustain healthy life. While this definition might sound straightforward, listing all the material things that people need can get very complicated. Therefore, different definitions of poverty can produce vast differences in how we operationalize poverty. The bottom line is that how we define this concept has a bearing on who will receive services.

Levels of Measure

Four levels are used to measure variables: nominal, ordinal, interval, and ratio. The first two levels of variables are called discrete variables, or categorical variables. Both nominal-level and ordinal-level variables are discrete because they are made up of distinct separate units or categories. The last two levels of a measure are called continuous variables because they are made up of a large (sometimes infinite) number of units. Both interval-level and ratio-level variables fall into this category. With each subsequent level of measure, we gain the ability to more precisely measure what we are studying. Keep in mind that we want to be as precise as possible in our measurement.

Discrete Levels of Measure

The first level of measurement we examine is the nominal-level variable. **Nominal-level variables** are mutually exclusive (i.e., responses fit into one category and cannot be in another) and are exhaustive (i.e., no other options are available). One type of nominal-level variable is a **dichotomous variable**, for which there are only two responses to choose from (e.g., yes or no, treatment group or nontreatment group). We can measure gender as a nominal-level variable (a person is either male, female, transsexual, or hermaphrodite). We can measure attitudes at a nominal level ("Do you like research—yes or no?"). We can measure religious affiliation as Catholic, Protestant, Jewish, Muslim, or other. One way to determine if a measure is nominal is to decide whether you can add or subtract from the measure. For instance, you cannot subtract a Catholic from a Muslim and get another religion. This highlights a problem with nominal-level variables—they are limiting. Say, for example, that eight people state on a survey that they are Catholic. This gives us no information about the extent of their involvement in their faith, such as church attendance, tithing, and praying. So we move up a level to ordinal-level data to gain greater detail.

With **ordinal-level variables**, in addition to being mutually exclusive and exhaustive, responses are rank ordered. For example, for the question "How much do you like research?" ordinal-level responses could range from "not at all" to "somewhat" to "very much." Notice how this provides more information than purely nominal-level responses (yes or no) for "Do you like research?" Nominal-level variables can tell us whether someone feels positively or negatively about something but not the degree to which they feel that way. By using rank ordering, we begin to establish different levels or degrees of responses. The limitation of ordinal data, however, is that it is not precise. For instance, the difference between "somewhat" liking research and liking research "very much" can be big or small. The next level of measurement begins to achieve greater precision.

Continuous Levels of Measurement

The next level of measurement is the interval-level variable. With **interval-level variables**, items are rank ordered and each step is mutually exclusive and exhaustive, and there are equal gradations between each step. This means that the difference between the responses can be determined through addition or subtraction. An example is IQ. One person's IQ can be 110, and another person's 140, for an increase in IQ of exactly thirty points. Another example is the range between −10 and −20 degrees Fahrenheit, which is the same as that between 50 and 60 degrees Fahrenheit, or exactly 10 degrees.

The fourth level of measurement is the ratio-level variable; this is the most precise level of measurement. **Ratio-level variables** have all the attributes of the other three levels (items are mutually exclusive and exhaustive, they are rank ordered, and there are equal gradations between steps). The main difference between interval and ratio measurement is that interval-level variables have no absolute or fixed zero point, whereas ratio-level variables have an absolute zero point. Items measured at this level might include such things as income (you could have no income) and number of children. Notice that both income and number of children would meet all the criteria: they are mutually exclusive categories that are rank ordered and have equal gradations and an absolute zero.

Keep in mind that variables are fluid because they can be viewed and used in various ways. In table 4.1, the researcher has taken what is a ratio-level variable ("How many days in the past week have you experienced episodes of crying?") because it has an absolute zero (zero to seven days) and is treating it like an ordinal variable by dividing it into categories. When this variable is treated as interval level, the results can provide more information, such as how many or what percentage of participants reported one or two days per week as opposed to three or four per week, five or six days per week, daily, or none.

In the following examples, indicate what level of measurement is being used:

- A student is polling other students on campus about their position on abortion. Students have the option of defining their position

TABLE 4.1: EXAMPLE FOR EACH LEVEL OF MEASUREMENT

ITEM (STIMULUS)	RESPONSE OPTIONS	LEVEL OF MEASUREMENT
Have you ever been treated for depression?	Yes No	Nominal
In the past month, I have thought about ending my life.	Not at all Sometimes Frequently	Ordinal
How many days in the past week have you experienced episodes of crying?	None 1–2 days 3–4 days 5–6 days Daily	Interval
How many times have you attempted suicide?	(Respondents enter a number)	Ratio

on the issue as "support abortion" or "do not support abortion." (Nominal)

- A substance abuse counselor wants to know how satisfied consumers are with the on-site Alcoholics Anonymous meetings. She administers a survey that asks respondents to indicate whether they are "very satisfied," "somewhat satisfied," or "not satisfied." (Ordinal)
- The supervisor of an after-school program needs to know in which grade each student is currently enrolled. (Ratio)

Standardized Measures

There are multiple standardized measurement instruments in circulation today. A **standardized measure** is one that has been given to enough people that we can compare one person's scores to those of other test takers. For example, you have probably taken the ACT or a similar exam. These tests have been normed or standardized so that your scores could be compared with those of other test takers. A similar example would be tests of intelligence quotient (IQ tests). Most people who take an IQ test score in the range of average intelligence (around 100). Some compilations of measures are described at the end of this chapter.

Standardized measures have limitations. To illustrate some important limitations, let us return to the example of the Michigan Alcoholism Screening Test. The MAST was normed on multiple groups: 116 hospitalized alcoholics, 99 people arrested for drunk driving, 98 people under review for revocation of their driver's licenses because of excess accidents and moving violations, and 103 controls (individuals who functioned as part of a control group). The groups were largely made up of white males between the ages of twenty-five and forty-four years. What are potential problems that might arise if the MAST is administered in the following situations?

- You are working with members of a gang who are in high school. Drinking alcohol appears to be an important part of gang culture.
- You are working with parents referred by Child Protective Services for alcohol abuse. The majority of these parents are women.
- You are working with Hispanic immigrants referred through the court system for charges of driving while intoxicated.

Standardized measures such as the MAST are used universally, regardless of the population for which they have been normed. Researchers should be informed of how standardized measures are normed so that they can avoid placing individuals into stereotypical categories that do not take into consideration issues of diversity such as culture, sex, age, and nationality.

Reliability and Validity in Measurement

Two of the factors that contribute to the credibility of a research study are the measurement's reliability and validity. **Reliability** is used to describe the stability and consistency of a measurement. For instance, a tape measure is a highly reliable measuring instrument because it does not change over time (i.e., it is stable), and it measures everything according to the same standards (i.e., it is consistent). There are four major categories of reliability for most instruments: test-retest, equivalent form, internal consistency, and interobserver reliability.

Test-retest reliability has to do with the consistency of your measure from one time to the next. When a researcher administers the same measurement tool multiple times to the same group following the same research procedures, does he or she obtain consistent results (assuming that there has been no change in what is being measured)? If so, the measure has test-retest reliability.

Equivalent form reliability is concerned with consistency between two versions of a measure. If a researcher wanted to develop a new measurement tool for anxiety, he or she could administer the new measurement tool alongside a more traditional measurement tool to the same group. If consistent results were found, it could be argued that the newer measurement tool had reliability for measuring the concept of anxiety. Another option is to create two new instruments that measure the same concept. This requires a long list of variables for the concept to be divided between the two instruments. Again, both instruments would be administered at the same time to the same group, and then the researcher would compare the scores from both instruments to determine whether they were equivalent.

Internal consistency is the consistency among the responses to the items in a measure. It is the extent to which responses to items measuring the same concept are associated with one another. This form of reliability is examined when a single measurement instrument is administered to a group of people on one occasion. Tests of internal consistency estimate reliability by grouping items in an instrument that measure the same concept. For example, you could write two sets of three questions each that measure the same concept (e.g., social isolation), and if the responses to those two groups of three questions were consistent, you would know that your instrument is reliably measuring that concept. For instance, if we were measuring the concept of social isolation, we might ask respondents whether the statements "I feel lonely at times" and "I never feel lonely" accurately describe their experiences, and we would expect those items to have opposite answers. Another practice used to determine internal consistency is called split-half reliability, which involves randomly dividing the items related to a concept into two groups. Then the scores of the two groups are compared to determine whether they are measuring the same concept. In this way, you are not developing two surveys, as required by the equivalent form method. The more items that are included and the stronger the consistency between the two groups of scores, the greater the reliability is.

Interobserver reliability must be measured when more than one observer uses the same instrument to rate the same person, place, or event. If different observers or interviewers use the same instrument to score the same thing, their scores should match. The more similar the ratings, the more reliable the findings are. For instance, four observers are using an observational assessment tool to measure the quality of interactions between a mother and her child on a playground. The rating scale of the tool ranges from 0 to 10, and two observers rate the mother as a 4, another observer rates the mother as a 2, and the final observer rates the mother as a 6. These scores are fairly similar to one another. This measure would be less reliable than if the ratings were more widely spread, for instance, scores of 2, 3, 6, and 10.

An alternative version of this type of reliability is called **intraobserver reliability**. This means that there is one observer rating a person, place, or event two or more times. As with interobserver reliability, the findings are compared to ensure that the measurement is consistently getting similar scores each time.

Validity is a term that is used to describe how much a measurement tool (e.g., scale, survey, poll, test) measures what it is meant to measure. It is the match between how a concept is conceptualized (defined) and how it is operationalized (measured). For example, if we are using a scale that measures depression, we would expect the scale to ask questions about changes in the person's eating and sleeping habits (either eating or sleeping more or less), number of suicidal ideations, and the like. If these were the questions that were asked, we might say that the scale had validity. Conversely, the measurement would not focus on other psychological traits such as anxiety, poor body image, or attention deficits. A few years ago, a national fast-food chain bragged that it had the best french fries in the world. This assertion was based on their claim to have sold the most french fries globally. How is the validity of this claim flawed? In this example, the focus was on the number of fries as opposed to the quality of taste. Think for a moment about the issue of availability. This fast-food chain has a global presence; the more stores it has, the more fries they sell. But this does not mean that the claim that the chain's french fries are better is valid.

The fact that a measurement instrument is reliable (it consistently measures the same thing over and over) does not mean that it is valid. For example, let us say that you want to measure your participants' level of depression. You select a measure that has been normed and is standardized. However, the instrument you select is a scale that measures how a person feels about him- or herself (a measure of self-esteem). Even though you are consistently measuring your participants' self-esteem, you may not be measuring their level of depression. This is an issue of validity.

Let us return again to the MAST instrument. The validity of the measure was established in the following ways:

- The MAST was able to classify respondents as alcoholic or nonalcoholic.
- Only 15 out of 526 people originally classified as nonalcoholic by the MAST were found to be alcoholic.

- The MAST correctly identified 92 percent of the ninety-nine respondents hospitalized for severe alcohol problems.

Consider the following questions:

1. The MAST classified respondents as either nonalcoholic or alcoholic. How do we know that these classifications are correct? (Think about what you have learned about operationalizing and defining measures.)
2. Should the study report how many people who were classified as alcoholic were actually nonalcoholic?
3. Does administering a survey to hospitalized alcoholics influence the findings?

So how do we establish validity? There are several types of validity: face validity, content validity, criterion-related validity, concurrent validity, and construct validity.

Face Validity

Face validity refers to whether a measure seems to make sense (i.e., be valid) at a glance. When a student asks another student to look over a paper to see whether his or her answers appear to be correct, the student is requesting a review of the face value of the paper. However, when the paper is evaluated by the standards of the instructor and the overall performance of the other students on their papers (the norm), the comments the student receives from the instructor may differ from those he or she received from the student who looked only at the face value of the paper. Therefore, caution must be taken when one is determining the validity of research based on the face value of what is presented. In fact, many researchers do not consider face validity a useful form of validity, and face validity should never be the only form of validity used to validate a measure.

The following are some issues that you can look for when you are examining the face value of a measurement tool:

- *Forced generalities*—These are questions that force a respondent to make generalizations. An example would be "Do you trust people in your community?" A yes answer implies blanket trust in everyone in the community.

- *Inapplicable items*—Some items do not apply to all people or their situations. For instance, the question "Are you close to your father?" implies that everyone has a living father.
- *Double-barreled questions*—A variable that asks two questions but only allows for one reply is a double-barreled question—for example, "On a scale from 1 to 5, how would you rate your satisfaction with your supervisor and colleagues?" In this situation, respondents may be happy with their supervisor but not with their colleagues.
- *Unclear items*—An unclear item may lead to responses that are unintended because the question was misunderstood. An example would be asking, "Do you visit your adviser regularly?" The interpretation of "regularly" is different for each respondent.
- *Leading questions*—A leading question is one that tries to lead a respondent to a particular response; for instance, "With the rising popularity of violent video games, do you think there should be mandatory ratings for children?"
- *Overdemanding recall questions*—"Have you been sent to the principal's office in the last week?" is a question that demands less recall than "How many times have you been sent to the principal's office in your lifetime?"

Content Validity

Content validity refers to how well the items in a measurement represent the concept that is being measured. For example, going back to the issue of conceptualizing child maltreatment, by reviewing the child maltreatment literature, a researcher developing a tool to measure child maltreatment would find that the measure would need to include the commonly identified types of both abuse and neglect.

As with face validity, there can be difficulties in relying solely on content validity. Experts may disagree about the range of content provided in a measure. For example, a scale measuring obsessive-compulsive disorder (OCD) that asked, "Do you have great difficulty discarding things even when they have no practical value?" would pose problems if experts do not agree that the item is representative of the concept of OCD. In this instance, while hoarding behavior can be related to OCD, many people without OCD hang on to items that they never use.

Criterion-Related Validity

Criterion-related validity refers to a measure's ability to make accurate predictions, and it is also referred to as predictive validity The name *predictive* comes from the fact that this form of validity is derived from how well the measure predicts an outside criterion. For instance, how well SAT scores predict college grades is an indication of the SAT's criterion validity. As another example, a scale measuring students' satisfaction with their educational experience at a university could be compared to how many incoming students stay at that university (graduation rate). In this case, student satisfaction predicts the criterion (graduation). This type of validity is difficult to establish because researchers may not be able to gain access to the criterion, such as the specific course grades or graduation rates of the sample.

Concurrent Validity

Concurrent validity refers to how well a measure correlates with some other measure of the same variable that is believed to be valid. For instance, if a researcher designed a survey to measure depression, he or she could compare it to another measure of depression to see whether they predict the same outcome. For example, if an instrument measuring the concept of job satisfaction gives results that are similar to those given by a job satisfaction instrument that has already been validated, the new measurement has concurrent validity. Therefore, when concurrent validity is being measured, the two measures are taken at the same time. This is different from measuring predictive validity, where one measure (e.g., a measure of job satisfaction) is meant to predict responses to a measure that is administered at a later time (e.g., a measure of job retention).

Construct Validity

Construct validity refers to the extent to which the items of an instrument accurately sample a construct. A **construct** is the concept or the characteristic that an instrument is designed to measure. Whereas measures of content validity ask whether an instrument measures the full range of possibilities within a concept (e.g., alcoholism), construct validity is the degree to which an instrument actually reflects the construct being measured. In other words, with content validity we are determining whether the instrument includes the items (content) that can accurately operationalize a concept, and with construct validity we are determining whether the overall instrument was constructed to measure a single concept such as alcoholism, and not OCD or social isolation. This type of validation is commonly used in social research when there is no existing criterion for validation purposes. There are two subtypes of construct validity, convergent validity and discriminant validity.

Convergent validity refers to how well the measures of a construct (e.g., depression or alcoholism) that you expect to be related to each other are indeed found to correspond to each other (measure the same construct). Conversely, **discriminant validity** refers to the situation when the measures of a construct that you would not expect to be related are indeed measuring different constructs.

Case Scenario

You have a part-time job during the summer working at a summer camp with adolescents who range in age from thirteen to sixteen. You have noticed that those teenagers who are active in sports in school tend to feel better about themselves, have more self-confidence, and in general are happier in life. You decide to test out your beliefs by developing a survey to distribute to the various attendees at the camp. You ask several demographic questions, including gender (male or female), age, and ethnicity. You ask as an independent variable their participation in school sports ("Do you participate in any organized sport at school?" with yes or no as possible responses). You also ask about the following dependent variables: "On the whole I am happy with myself," "Overall, I am a worthwhile person," "I am generally satisfied with who I am," and others. Each of these questions has a response of 1 (strongly disagree) to 5 (strongly agree) with categories in between of "agree," "neutral," and the like.

Critical-Thinking Questions

1. On which level are you measuring your independent variable?

2. On which level are you measuring your dependent variable?

3. Are you utilizing a standardized measure for your dependent variable? Why or why not?

4. Does your dependent variable have validity? How can you be sure of your answer?

Key Points

· Variables can be categorized into three groups: independent variables, dependent variables, and control variables.

- The dependent variable is predicted by another variable, or is said to depend on the independent variable.

- The independent variable is often thought of as a variable that is manipulated by the researcher.

- Conceptualizing a variable refers to how we translate an idea or abstract theory into variables that can be used to test hypotheses or make sense of observations.

- A control variable is any variable that the researcher wants to hold constant (control for).

- A confounding variable obscures the effect of another variable.

- A measure is a tool or instrument that is used to gather data.

- There are four levels of variables: nominal-level variables, ordinal-level variables, interval-level variables, and ratio-level variables.

- The term *operationalize* refers to how we define a concept so that it can be measured.

- Reliability refers to the ability of a measure to remain stable and consistent over time.

- Validity is a term that describes how much the instrument measures what it is meant to measure.

- There are several types of validity: face validity, content validity, criterion-related validity, concurrent validity, and construct validity.

Practice Exam

Multiple Choice

1. An independent variable is said to be:

    a. The variable that is predicted by another variable

    b. The variable that predicts a change in another variable

    c. A variable that stands alone (independent) of the other variables

    d. All of the above

    e. None of the above

2. A dependent variable is said to be:

  a. The variable that is predicted by another variable

  b. The variable that predicts a change in another variable

  c. A variable that stands alone (independent) of the other variables

  d. All of the above

  e. None of the above

3. In quantitative research, the literature review is:

  a. Used to support the hypothesis

  b. Used to reject the hypothesis

  c. Used to shape the hypothesis

  d. None of the above

Identify the Independent and Dependent Variables

4. Fathers who participate in classes to increase empathy are less likely to inflict physical injury on their children than fathers who don't participate.

5. Patients who jump rope a minimum of thirty minutes each day will be less depressed than those who do not jump rope.

6. Police officers who witness domestic violence are more likely to be in favor of mandatory jail sentences for perpetrators of domestic violence than those police officers who do not witness domestic violence.

7. Students who take the course Research Methods are more likely to correctly identify independent and dependent variables than those who do not take the class.

8. Adolescents who are prescribed medication for attention-deficit disorder are more likely to abuse stimulant drugs.

CHAPTER FIVE

Sampling

CSWE Core Competencies

IN THIS CHAPTER you will find the following Council on Social Work Education (CSWE) competencies:

Educational Policy 2.1.3—Apply critical thinking to inform and communicate professional judgments

Educational Policy 2.1.6—Engage in research-informed practice and practice-informed research

Educational Policy 2.1.9—Respond to contexts that shape practice

Educational Policy 2.1.10(b)—Assessment

So far, this book has mostly addressed the planning stages of research. Now we will move into the stage of choosing which variables to observe and gathering data. In this chapter, we investigate the issue of sampling. This chapter looks at different sample options and examines which ones are more or less likely to offer an adequate representation of a population. We discuss sample size, two types of sampling—probability and nonprobability—and several techniques for sample selection.

What Is Sampling?

One of the goals of research is to draw conclusions from a sample of observed cases in a population. In research, a population is a set of entities from which a sample can be drawn either to describe a subsection of that population or to generalize information to the larger population. Within a population there are individual members, called **elements**. In most studies it is impossible to study all pertinent cases in a population, so we must choose a sample of the elements within the population. For example, it is not possible to study every case of binge drinking on every U.S. college campus or even on a single campus. When we select a subset from a population, that group is referred to as a sample. Sampling allows the researcher to make the best use of time, money, and other resources.

A **sample** is a group of elements selected from a larger population in the hope that studying the smaller group will reveal important things about the group and may represent the larger population of that group. Sampling, then, is the process of selecting elements from which observations will be made. People do this every day; students take their first social work class and imagine what the rest of their social work classes will be like. Or you might meet a victim of domestic violence and make generalizations about other instances of domestic violence or domestic violence victims. Although people sample daily, they rarely think about good and bad sample experiences and can therefore come to inaccurate conclusions.

Social and behavioral sciences research is often conducted on individuals or groups (e.g., hospitals, schools, families). A **sampling frame** is a list of all elements or other units containing the elements in a population. For example, we want to survey all the students living in a dorm about the quality of food on campus, but we can obtain only a list of the rooms (not the residents) in the dorm. Therefore, we will draw our sample from the dorm rooms, which are called enumeration units, as opposed to the individual students in each dorm room, who are the elements. An **enumeration unit** contains one or more units to be listed in the sampling frame.

There are times when the researcher samples different elements within a sampling frame. For instance, we could sample the dorm rooms about the quality of food at the university and then sample individual students on campus about the quality of the food. Both the dorm rooms and the individual students would be sampling units. A **sampling unit** is a population selected for inclusion within a sampling frame. The dorm rooms are selected in the first stage of sampling and become the primary sampling units (they are also the elements in the study). The general student population becomes the secondary sampling units because they are not necessarily elements of the study, since some students do not reside on campus.

Random Selection and Random Assignment

Researchers can derive a sample using **random selection**, a means of selecting a sample from a larger population in which each member of the population has an equal chance of being selected for a study, or **random** assignment, the selection and placement of individuals from the pool of all potential participants to either the experimental group or the control group.

For example, let's say you want to know if studying in a group results in a better grade in research classes than studying individually. There are four sections of a research class offered this semester. Ideally, you would want to survey all the students in those classes, but for the purpose of this example, you randomly select half of them from the class rosters (e.g., every other person on the roster lists). This is random selection. Then, you randomly assign members into one of two groups (perhaps by drawing names out of a hat). One group (the experimental group) studies together, and the members of the other group (the control group) study on their own. This is random assignment.

Sample Size—How Many Is Enough?

As researchers, we need to be confident that our sample is representative of the population from which it was drawn. Representativeness is assumed when characteristics of the sample are similar to those of the population from which the sample was drawn. There are several ways that we can ensure representativeness. One of the easiest ways is to have a large-enough sample. We know that a very small sample can be misleading. For example, interviewing three survivors of Hurricane Katrina about their intent to return and rebuild their home might reveal that all three do not plan to return to their hometown; however, a larger sample may reveal that although some report no intention of returning, many more plan to return and rebuild. Unfortunately, there are no hard-and-fast formulas to use to determine the appropriate sample size. There are, however, some guidelines that you can use. One technique that is widely utilized (and has gained widespread acceptance) is simply counting the number of variables in your study and then selecting a certain number of cases for each variable. Different researchers have different opinions on what that number of cases should be, but most people agree that between ten and twenty cases per variable is adequate. Thus, if you had ten variables, you would need a sample size of between one hundred and two hundred subjects. Therefore, for many researchers the challenge is not having a large-enough number of variables in the study but recruiting enough subjects to participate.

External and Internal Validity

One goal of many research studies is to apply findings beyond the group from which they were drawn. For example, you study the activities of gang members in one city to try to understand gang activity in all cities. This makes sampling an important process in conducting research. **External validity** (sometimes referred to as *generalizability*) is the extent to which a study's findings are applicable or relevant to a group outside the study (often the population from which the sample was drawn). The more that a study can be generalized to a larger population, the more external validity the study has. **Internal validity**, in its simplest form, refers to how confident the researcher can be about the independent variable (as opposed to outside influences) truly causing a change in the dependent variable.

External Validity

External validity cannot be quantified in terms of a specific set of guidelines. However, it can be evaluated in light of several characteristics. One characteristic is whether the study is explained in enough detail that other researchers could duplicate the study if they wished. The more a study can be replicated, the more external validity it assumes. Two other characteristics of external validity are related to how the sampling was conducted: how the respondents of the measure were chosen and the size of the sample.

Internal Validity

Internal validity is different from the validity of a measure. Internal validity is a measure of the worth of the overall research design. It exists when a conclusion that A leads to or results in B is correct. When designing your research study, you need to keep in mind the following seven threats to internal validity:

1. *Extraneous and widespread events that coincide in time with your study*—For example, you are working with students in an afterschool program to teach seventh graders social empathy skills during the autumn of 2001. How do you know that the repercussions of 9/11 did not account for some of their increased social empathy?

2. *Maturation or the passage of time*—The passage of time during a study (especially for studies lasting months or years) can have an effect. For example, we know that people commit less crime as they become sick or weak. Therefore, if you were researching crime among older adults, factors associated with age alone may account for a lower incidence of crime in older respondents.

3. *Enhanced test-taking skills*—After taking a test the first time, respondents' performance on subsequent tests often improves. For example, imagine that we are conducting a workshop for consumers in a homeless shelter on effective job-interviewing techniques. We give participants a pretest and then provide a workshop on techniques for effective job interviewing. After the workshop, we give the participants the same test again (posttest). If they scored significantly better on the posttest, we might be tempted to argue that it was the workshop that made the difference. However, we cannot be certain that taking the pretest did not prepare participants to do better on the posttest.

4. *Instrumentation*—If different measures are used for the pretest and posttest, how do we know that the posttest is not easier than the pretest? For example, an easier posttest might inflate the difference in scores and thus affect the findings of the study. In other words, the results may be inaccurately reporting that the intervention was effective. Problems involving instrumentation can also develop when a researcher uses a measure that is not measuring what it is intended to measure or that is not normed for the population to whom it was given.

5. *Selection bias*—Selection bias refers to the differences between groups that are being compared that occur when group members choose which group (treatment or nontreatment group) to be in. The differences between the members of the two groups might explain away any change that occurred after the intervention. For example, participants who self-select into a treatment group dealing with attitudes toward feminism may already be more politically liberal. It is important to make sure that selection bias is eliminated as much as possible through randomization.

6. *Experimental mortality*—This refers to subjects dropping out of a study. This is one of the most common threats to internal validity and can affect sample size (you may not have enough respondents left at the end of the study to have a meaningful finding) and generalizability (your study no longer represents the characteristics of the population your sample came from).

7. *Ambiguity about the direction of causal inference*—To establish causation, the independent variable must precede (cause) the change in the dependent variable. For example, studies looking at substance abuse and mental health issues have established that there is a relationship between the two variables. What is not clear is which variable precedes the other.

One of the best ways to control for threats to internal validity is to use a group for comparison with the study group, which strengthens the study. By having a group to compare against the study group, the researcher can make a stronger argument that any change in the study group is due to the intervention, not to outside influences.

Probability Sampling

In probability sampling, each and every member of the population has a nonzero chance of being selected for the study (i.e., of being included in the sample). That means that every single type of person or thing has a greater-than-zero likelihood of being in a study. Probability sampling allows the researcher to make relatively few observations and generalize from those observations to the wider population. Probability sampling theory requires the researcher to select a set of elements from a population in such a way that those elements accurately portray the parameters of the total population.

Probability Sampling Techniques

There are four types of sampling techniques used in probability sampling: simple random sampling, systematic random sampling, stratified random sampling, and cluster sampling.

In simple random sampling, each person in the population is assigned a number, and then a sample is generated randomly from the population. This technique requires the compilation of a list of everyone in the population, such as all residents in a nursing home. The process for selecting the sample can be as simple as drawing numbers from a hat that will be matched to the names on the list. When drawing a sample from a population, one can return or not return subjects to the sampling space after each draw. Returning a number to the hat after it is drawn is called sampling with replacement and is a preferred method. When one is using sampling with replacement, each selection from the population is independent of the selections already made. For example, if your population at the nursing home had twenty-five individuals (elements) to select from and you were to randomly select individual number 4, that individual would become part of your sample. Then you go back to your original twenty-five elements and draw again, leaving the number 4 as an option. If you draw number 4 again, you return it to the hat and continue to draw until you get a different number to add to your sample. Drawing a sample without returning elements to the hat is called sampling without replacement.

For systematic random sampling, every nth number is selected at random (e.g., every third person, every tenth person). In essence, this is identical to simple random sampling but uses a more organized technique to produce the sample. Here simple random sampling is always used to select the first number. For example, if you want to draw a systematic sample of 1,000 individuals from a student roster containing 100,000 names, you would divide 100,000 by 1,000 to get 100, meaning that you would select every hundredth name on the list. You would start with a randomly selected number between 1 and 100. For example, if you started with the number 47, you would then select the 147th name, the 247th name, the 347th name, and so on.

Stratified random sampling is a method for obtaining a greater degree of representativeness. Remember, probability sampling theory requires the researcher to select a set of elements from a population in such a way that those elements accurately portray the parameters of the total population from which the elements are selected. To do this, you divide your population into subgroups, or strata (e.g., by sex), then you draw the sample from each stratum, using a probabilistic procedure.

Cluster sampling (sometimes referred to as multi-stage sampling) is a method for drawing a sample from a population in two or more stages. This is used when the researcher cannot get a complete list of everyone in the population but can get complete lists within clusters of the population (e.g., the population of a city from a phonebook). In general, the researcher wants to get clusters that are as diverse as possible, whereas in stratified random sampling, the goal is to find subjects who are as similar to one another as possible. Cluster sampling is accomplished through two basic steps: listing and sampling. Listing entails constructing a list of a subset of the population. Sampling occurs within your chosen clusters. The disadvantage of cluster sampling is that each stage of the process increases sampling error. In fact, the margin of error is larger in cluster sampling than in simple random or stratified random sampling. However, you can compensate for this error by increasing the sample size.

Perhaps you are examining child maltreatment reports by grade level in your thirteen-county region. You get a list of the schools for each county (primary cluster list) and identify a random sample of approximately 30 percent from each county (secondary cluster list). See table 5.1 for an example. You will then collect child maltreatment reports by grade level in each identified school. A sample of clusters will best represent all clusters if a large-enough number is selected and if all clusters are very much alike.

TABLE 5.1: EXAMPLE OF CLUSTER CODING BY COUNTY

COUNTY	NUMBER OF ELEMENTARY SCHOOLS IN EACH COUNTY (PRIMARY LIST)	IDENTIFIED SCHOOLS (SECONDARY LIST)
Fargo	6	Jefferson Elementary Jackson Elementary
Bishop	3	Washington Elementary
Johnson	7	Lincoln Elementary Carter Elementary
Sewer	5	Clinton Elementary Bush Elementary
Lake	8	Adams Elementary Buchanan Elementary
Lincoln	10	Johnson Elementary Kennedy Elementary Lincoln Elementary
Norman	2	Roosevelt Elementary
Tulane	6	Reagan Elementary Grant Elementary
Orange	5	Taft Elementary Garfield Elementary
Camargo	5	Fillmore Elementary Harding Elementary
Fisher	9	Hoover Elementary Hayes Elementary Tyler Elementary
Newman	5	Harrison Elementary Wilson Elementary
Angel	5	Nixon Elementary Reagan Elementary

Sampling Error

A **sampling error** is an error that occurs because only part of the population is directly contacted. With any sample, differences are likely to exist between the characteristics of the sampled population and the larger group from which the sample was chosen. Sampling error can be reduced in two ways. First, the larger the sample is, the smaller the sampling error. For instance, a sample size of 10 percent of the population will have less sampling error than a sample size of 5 percent of the population, because more of the original population is represented within the sample. Second, a homogeneous population produces samples with smaller sampling errors than does a heterogeneous population. Stratified random sampling is based on this second method. Rather than selecting your sample from the total population, you ensure that appropriate numbers of elements are drawn from homogeneous subsets of the population. This means that you break the sample into smaller sections with similar qualities such as age, sex, race, and occupation. For example, you want to measure client satisfaction with the services in a large social service agency. You suspect that race is a factor in consumer satisfaction, so you separate your participants according to race and then randomly select an appropriate number from each racial category (proportionate to the number of individuals in the category). For example, if you had one hundred whites and fifty African Americans, you might randomly select twenty whites and ten African Americans (one-fifth of each group) to sample. Again, stratified random sampling is used most often when a simple random sample cannot guarantee enough representation from small subgroups that are important to your study.

Nonprobability Sampling

Social work is often conducted in settings where it is not possible to use random selection of subjects or random assignment to an experimental or comparison group. This occurs for a variety of reasons. Often a list of possible respondents for a particular study does not exist. Also, a researcher is often only able to find subjects who are willing to volunteer for one group (e.g., the treatment group) as opposed to being randomly assigned. Sometimes finding participants willing to join either group can be a problem. So, a second form of sampling is available—**nonprobability sampling**. Any technique for selecting a sample in which every individual does not have a greater-than-zero chance of being selected is a nonprobability sampling technique. There are four sampling techniques used in nonprobability sampling: convenience, purposive, quota, and snowball.

Convenience sampling is sampling in which one relies on available subjects. That is, you get information from any source of data you can. This is one of the most frequently used sampling techniques in social work research. Some examples of researchers who use convenience sampling are a caseworker who studies her own agency, a college professor who studies students at his college, or a researcher who observes people in her own church. This type of sampling limits the generalizability of the research to the population from which the sample is drawn. Another drawback to this method is that it can be subject to sampling error because of researcher bias (selecting the sample that gives the best outcome).

Purposive sampling (also called judgmental sampling) is simply selecting a sample on the basis of one's knowledge of a population or drawing a sample with some predetermined characteristics in mind. For example, perhaps you are a caseworker at an agency that assists consumers in obtaining assistance with paying utility bills. You need to do a study for a grant that would help quantify the characteristics of your participants (e.g., whether they rent or own their homes, whether they are employed, education level, income level). Because your study must be completed soon and it is the middle of a cold winter, you decide to select those individuals who are requesting assistance for electric bills. You feel that individuals who seek assistance for electric bills reflect the majority of your clientele, as opposed to clients who seek assistance with telephone payments.

Quota sampling is a means of selecting a stratified nonrandom sample in which a researcher divides a population into categories and selects a certain number (a quota) of subjects from each category. Individual subjects from each category are not selected randomly; they are usually chosen on the basis of convenience and ease. Imagine that you are studying the treatment of individuals in a mental health setting. You want to see if professionals with different professional training treat clients in different ways. So your sample includes the psychiatrists, psychologists, and social workers who are willing to participate.

In snowball sampling, the researcher starts with one or more members of the group being studied to gain access to other members of the same group, through a referral system, for the purpose of building the sample. Snowball sampling is most appropriate when members of a population are difficult to locate. For example, if you are studying women who have children with disabilities and you are having difficulty locating such mothers, you may find that once you have established a relationship with one mother, she may be willing to introduce you to other women who have children with disabilities. Snowball sampling is also often used when the group being studied is engaged in an activity that is illegal or considered deviant. For example, to study members of a gang, you need referrals to members of the gang. The strength of this type of sampling is that it creates access that allows you to increase the sample. However, because friends and other associates usually have a similar worldview, may engage in similar "illegal" behaviors, and may be similar in terms of demographics, there may be little variation in the study.

Limitations of Nonprobability Sampling

Although nonprobability sampling may be more convenient, it is less likely to be representative of your population than probability sampling techniques. Remember that nonprobability sampling techniques do not require that every member have a greater-than-zero chance of being selected. Your study is affected if individuals not included in your sample differ in some way from the rest of the population. Therefore, a random sample will have more generalizability than a convenience sample or any sample in which subjects are self-selecting. For example, it might be misleading to apply the findings of a researcher who studies gangs only in Southern California to other areas of the United States because of differences in population size and characteristics, gang-related laws, law enforcement capabilities, and gang prevention programs. One question to ask is, "How much does the sample reflect the population from which it was drawn?" For obvious reasons, a larger sample size would be more generalizable than a smaller one because the study would be taking into account more of the actual population.

So when is nonprobability sampling most useful? Some examples are pilot studies in which you are doing a trial run, agency-based research, and qualitative investigations in which you are striving not for generalizability but rather to reproduce and understand real life.

Case Scenario

As part of your research class assignment, you and three of your fellow students have been assigned to work together in a group. You have been given the task of finding out whether there is any relationship between how much alcohol students consume on weekends and their choice of academic major. To determine this relationship, you and your group members wait outside one of the residence halls on campus, and as students enter and leave the building, you ask whether they would be willing to complete your survey.

Critical-Thinking Questions

On the basis of the case scenario, answer the following questions:

1. What type of sampling design would you and your group members be utilizing?

2. Would you consider your sampling to be probability or nonprobability? State your reasons for your answer.

3. What would you consider to be an adequate sample size? How did you arrive at that number?

Key Points

- Sampling is the process of selecting a group of subjects from a larger population in the hope that studying this smaller group (the sample) will reveal important things about the larger group (the population) from which it was drawn.

- Probability sampling is a method of sampling in which everyone in the population has an equal chance of being randomly selected for the study and randomly assigned to either the experimental group or the comparison group.

- There are four techniques for conducting probability sampling: simple random sampling, systematic random sampling, stratified random sampling, and cluster sampling.

- Nonprobability sampling is a method for selecting a sample whereby every member does not necessarily have a greater-than-zero chance of being selected.

- There are four techniques for conducting nonprobability sampling: convenience, purposive, quota, and snowball sampling.

- Internal validity refers to how confident the researcher can be about the independent variable truly causing a change in the dependent variable. There are seven threats to internal validity: extraneous events, passage of time, testing effect, instrumentation problems, selection bias, mortality of sample, and lack of causal direction.

- External validity (referred to as generalizability) is the extent to which a study's findings are applicable or relevant to a group outside the study. Characteristics of external validity include the possibility to be duplicated by other researchers, how the respondents of the measure were chosen, and the size of the sample.

Practice Exam

True or False

1. In research, a population is a set of entities from which a sample can be drawn to either describe a subsection of that population or generalize information to the larger population.

2. Probability sampling means that there is a high probability that someone will be selected for a study.

3. A random sample will be more generalizable than a convenience sample or any sample in which subjects are self-selecting.

Multiple Choice

4. Selecting subjects on the basis of predetermined criteria is known as:

   a. Quota sampling

   b. Probability sampling

   c. Sampling frame

   d. Sampling error

   e. None of the above

5. External validity is also known as:

   a. Reference sampling

   b. Generalizability

   c. Sampling error

   d. Criterion validity

   e. None of the above

6. There are four techniques for conducting nonprobability sampling:

   a. Convenience, purposive, quota, and snowball sampling

   b. Confrontational, purposeful, snowball, and external

   c. Random, obtrusive, intrusive, and personable

   d. None of the above

7. Snowball sampling is useful when:

   a. A researcher doesn't know what else to do

   b. A researcher is investigating hidden or illegal activity

   c. A researcher wants to remain anonymous

   d. A researcher is new in town

   e. None of the above

8. "Convenience sample" means:

   a. The researcher doesn't want people to know that they are involved in the research process

   b. The researcher doesn't have time to collect the data him- or herself

   c. The researcher is using who he or she has access to

   d. The researcher is afraid subjects will not be truthful with answers if they know who is collecting data

   e. None of the above

CHAPTER SIX

Qualitative Research Designs

CSWE Core Competencies

IN THIS CHAPTER you will find the following Council on Social Work Education (CSWE) competencies:

Educational Policy 2.1.3—Apply critical thinking to inform and communicate professional judgments

Educational Policy 2.1.6—Engage in research-informed practice and practice-informed research

Educational Policy 2.1.9—Respond to contexts that shape practice

Educational Policy 2.1.10(b)—Assessment

As we discussed in chapter 1, research studies use either qualitative or quantitative methods, or a combination of both methods. The type of research you choose is governed mostly by the research questions that are posed. For example, a social worker may meet someone who is a child-welfare worker and begin to ask questions such as "How did you become a child welfare worker?" or "What is it like for you to investigate a child abuse case?" These exploratory questions may lend themselves to a qualitative study because little is known about the experiences of child-welfare workers. In this chapter we examine the fundamentals of qualitative research. We discuss what qualitative research means and how it is conducted, and some basic strategies for conducting a qualitative research study.

How Is Qualitative Research Used?

Qualitative research is used if little or nothing is known about a subject. To develop a greater understanding of an issue, we need to use methods that allow us to investigate a phenomenon through the use of researcher observation and assessment. All research methods are equally useful and very necessary; however, they utilize different strategies and ask different research questions to gain knowledge. Two strategies that qualitative researchers use are describing the information collected (descriptive inquiry) and speculating on the information collected (speculative inquiry).

Descriptive Inquiry

Descriptive inquiry is the strategy used in qualitative research to develop a greater understanding of issues by describing individual experiences. For instance, some research examines issues related to lifestyle, such as Sinetar's *Ordinary People as Monks and Mystics: Lifestyles for Self-Discovery* (1986), which describes the quest of many people to find spiritual meaning in a materialistic universe. Other qualitative research may build on existing knowledge, such as Barton's *Stripped: Inside the Lives of Exotic Dancers* (2006), in which the author uses the participants' experiences to engage long-standing debates over the meanings of femininity and sexuality. These studies distinguish themselves by examining symbolic understandings through the words of the informants. These studies might typify respondents' attitudes, but they often address patterns in the samples. In both of these cases, the researchers are exploring the individual level of understanding (how each individual describes his or her experiences) as well as the collective level of understanding (what is common and not common about the experiences).

Social workers frequently use the strategy of descriptive inquiry in agency practice. For instance, in documentation it is valuable to record the client's statements ("I am always tired, and I cry easily") as evidence to support an impression (the client is depressed). Client assessments are the recorded descriptions of clients' statements as well as social workers' observations and impressions. Soliciting feedback, such as clients' verbal and written comments, is another important source of descriptive inquiry. Two ways to get verbal comments from clients are to interview them individually or to hold a focus group. A **focus group** is an open discussion in which individuals share their opinions about or emotional responses to a particular subject. For instance, a focus group can be used to gain information on what residents think about the current living conditions at a shelter. This information can be used to get a better understanding of their experiences or to meet the individual needs of residents, for example, by installing a sliding shower head for a resident who is very tall or very short. Researchers at a shelter might collect written information by asking residents to journal their thoughts, feelings, and experiences or by implementing a system that allows residents to offer written comments, like a comment box.

It is not uncommon for agencies to use data collected from assessments and from consumers' feedback to describe the issues related to the population they serve in reports to boards of directors and in presentations to the public. These reports and presentations create a greater understanding of clients' experiences and empathy for them among others who have never had the experiences themselves. This can also provide knowledge that is useful in supporting a request for a program or resources from grant-funding sources to improve the lives of clients.

Qualitative researchers want to discover more about the interactions between people and their environment. They want to gain an in-depth understanding of what a person is feeling, thinking, and experiencing. For example, people who want to fully understand the perspectives of someone addicted to gambling can learn a great deal by reading an addict's comments on the many lures of the games. It is not important to be able to make generalizations to all people, just to know what a particular person is experiencing.

Speculative Inquiry

In qualitative studies, data analysis is a process of **speculative inquiry**, in which the collected information is used to generate common themes. For instance, we might ask, "What has this been like for you?" As we ask several different participants the same question, we can begin to review their answers to see whether any common themes emerge; that is, we can see whether people say similar things about the same topic. This inductive method of going from the individual to the collective can lead us to generate new hypotheses and theories based on the knowledge we have gained.

The process of speculative inquiry is a form of **inductive research**, which is the gathering of information on the basis of observations and quotes that are organized into common themes. As more information is acquired, we increase our understanding and can develop research questions about the phenomenon at hand. **Deductive research** is the process of reasoning that moves from a general hypothesis or theory to specific results through the use of quantitative methods.

Qualitative Research Methods

A discussion of qualitative research needs to begin with the various types of qualitative designs. Essentially, there are five main research designs in qualitative research: ethnography, grounded theory, phenomenological study, case study, and biography. Biography is based on a single person's life reflections and is not widely used in social and behavioral sciences research. For that reason we confine our discussion to the four other designs. Whereas phenomenology uses descriptive inquiry as a strategy for understanding and grounded theory uses speculative inquiry, ethnography and case study use both descriptive and speculative inquiry strategies. At times, it may seem that some of the designs overlap and duplicate others. We try to make these distinctions as clear as possible.

Phenomenological Design

Phenomenology is a type of research design that seeks to understand the lived experience of the individuals who are being studied (i.e., their perceptions, thoughts, ideas, and experiences). Phenomenological research, in some ways, embodies the field of qualitative research because it is concerned with gaining an in-depth understanding of the experience of the individual under study. Phenomenological research uses descriptive inquiry. Sometimes researchers become research participants themselves to gain firsthand knowledge. When researchers employ this technique, they make no attempt to be detached; rather, they immerse themselves in the experience. They then rely on their own interpretation of the experience (i.e., they use introspection) to make sense of what they experienced. This is called participatory research.

Perhaps you are working in an agency where many of your clients are referred for welfare assistance and you want to be able to explain what they can expect when they apply. You could conduct a study in which you make an appointment at the local public assistance office and go through the process of applying for public assistance. At each step of the process, you would keep careful notes of your experiences, feelings, and reactions. You would encounter others going through the process and could gather information from their comments. You then could use this experience to share with clients what it was like for you to experience the application process for welfare assistance. This would be an example of a descriptive inquiry as part of a phenomenological study.

Grounded Theory Design

Grounded theory is a type of research design that utilizes a recursive form of question and analysis. The researcher begins with a set of questions often referred to as **grand-tour questions**. These are large, overarching questions that identify the broad intent of a research study and are based on the existing knowledge (e.g., experience, knowledge from others, tradition, prior research). The questions or requests are open ended, for example, "Describe for me what it was like for you," and "What was it like for you?" In the interviews, the researcher collects the information from participants. A review of the information often leads to more specific questions, thus resulting in a speculative inquiry.

In social work practice grounded theory is used to identify primary issues or problems. For example, often a family will seek help only after bearing the burden of a problem for a long period of time. By that time, many more problems and issues have emerged, and it is difficult to identify the primary or precipitating issues. Therefore, you start out by asking a broad, open-ended question, such as "What brings you here today?" You listen to a plethora of concerns and then ask for something more specific, for example, "What would you say are your top three concerns?" This leads to more specific questions, such as "What have you done in the past to get relief?" and "Have you experienced this problem before?" After collecting enough answers from family members and adding your own observations and practice experience, you can develop common themes to use to identify the primary or precipitating problems (going from specific to general).

Ethnographic Design

Ethnography is a research design centered on cultural behavior. Ethnographic research seeks to record the cultural aspects of a group (including such aspects as language, dress, social norms, and behaviors). It is concerned with the organization of society and the study of humans. Ethnography uses both descriptive and speculative inquiry to advance understanding.

An ethnographic design might be useful in work with subcultures, such as teen gangs. A social worker working with gang members would want to find out as much as possible about the culture of various gangs—for instance, colors, gang signs, and common clothing; how members are initiated into the gangs and how they can get out; which gangs are rivals; and which gangs use violence. These are important cultural questions that can be explored to help social workers studying gang-related practices. Trial and error shapes and reshapes many cultural practices, which makes it difficult for members of a group to identify, describe, or define what they do. Rules are sometimes more implicit than explicit. Thus, ethnography relies as much on observations as on interviews.

Case Study

A **case study** is a detailed analysis of a single person or event (or sometimes a limited number of people or events). Case studies are interesting because of the uniqueness of the case under study. This creates a limitation because the case is not representative of other cases. The data you collect from a former foster child living in a rural area whose foster parents paid no attention to her might be similar to other foster children in the same situation, but they might not accurately reflect the experiences of foster children from urban areas or more attentive families. Another problem with case studies has to do with objectivity. The person who is presenting the case usually has some preconceived bias (opinion based on knowledge from his or her own experiences, knowledge of the experiences of others, or tradition). Otherwise, why choose to study this particular case? However, it is acceptable in case studies for a bias to play a role in the interpretation of events and the selection of the facts to include in the case.

Let's say that you are a mother of twins and that you want to do a case study of one mother with twins and her weekly routine. While collecting information (observations and comments), you use your own experience to interpret what is happening. For instance, while one twin is talking to her mother, the mother is giving the other one a forbidden cookie. Some people may interpret this as a mother not being able to be in two places at once. However, as a mother of twins, you have experienced similar scenarios that have led you to believe that the twins might be working together to reach a goal. The following are some types of case studies.

Illustrative Case Studies

Illustrative case studies describe a domain; they use one or two instances to analyze a situation. This helps researchers interpret other data, especially when they have reason to believe that readers know too little about the study parameters. Illustrative case studies serve to make the unfamiliar familiar and to give readers a common language to use to discuss a topic. The chosen site for inclusion should typify important variations and contain a small number of cases to sustain readers' interest. The use of illustrative case studies may involve some pitfalls. Such studies require presentation of in-depth information on each case, but the researcher may lack time on-site for in-depth examination. In addition, in may be difficult to hold the interest of those being interviewed in order to gain the in-depth information desired. The most serious problem involves the selection of instances. Cases must adequately represent the situation or program under study. For instance, a researcher wanting to illustrate the role of a foster parent would not want to select only new parents to observe or interview, as the participants in the study would not provide enough in-depth information on what this role entails.

Exploratory Case Studies

Exploratory (or pilot) case studies can be conducted before the implementation of a large-scale investigation. For instance, where considerable uncertainty exists about a program's mission, goals, and services, an exploratory case study can help researchers identify questions, select measurement samples, and develop measurement tools. The greatest pitfall in the exploratory study involves premature conclusions: the findings may seem convincing enough, but they are inappropriate for release as conclusions. For instance, an exploratory study soliciting workers' opinions regarding clients' failure to show up for appointments might lead to conclusions that clients are not motivated, that the client-worker relationship was never formed, or that the worker was overburdened with cases and could not devote the time necessary to the client. However, if the study solicited clients' opinions, the results might show that lack of transportation, lack of available child care, and lack of money to purchase gas or pay for child care are predominant factors in no-show rates. Other pitfalls include researchers' tendencies to extend the study beyond the point of gaining new information and inadequate representation of diversity in the study.

Critical-Instance Case Studies

Critical-instance case studies examine one or a few sites for one of two purposes. For instance, a researcher might want to observe the roles of social workers and patients in an emergency room. A very common application involves the examination of a situation of unique interest in which the researchers have little or no interest in generalizability. In the case of emergency room observations, the purpose might be to examine the interactions between social workers and families when a patient has died. A second, rarer application entails calling into question a generalized or universal assertion and testing it by examining one instance. Again, in the emergency room scenario, this could involve testing a specific crisis intervention technique that social workers use with families when a patient has died. This method is particularly useful for answering cause-and-effect questions about the instance of concern (e.g., Does the crisis intervention technique reduce the effects of the crisis as intended?). Inadequate identification of the evaluation question is the most serious pitfall in this type of study. Correct application of the critical-instance case study involves recognizing the underlying concerns. In the emergency room scenario, studying a crisis intervention technique used with a family whose member died in a car accident would be a correct application, whereas grief counseling would be a better technique for a family who has prepared for the death of a family member who died from a long-term illness.

Program-Effects Case Studies

Program-effects case studies can determine the impact of programs and make inferences about reasons for success or failure. Data rely on observations and/or structured materials, which are often gathered through mixed-method research designs. In this type of case study, the researcher uses multiple sites to investigate why things happen and the cause of the problem. The program-effects case study uses predetermined themes, and findings are usually thematic and describe site differences. Pitfalls include failure to collect enough data, failure to examine a diverse number of sites, insufficient training of evaluators, and difficulties in giving evaluators enough latitude in collecting data to obtain insight without risking bias. One solution to these is to conduct the case studies in a set of sites chosen for representativeness and then verify the findings from the case study through targeted examination of administrative data, prior reports, or a survey. This type of case study utilizes methods derived from program evaluation that are discussed in chapter 8.

Prospective Case Studies

In a prospective case study, the researcher formulates a set of theory-based questions in relation to a social or cultural issue under review and then examines these questions at a predetermined follow-up time by using pattern matching or a similar technique to examine observed outcomes in light of the questions that were formulated at the beginning of the study. This type of study usually involves taking a cohort of subjects and watching them over a long period. For instance, you hypothesize that the longer a foster child stays in a foster home, the fewer behavioral problems he or she will exhibit. Therefore, you observe the behaviors of a foster child in care over several months. This type of case study predominantly uses quantitative methods.

Cumulative Case Studies

Cumulative case studies bring together the findings from case studies done at different times. In contrast to the program-effects case study, the cumulative case study aggregates information from several sites collected at different times and even over quite extended periods. The techniques for ensuring sufficient comparability and quality and for aggregating the information are what constitute the "cumulative" part of the methodology. The cumulative case study can have a retrospective focus, in which information across previous studies is collected. For instance, this can be useful for examining types of interventions used with a particular behavioral problem to identify best-practice outcomes. Or a cumulative case study can have a prospective outlook, including a design that features a series of investigations for different times in the future.

Narrative Case Studies

Narrative case studies present findings in a narrative format. This involves presenting the case study as events are unfolding. For instance, a narrative case study can relay the events that occur when an individual discovers that he or she was adopted, by reporting the comments that are made during the discovery process. This can include comments as the person finds each new family member (e.g., mother, brother, sister). While the findings cannot be generalized, they can be used to identify issues confronting the individual during the discovery process, and that knowledge might be beneficial to other individuals going through the same thing or to professionals working with these individuals.

Data Collection

Once you have created a working research question and selected a design, the next step is to begin developing the data collection method. Two of the most common ways data can be collected are through observation and through interviews.

Observations

Observations are used to describe the behavior of individuals or groups in their natural settings. Researchers must choose whether to identify themselves as researchers and explain the purpose of their observation. For instance, in one study, a researcher lived in a slum district of Boston to observe first- and second-generation immigrants from Italy (Whyte, 1955). This is called overt observational research. The problem with this approach is that, unless the observation is unobtrusive, there may be some subject reactivity. In other words, subjects tend to modify their behavior when they know they are being watched. They portray their ideal selves rather than their true selves. The issue of reactivity is especially problematic if those being watched are engaged in a behavior that is illegal or considered unacceptable by others (e.g., cheating on a test, stealing from a parent, breaking the confidentiality of a client). This effect often decreases with time, as after a while the subjects forget they are being observed. This is called habituation.

In covert observational research, the researchers do not identify themselves as researchers. They either mix in with the subjects or observe from a distance. Some famous covert research studies have involved a researcher becoming a maid without revealing her true identity to her employers (Ehrenreich, 2010) and a researcher who checked into a psychiatric facility incognito (Vincent, 2008). The advantages of this approach are that it is not necessary to get the subjects' cooperation, and the researcher's presence will not contaminate subjects' behavior. Some researchers have ethical misgivings about the deceit involved in this approach. Determining whether potential harm to those being observed can occur is an important factor to consider before conducting covert research.

The degree to which researchers involve themselves in the study makes a difference in the quality and amount of data that they will be able to collect. There are four observation roles a researcher can assume:

1. The complete participant is a member of the group being studied and conceals his or her role as a researcher from the group to avoid disrupting normal activity. The disadvantages are that the researcher may lack objectivity; the group members may feel distrustful of the researcher when the research role is revealed; and the ethics of the situation are questionable, since the group members are being deceived.

2. In the participant-as-observer role the researcher is a member of the group being studied, and the group is aware of the research activity. The advantage is that the researcher is a member of the group. This role also has disadvantages, in that there is a trade-off between the depth of the data revealed to the researcher and the level of confidentiality provided to the group for the information they provide.

3. The observer as participant enables the researcher to participate in the group activities as allowed by group members, yet the main role of the researcher is to collect data, and the group being studied is aware of the researcher's observation activities. In this role, the researcher is an observer who is not a member of the

group; he or she is interested in participating only as a means of conducting better observation and thus generating a more complete understanding of the group's activities. This peripheral membership role enables the researcher to observe and interact closely enough with members to establish an insider's identity without participating in those activities that constitute the core of group membership.

4. The complete observer is completely hidden from view while observing or is in plain sight in a public setting, yet those being studied are unaware that they are being observed. In either case, the observation in this stance is unobtrusive and unknown to participants.

Of these four stances, the most ethical approach to observation is the role of the observer as participant, as the researcher's observation activities are known to the group being studied and the researcher's emphasis is on collecting data rather than participating in the observed activity. However, all research roles can be ethically assumed if there is assurance that the potential risks outweigh the benefits for the participants of a study.

Researchers may decide which observational role they assume on the basis of the type of observation required to gain the information they desire. For instance, in descriptive observation, researchers assume that they know nothing, and they observe anything and everything; the disadvantage is that this leads to the collection of information that may or may not be relevant to the study. The second type of observation, focused observation, involves information that is culled from observation and supported by interviews in which participants' insights guide the researcher's decisions about what to observe. The third type of observation is selective observation, in which the researcher focuses on different types of activities to delineate the differences between those activities.

The following are tips for conducting observational research:

- Be unobtrusive in your dress and actions.
- Become familiar with the setting before beginning to collect data.
- Keep your observations short at first to prevent becoming overwhelmed.
- Be honest but not too technical or detailed in explaining to participants what you are doing.
- Use memory tools to remember information, such as remembering keywords or the first and last remarks in conversations, especially if you are recording data after participation takes place.

- Actively observe the details you want to record later, such as the interactions occurring in the setting, including who talks to whom, whose opinions are respected, and how decisions are made. Also observe where participants stand or sit, particularly those with power versus those with less power, or men versus women.
- Keep a running observation record.
- Be tolerant, adaptable, and flexible.

Interviews

The main task in interviewing is to understand the meaning of what the interviewees say. Interviews are particularly useful for getting the story behind participants' experiences; therefore, the interviewer can pursue in-depth information around the topic. In mixed-method research, interviews may be useful as follow-up to questionnaires or other quantitative data collection methods to further investigate participants' responses. In the personal interview, the interviewer works directly with the respondent and is considered a part of the measurement instrument.

The conversational interview has no predetermined questions; this allows the interviewer to remain as open and adaptable as possible to the interviewee's nature and priorities. During the interview, the interviewer "goes with the flow." With the interview-guide approach, interviewers have some basic questions intended to ensure that the information in the same general areas is collected from each interviewee; this provides more focus than the conversational approach but still allows the researchers a degree of freedom and adaptability in getting information from the interviewee. The open-ended interview asks the same open-ended questions of all interviewees; this approach facilitates fast interviews that can be easily analyzed and compared. Finally, the fixed-response interview asks the same questions and requires interviewees to choose answers from among the same set of responses. This format is useful for those not experienced in interviewing.

The interviewer has to be well trained in responding to any contingency. The following are tips for interviewing:

- Be familiar with the topic.
- Choose the setting with the least distraction.
- Explain the purpose of the interview.
- Address terms of confidentiality.
- Outline the procedure of the interview.
- Indicate how long the interview should take.

- Provide the interviewer's contact information.
- Allow the interviewee to ask questions or express doubts about the interview.
- Prepare a method for recording data, such as audio recording or note taking.
- Use simple, easy, and short questions.
- Speak slowly and clearly.
- Be tolerant, sensitive, and patient when the interviewee expresses provocative or unconventional opinions.
- Avoid digressions from the topic.
- Clarify the responses to test the reliability and validity of what the interviewee says.

Finally, make respondents comfortable in the interview as soon as possible by asking for some facts before asking about controversial matters. Intersperse fact-based questions throughout the interview. Ask one question at a time, and ask questions about the present before questions about the past or future. Attempt to remain as neutral as possible, and provide transitions between major topics or when the respondent has digressed from the topic on which you wish to focus. You might formulate the last interview questions to provide any other information that respondents' want to add and their impressions of the interview.

An Example Qualitative Study

Health-care workers have noticed a substantial increase in twin births over the past two years. As a social worker in this field, you are interested in preparing parents to deal with issues unique to rearing twins. To do this, you decide to do research to identify common experiences among mothers of twin children. You discover from a brief literature review that studies related to social work have been published on the issue. So, you begin by selecting a qualitative design. You may decide to select a grounded theory approach, which will allow you to start with some questions that address basic assumptions and expand your questions over time. You begin by developing an outline for completing the study.

Research Outline

You have already chosen the purpose and design of the study; now you can complete an outline for your study. An outline is basically a proposal that addresses the purpose of the study, how you will gain access to subjects, selection of participants (who and how many), protection of subjects' rights, your research questions, and the collection and analysis of information. As you can see in example 6.1, an outline is a carefully laid-out plan for the various parts of the study, with a timeline for completing the study. Thinking through your project is critical; researchers who do so have a better rate of completing their studies successfully and within time constraints.

Interview Questions

The grand-tour question in this study is intended to identify common experiences of mothers who are parents of twins. Thus, your grand tour question will be "What differences have you experienced in your life since having multiple-birth children as opposed to a single-birth child?" In this sample study, you make four assumptions. That is, you expect that participants will discuss issues of personal experiences, financial experiences, family experiences, and social experiences. Therefore, you will ask questions on these topics during the interviews to jump-start the conversation and keep the momentum going. For example:

- "In what ways has being a mother of multiples affected you personally?" (personal experience)
- "In what ways has being a mother of multiples affected your finances?" (financial experience)
- "In what ways has being a mother of multiples affected your family life?" (family experience)
- "In what ways has being a mother of multiples affected your social life?" (social experience)

These initial questions are used to generate additional questions and emergent lines of conversation. This is called a **semistructured interview,** in that you have research questions to start the interview process but will solicit additional information depending on the responses to your initial questions, whereas a **structured interview** is limited to the research questions the researcher brings to the interview.

Gaining Access

The issue of gaining access to subjects is particularly important when conducting qualitative studies. When the sample size is small, having the

EXAMPLE 6.1: MOTHERS OF MULTIPLES: RESEARCH OUTLINE

PURPOSE OF STUDY: To identify common experiences for mothers of twin children

RESEARCH DESIGN: Grounded theory design

GAINING ACCESS: Letter to Mothers of Multiples support group and phone call to president of group

SELECTION CRITERIA OF PARTICIPANTS: Sampling will be by convenience. Participants must:
- be mothers of twins
- have a single-birth child
- have twin children between the ages of three and six
- be able to complete all aspects of study by [date here]

SELECTION AND DESCRIPTION OF SITES:

Individual interviews will be conducted at each participant's home or a public library (participant's choice for comfort). Focus group will be held at either the university or a participant's home, depending on majority preference.

SAMPLE SIZE: 4–10

GRAND TOUR RESEARCH QUESTION: "What differences have you experienced in your life since having multiple-birth children as opposed to a single birth child?"

TIME LINE:
- Recruitment completed by:
- Interviews completed by:
- Focus group completed by:
- Paper completed by:

HUMAN SUBJECTS PROTECTION: See informed consent form—approved by [Instructor's name here].

DATA COLLECTION: Individual interviews will be audiotaped. Participants will edit results of study (to increase credibility).

DATA ANALYSIS: Content comparison for common themes

THEORETICAL FRAMEWORK: Inductive

DEMOGRAPHIC DATA TO COLLECT: Mothers' age, race, education, marital status, age at time of the twins' birth, and employment; whether or not mothers receive public assistance; number of children in the home; weight of twins at birth; whether or not fertility drugs were used to conceive; whether or not mothers want more children; whether or not mothers attend support groups; type of twins (identical or fraternal) opportunity to interview your subjects in depth is of vital importance. This usually means spending several hours talking with each person. As a researcher, it is important for you to spend time thinking about how you may gain access to a particular population. There are several methods for doing this, and you as the researcher have to decide which is best for you. For example:

- You may identify several places where mothers of twins congregate, such as support groups or parenting classes specific to mothers with multiple-birth children (convenience sample).
- You could gather contact information on women who delivered twins from your community fertility clinic, where you could also find subjects for your study (purposeful sample—looking at women who conceived through fertility).
- You might be able to identify someone who is a mother of twins. Once you have established a relationship of trust with her, she may be willing to introduce you to other women who are also mothers of twins (snowball sample).

The bottom line is that the researcher needs to go where the action is (the research site). In this study, you locate a support group called Mothers of Multiples and decide to send a letter to the president of the group to recruit volunteers (see example 6.2).

Selection Criteria

The next step is to decide how many people to interview. Qualitative research is not as concerned with sample size as quantitative research is, but this does not mean that sample size is not important. As a researcher, you will need to include enough people in your sample to gain an in-depth understanding of what parenting is like for mothers of twins. In addition, while the experiences of one or two mothers are unique and valuable, in a grounded theory design you must find common experiences among several women to increase the credibility of your findings. For instance, a mother tells you her twins have opposite personalities. Until you hear it from other mothers of twins, this is only one person's experience. This finding is appropriate for a phenomenological design; however, in a grounded theory design, your goal is to capture the shared experiences of mothers of twins. Therefore, you are hoping to recruit four to ten participants for your study.

In your study, you have chosen four specific criteria for selecting participants. First, you believe that mothers and fathers perceive the parenting

---

EXAMPLE 6.2: MOTHERS OF MULTIPLES: RECRUITMENT LETTER

Dear Mothers of Multiples,

I am a student in the School of Social Work at [name of university]. I am conducting a research project to help describe the experience of mothers raising twins. I am looking for mothers to volunteer to participate in this study and who are available to complete the study process by [date]. The study consists of three parts:

1. A personal interview lasting no more than one hour and consisting of five initial questions, conducted in your home, or at a quiet public place, such as a library (without children)
2. A brief questionnaire asking demographic information (such as your age, age of children, income, race, employment, marital status, education)
3. A group meeting with the other mothers in the study to go over the findings for clarification, additions, and accuracy (about one hour, location to be determined)

I am looking for mothers who have twin children between the ages of three and six years old and have at least one single-birth child in their family. This is so I can capture any differences between the experience of raising multiple-birth children and singletons. I need prospective volunteers to contact me by [date]. Please feel free to spread the word to other mothers who might be interested.

---

experience differently. Therefore, you are interested only in understanding the experience of parenting from a mother's point of view. Second, you want mothers who have a single-birth child in the home because you want to ensure that the experiences they discuss are unique to parents of twins, and not just the experiences of parents in general. For instance, losing sleep and having less personal time are inconveniences that almost every parent experiences. How would someone know whether having twins has caused her to have even less sleep and less personal time unless she can compare it to her experience of parenting a single-birth child? Third, you want mothers of twins who are at the same developmental age. By selecting mothers with twin children between the ages of three and six, you increase the likelihood that the children of your respondents will have had some similar developmental experiences. Finally, you will select only mothers who are available to complete the interviews within the established time frame. This will reduce the likelihood of participants dropping out of the study. For instance, you may contact a volunteer to schedule an interview but find that because she was unaware of the study's timeline, she has planned a vacation for the time during which you will be interviewing your subjects. As a final note, keep in mind that limited availability and strict access requirements are always issues that can shrink a projected sample size.

Ethical Considerations

It is important to keep in mind our discussion of ethics and the ethical considerations raised in chapter 2. In research with people, it is important to safeguard their anonymity and their confidentiality. Although the individuals in your grounded theory study may not be anonymous, they can have the assurance that their personal information will remain confidential.

It is also important that research participants understand their rights as subjects in the study. We strongly suggest that you develop an informed consent form, have it approved by the school's institutional review board, and then have your participants sign the form. You can use example 6.3 for grounded theory research.

Recording Information

Once you have identified the research questions to be asked and have found subjects to participate in your study, the next step is to decide how you will record the information. Some researchers prefer to audiotape their interviews and then transcribe the tapes later. Others prefer to use videotapes to record their subjects' responses. Still others record information in notes or collect information from journals and written comments. Regardless of the format that you decide to use, it is important to remember to protect the confidentiality of the participants in your research.

Analysis

For some researchers, the analysis is the most difficult portion of the qualitative research process. The researcher can end up with pages of notes, and the classification and categorization of so much evidence can lead to confusion, overload, and uncertainty. Therefore, after you have finished collecting information, you will compile the information in a word-processing program (see example 6.4). This provides you with a hard copy of the subjects' spoken words and allows you, the researcher, to begin to analyze what has been said.

You can increase the credibility of the findings by verifying the information you collect. You can clarify individual answers during the interview

---

EXAMPLE 6.3: MOTHERS OF MULTIPLES: INFORMED CONSENT FORM

You are being asked to participate in a research project. This research project is part of the requirements for an undergraduate social work degree at [name of university]. You will be asked to participate in an interview, and as part of this interview you will be asked questions about your experience being a mother of twin children. Your participation will require approximately sixty minutes of your time.

The principal investigator in this research project is [your name], who is currently a student at the [name of university]. **All research projects that are carried out by the investigator are governed by requirements of the university and the federal government.**

There are no reasonable foreseeable risks or discomforts that can occur to you while you participate in this research. You may discontinue your participation at any time.

As part of this research, audiotaping will be utilized to record your statements. By signing this statement, you give the researcher permission to record your conversation. The tapes will be transcribed and then destroyed. Your name will not be used, and in no way will you be identified. Any reference to you will be deleted from the transcript and replaced with a fictitious name.

Your participation is completely voluntary. You will receive no special consideration, reward, or compensation for participating.

[Your name]   or   [Your instructor's name]

Tel.: xxx-xxx-xxxx   Tel.: xxx-xxx-xxxx

_____   _____

Name (please print)   Date

---

by repeating what you heard to ensure accuracy. In your study on twins, the mothers agree to review the narratives collected from their interviews to ensure their accuracy. This is especially helpful when you have taken notes as opposed to using an electronic recording device that captures exact wording.

Literature Review

In the qualitative research design, the literature review is used to shape the study not so much on the basis of what others have found but rather on what others have not explored. Therefore, literature reviews can occur

EXAMPLE 6.4: MOTHERS OF MULTIPLES: INTERVIEWS

PARTICIPANT 1: People stop us all the time. I find myself getting almost ugly with people sometimes. You just can't walk into the store; like at Walmart, people will ask, "Are they twins?" And they try to reach out and touch them. I am trying to teach them not to be too friendly with strangers, and it makes that job really hard. "I am glad it is you and not me"—I hear that a lot. It's not just because I have twins but because I have four kids. Some people will say, "Oh my God, are they all yours?" Others will say, "You're not going to have any more, are you?" I can't believe people have the nerve to say that. What gives people the right to say whatever they feel? I can't believe it. Some people will come up because they have twins in their own family. When my husband is with me he will say, "You don't have to be ugly." Everyone has a comment. I have gotten to the point where I learn not to look at people so I don't encourage contact. One lady walked by and said to her mother, "Come look at the kids!" and called her mother over, and then she said, "That's what I am afraid is going to happen to me." One woman said, "Oh my God, bless your heart." And I said, "Yes, he [God] really has." So, I am having trouble with that; it has been a big adjustment for me.

PARTICIPANT 2: The real big difference is the attention you attract in public. That has been just such a basic thing; it's just everywhere you go, you have to stop and talk. Not everybody, but it seems like it, almost. You can't go anywhere quickly, just because [of] how tedious it is to get everyone in and out, and you have to stop and talk along the way. Everybody says, "Oh, you have your hands full." That's probably the thing I have heard the most. And then, uh, people comment about, uh, they make comments about the four boys, all the time. We get the "double trouble" that you hate, you know. You get that comment all the time. And, uh, "We don't see how you do it." Personal questions: "Are you going to have any more children" and "When are you gonna have a girl?" You know. People ask a lot, right off the bat, "Are they twins?" They're identical. People often ask their names. People ask so much more with twins, I find there is really a fascination with multiple births by just the general public, even though it's more common now than it used to be with fertility drugs and stuff. Still, it is a real fascination with it, um, I never realized that. People often stop to chit-chat, just all sorts of things; people might even stop you in a store and call somebody over to see the twins.

EXAMPLE 6.4: (CONTINUED)

PARTICIPANT 3: It's a parade. You're a spectacle. I have had several people come up and say, "Are they twins?" So, I decided to put them in the same outfit and different colors. When my husband and I are together, we can buy groceries in forty-five minutes. But it takes an hour and a half easy when the twins are with us. Because people stop and say, "Aren't they the cutest kids" and "I always wanted twins," and it goes on and on. When my husband goes with us, he usually takes one of the twins and I take the other. You hear a lot of "I always wanted twins." You hear a lot of family stories. But the thing that irritates me is "Better you than me," and the one that kills me is "Do you have a favorite?" and I always say, "Uh-huh, the one that is not crying." They want to know things like "How much did they weigh?" They think they have the right to know the whole personal history. "Are they identical?" "Are they boys?" And then they ask, "Were you on fertility drugs?" And I say, "And your name is?" People don't normally ask others if they are on drugs, but I get that all the time. But people mostly ask, "Are they twins?" And being president of the Mothers of Multiples Club, when I see someone with twins, I will say, "Oh, how old are the kids?" and that will tell me right away whether or not they are twins.

PARTICIPANT 4: A lot of people comment about the twins at the mall. There is more attention attracted to twins than to single babies. We do have a lot more people stopping us. I am glad for the twins club because it is not that big of a deal. They are all in the same boat.

before and after you have collected information. A review of the literature before a study enables the researcher to determine what general knowledge is available and is not available. In the example study, you discover from a brief literature review that very few studies related to social work have been published on the issue of parenting twins (see example 6.5). This prompted you to do a qualitative study. After you conduct the study, you go back to the literature to research the common themes that were found. In this way, you are adding to any existing knowledge.

Writing the Report

The qualitative researcher is concerned with providing a detailed and accurate description of the subject's experience rather than an objective

---

EXAMPLE 6.5: MOTHERS OF MULTIPLES: LITERATURE REVIEW

The U.S. Department of Health and Human Services reports that for 1996 there were 1,000,750 live births of twins, a 150 percent increase over the past ten years (Kogan et al., 2000). This rapid increase in multiple births is largely due to the use of fertility drugs and better medical interventions (Kiely & Susser, 1992). Multiple-birth children are more prone to health-related risks, such as being born premature, and associated health-related problems can create a large increase in medical costs for the family. This stressor and others associated with parenting fragile multiple-birth newborns are diverse and unmet by health-care professionals. This may be due to a lack of awareness of the needs that exist for these families.

Walton, Collins, and Linney (1994) report that parents of multiple-birth children feel that health caregivers are not aware of the stresses they experience and are unsure how to advise them. Some specific stressors for parents of multiple-birth children noted by Malmstrom and Biale (1990) are sleep deprivation, economic hardship, lack of time for parents to be alone, and lack of in-home help. In addition, Papiernik, Alexander, and Paneth (1990) calculate the cost of multiple births due to extensive perinatal care and a higher rate of handicaps to be ten times greater for twins than for single-birth children. The bottom line is that physicians, social workers, and other caregivers need to understand the special needs of multiple-birth families in order to provide psychosocial services (Bryan, 1997).

---

and dispassionate overview of the findings (as would be expected in a quantitative report). You may spend a great deal of time and energy telling a narrative that will help the reader understand the subject's experiences. In your grounded theory study, you would try to find general themes in all the interviews and use quotes to illustrate those themes in your report. The report is organized to summarize common themes regarding each assumption as well as additional themes that were not presumed. For example, one of the recurring themes in the narrative of each subject in your grounded theory study is the issue of the public's reactions to twins. This may lead you to formulate a new hypothesis that being a mother of twins requires one to have more interactions with others in public than being a mother of single-birth children does. Example 6.6 is an example of a summary of the assumptions concerning social experiences discussed by the mothers of twins.

EXAMPLE 6.6: MOTHERS OF MULTIPLES REPORT

Social experiences were a predominant theme in the study. All four women reported a lack of privacy in public as a result of stranger curiosity. The comments and questions most encountered were "Are they twins?" "You're not having more are you?" and "I'm glad it's you and not me." One mother summed up her frustration concerning public curiosity in this statement: "They want to know things like how much did they weigh. They think they have the right to know the whole personal history."

Another common experience for all four mothers was the additional time it takes in public when they have their twins with them. "You can't go anywhere quickly, just because of how tedious it is to get everyone in and out, and you have to stop and talk along the way"; "We do have a lot more people stopping us"; "People stop us all the time"; and "When my husband and I are together, we can buy groceries in forty-five minutes. But it takes an hour and a half easy when the twins are with us."

The literature reports that families with multiple-birth children suffer economic hardships, medical problems, and multiple stressors. What literature fails to identify are the *specific* stressors and hardships facing these families. In this study, specific information has been captured to help ferret out the unique social struggles these four women experienced.

One recommendation for practice is to educate families about the social impact of twins in public. With the overexposure of quintuplets and sextuplets in the media, the mothers of twins in this study felt their privacy was invaded in public, but they felt neglected in supportive donations such as those seen with families of quintuplets.

If your research outline includes collection of demographic information in addition to narrative data, you will want to compile the data. This information may be useful when you are writing the report. Table 6.1 shows the demographics that were collected for our sample study.

Case Scenario

You are employed as a case manager in an agency that provides monetary assistance, help with utility bills and rent, and other services for indigent clients. Your supervisor has noticed that there has been a dramatic increase in consumers who are illegal immigrants and are employed at a local factory. Your supervisor has charged you with conducting a qualitative study

TABLE 6.1: MOTHERS OF MULTIPLES DEMOGRAPHICS

	MOTHER #1	MOTHER #2	MOTHER #3	MOTHER #4
AGE	33	39	27	36
RACE	White	White	White	White
EDUCATION	3 years college	Bachelor's	High school diploma	Master's
MARITAL STATUS	Married	Married	Married	Married
PUBLIC ASSISTANCE	None	None	WIC	None
EMPLOYMENT	Full time	None	Part time (at home)	None
FAMILY INCOME	$62,000	$120,000	$36,500	$75,000
NUMBER OF CHILDREN IN THE HOME	3	4	4	4
AGE/SEX OF CHILDREN	34mo/male 34mo/male 19mo/male	6yr/female 5yr/male 34mo/male 34mo/male	8yr/female 5yr/male 32mo/male 32mo/male	5yr/male 3yr/male 14mo/male 14mo/male
WEIGHT OF TWINS AT BIRTH	4lbs, 0 oz 4lbs, 10 oz	7lbs, 6 oz 8lbs, 1 oz	6lbs, 13 oz 6lbs, 4 oz	5lbs, ½ oz 5lbs, 14 ½ oz
MOTHER'S AGE WHEN TWINS WERE BORN	29	36	25	35
FERTILITY DRUGS USED WHEN TWINS WERE CONCEIVED	Yes	No	No	No
WANT MORE CHILDREN	No	No	No	Maybe
SUPPORT GROUPS USED	AMOM	AMOM	AMOM Church	AMOM Church PTA
TYPE OF TWINS	Identical	Identical	Identical	Identical

to try to understand more about these clients, why they have chosen to relocate to your area, and how your agency may better serve them.

Critical-Thinking Questions

On the basis of the case scenario, please answer the following questions:

1. What qualitative inquiry method would you employ to conduct your research? Give your reasons for your choice.

2. What sampling technique would you utilize?

3. What would be your sample size?

4. According to the type of inquiry method you would use, how would you report your findings?

Key Points

- The four most common qualitative research designs are ethnography, grounded theory, phenomenology, and case study.

- Ethnographic research designs are centered on cultural behavior and seek to record the cultural aspects of a group.

- Grounded theory is a type of research design that utilizes a recursive form of question and analysis. The researcher begins with a set of questions that lead to further questions and identifies common themes from the individual information collected.

- Phenomenological research designs seek to understand the lived experience of those who are being studied.

- A case study is a detailed analysis of a single or limited number of people or events. A case study can be illustrative, exploratory, a critical instance, program effects, prospective, cumulative, or narrative.

Practice Exam

Multiple Choice

1. Qualitative research techniques are used:

    a. When we want to draw correlations between variables

    b. When we know a great deal about a subject and there is literature to support our findings

    c. When we know very little about a subject or phenomenon

    d. When we are sure about our outcomes and simply want to verify our hypothesis

2. When conducting qualitative studies, the ability to interview a subject in depth:

    a. Is of vital importance

    b. Is of little or no importance

    c. Should not be done, because you might frighten your subject

    d. None of the above

3. Sample size, in qualitative research, is:

    a. Of more importance than in quantitative research

    b. Not considered at all

    c. Of less importance than in quantitative research

    d. None of the above

True or False

4. Ethnographic research designs are centered on cultural behavior.

5. The four most common qualitative research designs are ethnography, grounded theory, phenomenology, and single-subject design.

6. Phenomenological research designs seek to understand the lived experience of those who are being studied.

7. In the qualitative research design, the literature review is used to shape the study not so much on the basis of what others have found but rather on what others have not explored.

8. In research with people, it is important to safeguard their anonymity and their confidentiality.

CHAPTER SEVEN

Quantitative Research Designs

CSWE Core Competencies

IN THIS CHAPTER you will find the following Council on Social Work Education (CSWE) competencies:

Educational Policy 2.1.3—Apply critical thinking to inform and communicate professional judgments

Educational Policy 2.1.6—Engage in research-informed practice and practice-informed research

Educational Policy 2.1.9—Respond to contexts that shape practice

Educational Policy 2.1.10(b)—Assessment

This chapter focuses on the process of conducting quantitative research, or using research designs that attempt to explain the relationship between two or more variables. In this chapter we look at developing a testable hypothesis, the differences between correlation and causation, cross-sectional and longitudinal designs, and group research designs.

Getting Started

We know that all social work research should be subjected to the "so what" rule (So what does this have to do with social work or what is the value to social work?). Provided you can adequately answer this question, you then proceed to the second issue—ethical considerations. In chapter 2, we reviewed ethical considerations, and you may recall there was one overarching principle—all research must be careful to ensure that no harm is done to human subjects. This extends to protecting subjects' anonymity and their confidentiality. Once these considerations have been satisfied, you are ready to proceed with the literature review.

When researchers start their literature review, they must address several questions. These questions are as follows:

1. What is known about the subject? What research has been conducted to date? What has been discovered thus far?

2. What level of knowledge exists? Are we at a level that suggests exploratory studies are needed (because little is known about something)? Or has enough information been acquired that we can draw some tentative conclusions (i.e., conduct descriptive research)?

3. Have enough studies been published that we can begin to postulate research questions about the relationships between variables (i.e., conduct explanatory research)? Moreover, do the studies agree or disagree on how one variable influences another variable or even which variables are important?

Let us assume that after conducting our preliminary literature review and answering these questions, we have discovered that enough information exists for us to design a quantitative research study. As a result of our search of the existing literature, we have been able to develop some tentative research questions. These questions are designed to address a gap in existing knowledge.

Developing a Testable Hypothesis

You may remember from chapter 1 that hypotheses are generally defined as testable statements that predict a relationship between at least two variables. In later chapters we discuss how to test hypotheses, and we examine some statistical methods for determining whether our hypotheses are indeed supported (i.e., whether they can be accepted or rejected). In the meantime, we discuss the issue of establishing research hypotheses for a quantitative study.

When researchers are developing a research hypothesis, they turn to the existing literature. Quantitative research is deductive; that is, it is driven by the findings of other studies (either qualitative or quantitative) and what is already known. You, as a researcher, should not be developing hypothesis statements based on a guess or opinion; rather, you should be guided by what other researchers have found. For instance, some studies have found that people who accept racial stereotyping are less inclined to support increased funding of welfare. With that in mind, you can develop a hypothesis about the relationship between these variables with different sample characteristics (e.g., whether this applies to all races). Then you will read more research to build more hypotheses.

Since numerous factors drive human behavior, each explanatory study can have several independent variables. For example, a married couple may get a divorce because of boredom with each other, fights over money, arguments over how to deal with children or in-laws, or infidelity. If researchers want to examine each of these variables, they should write a hypothesis for each independent variable; for instance, "Couples who bicker over finances are more likely to divorce" and "Divorce occurs more frequently when one of the spouses has a sexual encounter outside the marriage."

What Is Descriptive Research?

The concept of description has a much different meaning in a quantitative design from when it is employed in a qualitative design. Description is used in qualitative or inductive research to help the reader understand the lived experience of people experiencing a phenomenon. Description is used to convey the feeling of being there and to help the reader understand the experience from the person's own perspective. In qualitative research, one of several **nonstandardized methods**, or informal methods of collecting data, such as the use of broad and open-ended questions (recorded for accuracy) or a journal or field notes, may be used to do this.

Descriptive research is used to obtain information concerning the current status of a phenomenon in order to describe variables or conditions in a situation. The quantitative methods that can be used range from correlational studies that describe the relationship between variables and surveys, which are used to describe the status quo (both discussed later in this chapter), to evaluative studies (discussed in chapter 8), which can evaluate specific characteristics of a program within an agency. Quantitative research methods handle descriptive data by systematically recording information that describes characteristics about the population or phenomenon being studied. This may involve the use of standardized methods of data collection, such as surveys in which data are recorded in a quantifiable fashion or are collected from case records.

Correlation versus Causation

When you are conducting quantitative research, you are attempting to determine whether any relationship exists between variables, and if so, what kind. The relationship can be causal (one variable is causing a change in the other), which tends to be difficult to demonstrate, or it can be a **correlational relationship**, in which two (or more) variables are linked. A change in one variable may be associated with some degree of change in the other variable. For example, husbands who embrace traditional gender roles may be more likely to hit their wives than husbands who embrace nontraditional gender roles. Likewise, social work students whose parents are politically active usually find their policy classes more pertinent than do their peers whose parents are not politically active. However, to say that one variable is correlated with another does not mean that one caused the change in the other. When a study finds associations or correlations between its variables, one cannot automatically conclude that the indepen-dent variables produced the change in the dependent variable. A **causal relationship** requires that three conditions be met: (1) the independent variable must come before the dependent variable (known as temporal ordering), (2) the independent and dependent variables must be correlated, and (3) the impact of another variable cannot explain the correlation between the independent and dependent variables. The absence of one of these conditions destroys the chance of causation. Thus, to demonstrate causality, one must show that traditional gender roles affect abuse by themselves and that there are no hidden (confounding) variables. For instance, we must rule out the possibility that other factors such as having an abusive father, working in a male-dominated occupation, and taking classes on domestic violence may also have an effect on spousal abuse. In addition, we must prove temporal ordering—that is, did men embrace traditional gender roles before they hit their wives? It is possible that hus-bands hit their wives before they espoused traditional gender roles and that they began to use the statement "Wives, obey your husbands" after the fact as justification. One truism in research is the axiom "Correlation does not imply causation." The fact that two things are correlated does not mean that one causes the other.

Data Collection

Once you have created a working research hypothesis, the next step is to begin developing the data collection method. Two common methods of collecting quantitative data are through archives and other preexisting data and through surveys.

Archival or Retrospective Research

Archival or retrospective research, sometimes referred to as secondary research, relies on preexisting data or records. This research method often involves content analysis, a qualitative analysis of material in which the content of the data is examined and themes are identified. In quantitative research, researchers use archival research to determine the information they want to collect or what the variables in the study will be.

Perhaps you are a caseworker for Child Protective Services and are interested in conducting a descriptive study of therapeutic foster-care placements during the past twelve months. You would create a sample study employing a quantitative descriptive design from case files over the past twelve months. You would begin by identifying some data that you want to collect, such as each child's age, sex, race, reason for placement (defined as type of maltreatment), length of placement, and placement upon discharge from foster care. These and other variables begin to form the basis of your research to describe therapeutic foster-care placements during the past twelve months.

Cross-Sectional and Longitudinal Designs

A **cross-sectional design** is a research design that looks at a cross-section or subset of a population at one point in time. For example, let's assume that you are conducting a study on the attitudes toward illegal drug use among two groups—one group with members between the ages of sixty-five and seventy, and one group with members between the ages of twenty and twenty-five. You may find that the older group has stronger opinions about drug use and feels that drug use is detrimental to individuals who engage in it. However, one cannot assume that the younger group will have the same attitudes when they are older.

The cross-sectional method of investigation is useful when the research goal is to compare developmental levels of people at various ages or from various backgrounds. Many children at different ages are studied in groups according to their age, and the results on the same sets of measures are compared for the groups. For example, by observing the behavior of groups of children from birth until the age of about fifteen months, one can determine the approximate age at which an infant can be expected to roll over, creep, crawl, pull him- or herself up to a standing position, and walk unaided. If we study a group of one-month-old infants, another group of two-month-olds, and so forth, up to the age of fifteen months, we have a cross-sectional research design.

One must be careful not to infer too much from the results of cross-sectional research designs. For instance, cross-sectional research cannot deal with the issue of temporal ordering. If a researcher finds a correlation between independent and dependent variables in a onetime study, he or she cannot determine which factor precipitated the other. For example, a social worker may find that delinquent teenagers often have delinquent friends. This may be true, but it is impossible to know whether the friends' behaviors motivated the teenagers to engage in illicit activities or whether the teenagers chose only friends who supported their illicit behaviors.

A **longitudinal design** is a research study that follows one cohort over a period of time (usually several years or even decades). Whereas the cross-sectional design looks at one group at one point in time, the longitudinal design is interested in how the same person or group changes over time. Longitudinal research can address issues and support methods in ways that are not possible with traditional cross-sectional approaches. It is particularly valuable in a number of research areas, including the following:

- when the focus is directly on change and the phenomenon being studied is itself inherently longitudinal—for example, the dynamics of poverty, employment instability, social mobility, and changing social attitudes
- when investigating causal processes—for example, the effects of unemployment on mental health or of child poverty on later-life chances of poverty
- when social change is being studied and the researcher needs to separate age, period, and cohort effects
- when establishing the effect of a treatment by following participants involved in an experimental or quasi-experimental design (discussed later) or comparing periods before and after the introduction of public policy such as a ban on smoking in public buildings

For obvious reasons such as cost, time commitment, and the difficulty of tracking a group over time, longitudinal studies are rarely undertaken. Some examples of this research are studies looking at people's attitudes toward rape, marijuana use, and the division of labor in families, all of which have changed over the past fifty years.

Group Research Designs

Social workers practice with a variety of groups in multiple settings. Because research always deals with comparisons of patterns within groups of people or things, researchers must rely on different types of group research designs. There are three major types of group research designs: preexperimental, quasi-experimental, and experimental. Each involves a different type of research, and a researcher's decision of which to use depends on the purpose and resources available.

Preexperimental Designs

Preexperimental research designs can be useful when the research question is fairly simple and it is impossible to set up experimental conditions. Many social scientists rely on this design because they want to study human habits in the setting in which they occur without using a comparison group. That is, rather than taking a person to a structured environment, researchers study people in, for example, the schools, agencies, and places of religious worship where the behavior they are studying actually occurs. In fact, many social scientists believe that this is the best way to study human behavior because these naturalistic approaches allow them to capture information in situations that are closest to real life. But it is important to note that a limitation of this research design is that it may pose many threats to internal validity.

The preexperimental approach is used frequently in social work practice. Let's imagine for a moment that you are offering a class to sixth graders on the effects of alcohol on the body. As a researcher, you can develop the following hypothesis: "Sixth-grade students who attend an alcohol awareness course will increase their knowledge of the effects of alcohol on the body." This is a testable hypothesis; therefore, it is possible to design a study to accept or reject it. Your first task is to develop a lecture that will convey information about alcohol and its effects on the body. Then you explore the factors that may either facilitate or block students' understanding of the material, such as "Is the material age appropriate?" "Will the presentation be too lengthy?" and "Will there be interruptions?" Next, you develop a short quiz to measure the information covered in your presentation. You include in the quiz some questions on factors that may affect the students' learning (i.e., confounding variables). For instance, you may ask the students whether they understood the material, whether they thought the lecture was too short or too long, or whether there were interruptions during the lecture that distracted them. Next, you present the material about drinking and how it affects the body over the course of about forty minutes. At the end of the class period, you give the students the quiz to measure what they have learned. This is a one-group posttest-only design. In research notation this would be described as:

$$X \quad O$$

Here the X represents the service or intervention, and the O represents the observation or response of the participant. In this case, the X represents the lecture content on the effects of alcohol, and the O represents the quiz score at the end of the class. It is simply measuring what the students learned post-intervention (i.e., after the intervention). It could be argued that perhaps these students had an exceptional amount of knowledge about the subject before the class started.

Another preexperimental design is the one-group pretest-posttest design. Let's imagine that you administered the quiz before the start of the class to measure students' baseline level of knowledge. You then presented the material over the next forty minutes and then tested them again with the same quiz (this is classical educational methodology). You could then compare the pretest scores with the posttest scores. If students' scores improved, it could be logically argued that the improvement was due to what they learned in class. Research notation would diagram this design as follows:

$$O \quad X \quad O$$

It should be clear at this point that the first O represents the pretest, and the X represents the class lecture. The second O represents the posttest. The most obvious limitation of this design is that there is no comparison group. Critics could argue that perhaps the students' scores were random or occurred by chance. Thus, it is difficult to determine the true effect of the intervention on students.

Quasi-Experimental Designs

Quasi-experimental designs are designs in which there is a comparison group but it is either not possible or not feasible to use random assignment to assign participants to groups. Random assignment, discussed in chapter 5, increases internal validity and reduces the likelihood of bias because each subject has a nonzero probability of being placed in each group. For example, it would not be ethical to recruit a group of volunteers for a study about homelessness and then randomly assign one group to a condition of homelessness for a period of time. You might, however, be able to find a group of individuals who are currently homeless and compare them to a group of people who are living in permanent housing.

Thus, without a comparison group of students who did not have the alcohol education class in our example, we would be unsure whether the class itself led to the results on the quiz. To deal with this, you might also give the quiz to several other students who did not participate in the class. In other words, you would use a comparison group that had no access to the material to control for these issues. This would be an example of a slightly more sophisticated design known as posttest-only with nonequivalent group. In research notation it would be as follows:

$$X \quad O$$
$$O \text{ (different group)}$$

Again, X represents the class lecture, and O represents the posttest. Now, if the students in the class who received the lecture scored much higher on the quiz, you could assert that maybe they did so as a result of the lecture. We cannot be certain, however, that there are not inherent differences between the two groups. Confounding variables such as family experience with alcohol abuse, religious beliefs, and gender may have an impact on the level of knowledge each group has concerning the effects of alcohol on the body.

Let's imagine for a moment that you are a case manager working with adults in a community mental health agency. You have been offering a support group for your consumers in which you discuss issues such as daily living skills, money management, and other skills necessary for independent living. The group begins every eight weeks and meets once a week for the two-month period. You have noticed that several of your consumers seem to feel better about themselves after participating in the group. Perhaps you review the literature and find several studies that suggest that support groups are an effective way to increase the self-esteem of consumers. After completing your literature review, you develop the following hypothesis: "Participants will report an increase in self-esteem following an eight-week support group."

To test this hypothesis, you ask the participants who begin the following eight-week period to complete a self-esteem measurement instrument before the beginning of the first class. As a comparison, you ask an equal number of participants (who are not attending the group but who are consumers at your agency) to complete the same instrument. At the end of the eight weeks, you ask both your support group and the comparison group to complete the self-esteem questionnaire again. In research notation this would be as follows:

O   X   O
O   O

The Os represent the pretest and posttest, and the X represents the support group (the intervention). We could argue that if the experimental group (the group that participated in the support group) had remarkably higher scores on the self-esteem scale after completing the support group (compared to the scores on the pretest), then the difference may be attributed to the support group itself. The scores of the comparison group would strengthen this argument if the comparison group's scores remained similar from the pretest to the posttest (i.e., their scores did not increase or decrease over time).

All research designs have inherent limitations, and the pretest-posttest nonequivalent comparison group design is no exception. Logic would dictate that we could not rule out any alternative explanations for the perceived changes in the experimental group. How do we know, for example, that something else outside the group did not happen to cause the group to feel better about themselves? Perhaps all the members of the group suddenly found new jobs, received promotions, or felt that the climate at their places of work became friendlier toward them. Any number of variables could account for a change in the group outside the influence of the support group itself.

Time-series designs are slightly more rigorous than simple quasi-experimental designs such as the pretest-posttest nonequivalent group design outlined earlier. Imagine again that you are working as a case manager at a community mental health agency. You are working with adults who participate in your support group. This time, instead of recruiting other consumers to serve as a comparison group, let's imagine that all the consumers in your agency are participating in your support group, which effectively eliminates the chance to have a comparison group. One solution is the time-series design. To use this design, you, the researcher, would simply give the same self-esteem questionnaire at several points in time before the support group begins. Perhaps you would ask respondents to complete the questionnaire every other day for a week. Then the support group would begin, and after its completion, you would ask participants to complete the same questionnaire again every other day for a week. You could then compare the three pretests to the posttests. In research notation, this research design would look like this:

O   O   O   X   O   O   O

Again, the Os represent the self-esteem questionnaire, and the X represents the support group. Because there is no comparison group, the researcher uses the self-esteem questionnaires at various points in time as a comparison group by comparing the groups' overall scores over time. If, over the course of a week, the pretests seem to reflect a low level of self-esteem but then the group's level of self-esteem dramatically improves after participants complete the support group, you could argue that the intervention may be correlated with the increase in self-esteem. Notice, however, that we are not saying that the intervention *caused* a change in self-esteem; we are simply stating that there is a correlation.

The next design we examine is the time-series design with nonequivalent comparison group. This is simply a variation of the time-series design discussed already. Perhaps you are able to find a group of consumers who are not willing to participate in your support group but are willing to serve as a comparison group. You may ask both groups to fill out the self-esteem questionnaire a total of three times over the course of seven days before the support group begins and then again three times over seven days after the end of the support group. In research notation, this would look like this:

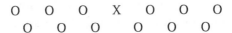

The Os represent the self-esteem questionnaire, and the X represents the intervention. We said that the strength of the time-series design was that the questionnaire repeated over time served as its own comparison group. When you include the additional component of the comparison group, your design is strengthened. You can now compare the pretest scores with the posttest scores, and you can evaluate these against those of the comparison group. Let's assume for a moment that the comparison group's scores stayed fairly similar over time. Logic would tell us that there is a strong possibility that the support group was effective (assuming that the scores of the experimental group increased after the intervention, of course).

Like all research designs, quasi-experimental designs have both strengths and weaknesses. On the one hand, they are methodologically stronger than preexperimental designs because they use a comparison group with pre- and posttests and/or test the findings at several points in time. However, they cannot rule out alternative explanations for any observed changes in groups. For instance, the members of one group may have much higher IQs than the other group or may have been more motivated to participate in the study. Each of these could be an alternative explanation for observed changes in groups.

Experimental Designs

The one aspect that differentiates the experimental design from the quasi-experimental designs is the assignment of subjects to groups. In true experimental designs, subjects are randomly assigned to either the experimental group or the control group. Up to this point, we have been discussing the use of a comparison group. In quasi-experimental research, the group that receives no treatment (the intervention) is referred to as the comparison group (or sometimes as the nontreatment group). The term *control group* is used only for experimental research.

It is often difficult to randomly assign subjects to one group or the other, for a variety of reasons. First, there are ethical considerations. Much of what is done in social work research precludes the social worker from assigning subjects to a particular group (as that might mean that they are not receiving services that could benefit them). Second, random assignment of subjects can increase the cost of a study (and many researchers have limited resources). Third, researchers might be studying an event that has already transpired (such as the effects of the 9/11 terrorist attacks), which makes a random assignment impossible. However, for the sake of discussion, let's pretend for a moment that you are continuing with your study on the support group. Let's also assume that you have the luxury of assigning participants to the experimental group and to the control group. Your research design then would be:

$$R \quad X \quad O$$
$$R \quad \quad O$$

In this design, the Rs represent random assignment of subjects (all subjects have an equal chance of being in either group). As before, the Os represent the self-esteem questionnaire, and the X represents the intervention. Because all consumers have an equal chance of being in either group, you can compare the posttest scores of the experimental group with those of the control group. If they are vastly different, then you could argue that the intervention must have worked (even without a pretest for the control group). However, adding a pretest for the control group makes the design even stronger. This is the classic research design known as the pretest-posttest control group design:

$$R \quad O \quad X \quad O$$
$$R \quad O \quad \quad O$$

In this design, the Rs represent random assignment of subjects, the Os represent the pretest and posttest questionnaire (the self-esteem instrument), and the X represents the intervention (the support group).

The last research design we discuss here, called Solomon's four-group design, is the highest standard in experimental group research designs, because the researcher can be confident that a change between the pretest and the posttest is truly due to the intervention. In research notation, this is described as follows:

$$
\begin{array}{llll}
R & O & X & O \\
R & O &   & O \\
R & X &   & O \\
R &   &   & O \\
\end{array}
$$

As you can see, this complex design combines the designs of pretest-posttest control group and posttest-only control group. The major advantage of the Solomon design is that it can tell us whether changes in the dependent variable are due to some interaction effect between the pretest and the treatment. For example, let's say we wanted to assess the effect of positive information about a group of child welfare workers' community service work (the independent variable) on people's attitudes about child protection workers (the dependent variable). During the pretest, the groups are asked questions regarding their attitudes toward child protection workers. Next, they are exposed to the experimental treatment: newspaper articles reporting on the civic deeds and child-rescue efforts of child protection workers. If treatment group 1 scores lower on the posttest than control group 1, it might be because of the independent variable. However, it could also be that filling out the pretest questionnaire sensitized people to the difficulties of being a child protection worker. The people in treatment group 1 have been alerted to the issues and react more strongly to the experimental treatment than they would have without the pretest. If this is true, then experimental group 2 should show less change than experimental group 1. If the independent variable has an effect separate from its interaction with the treatment, then experimental group 2 should show more change than control group 1. If control group 1 and experimental group 2 show no change but experimental group 1 does show a change, then we know that change is produced only by the interaction of pretesting and treatment.

Researchers often bypass the Solomon design because it requires twice as many groups. This effectively doubles the time and cost of conducting the experiment. Many researchers decide that the advantages are not worth the added cost and complexity.

Case Scenario

You are employed as an alcohol and drug substance abuse counselor in an outpatient facility. You notice that the more your clients get involved in twelve-step support groups like Alcoholics Anonymous and Narcotics Anonymous tends to have a direct effect on the length of time they stay clean and sober. You develop a research question: Is there a correlation between the number of twelve-step meetings a recovering addict attends and his or her length of sobriety? To test your question, you begin tracking the number of meetings that clients attend (independent variable) and the number of days they go without using any alcohol or other drugs (dependent variable).

Critical-Thinking Questions

On the basis of the case scenario, answer the following questions:

1. What type of research design would you be employing (preexperimental, quasi-experimental, experimental)?

2. Would you consider your findings to be causal? Why or why not?

3. What are the strengths of this design?

4. What are the limitations of this research design?

Key Points

- Causal relationships exist when one variable causes a change in the other, and correlational relationships exist when one variable may be associated with some degree of change in the other variable.

- Cross-sectional research looks at a slice of the population at one point in time.

- Longitudinal studies follow the same cohort of individuals over time.

- There are three main types of group research designs: preexperimental, quasi-experimental, and experimental designs.

- A comparison group (sometimes called nontreatment group) is used in quasi-experimental research; this is the group that receives no treatment (intervention).

- A control group is used in experimental research. In studies that use a control group, subjects have been randomly assigned to either the experimental group or the control group.

Practice Exam

True or False

1. Longitudinal studies follow the same cohort of individuals over time.

2. Causal relationships exist when one variable causes a change in the other.

3. In studies that use a control group, subjects have been randomly assigned to either the experimental group or the control group.

Multiple Choice

4. Solomon's four-group design:

   a. Is considered the highest form of research

   b. Is a myth

   c. Is a form of preexperimental research

   d. Is not considered a valid design

   e. None of the above

5. The phrase "control group" implies:

   a. That subjects are under the researcher's control

   b. That subjects have no control over the outcome of the research

   c. That subjects are randomly assigned to one group or another

   d. None of the above

6. All research designs:

   a. Have built-in limitations

   b. Are predetermined by how the researcher structures the design

   c. Are doomed to fail

   d. Should be viewed with skepticism

7. Research designs are grouped into the following categories:

   a. Preexperimental, quasi-fundamental, and fundamental

   b. Prefundamental, fundamental, and quasi-fundamental

   c. Preexperimental, experimental, and random

   d. Preexperimental, quasi-experimental, and experimental

CHAPTER EIGHT

Survey Research

CSWE Core Competencies

IN THIS CHAPTER you will find the following Council on Social Work Education (CSWE) competencies:

Educational Policy 2.1.3—Apply critical thinking to inform and communicate professional judgments

Educational Policy 2.1.6—Engage in research-informed practice and practice-informed research

Educational Policy 2.1.9—Respond to contexts that shape practice

Educational Policy 2.1.10(b)—Assessment

Defining Survey Research

Surveys are a research design in which a sample of subjects is drawn from a population and studied (usually interviewed) to make inferences about the population. Surveys pose statements or questions to which subjects are asked to respond. They may be used for descriptive, explanatory, and exploratory research. They can be limited to one point in time in cross-sectional surveys, or they can be repeated at different points of time in longitudinal surveys. Surveys are chiefly used in studies that have individual people as the unit of analysis. Even though they can be used for groups such as families or organizations, it is still important to have one individual as the chief respondent.

Surveys are a relatively inexpensive way to reach a large number of people quickly, as well as to describe a small population or an individual.

Suppose, for example, that you want to find out to what extent subscribers are satisfied with a quarterly newsletter that your agency publishes. You may choose to interview subscribers in person, or by phone, using a survey tool. Unfortunately, interviews are often difficult to arrange because people's schedules do not always coincide, and their time is limited. Also, interviewers must be trained—a costly and time-consuming process—if they are to obtain reliable information. Even with printing and mailing charges, surveys cost considerably less than interviews administered to the same number of people. Many people are familiar with surveys and are accustomed to completing them. Mailed surveys may be particularly easy to complete, since people are under no pressure to finish all the questions within a certain amount of time, but these can fail to provide a good response rate of return.

Appropriate Survey Topics

Surveys are most appropriate for measuring people's attitudes, beliefs, and behaviors. Some things are impossible to measure. For example, asking about the *best* type of therapy is not a question that can be answered. The "best" is a value-laden question and depends on many factors, including the problem for which the social worker is trying to intervene, who the consumer is, and the setting in which the social worker is employing the counseling strategy. For example, let us consider the issue of depression. Research studies have demonstrated that for people who are suffering from depression, the most effective strategy is to employ cognitive-behavioral therapy combined with pharmacology (specifically some type of antidepressant). But even this approach has been demonstrated to be most effective with individuals who have a high level of cognitive functioning. Conversely, cognitive-behavioral therapy has not been well researched with people of color, and so it is not known how effective this type of therapy is with people who are not Caucasian. To summarize, it is impossible to state what the *best* type of therapy is—all we can state is that one type of therapy has been demonstrated to be effective with certain populations. In the next section, we turn to the issue of constructing a survey.

Developing a Survey

Before we delve into some of the specifics of survey construction, we must interject a note of caution. You, as the researcher, will ultimately have to make some decisions about your survey—what to leave in, what to take out, and how to phrase the questions. Part of what makes research so difficult is that there are no absolutes. We, as the authors, will provide you with some guidelines, and we will point out some of the common pitfalls to avoid, but you will be the final judge of how you implement your study.

Constructing surveys for a large sample or population is not easy and requires many skills. The directions and the questions should be written clearly and easy to read, and the survey should be easy to complete and return. The authors suggest using the **rule of parsimony** when constructing a survey. The rule of parsimony simply means eliminating all unnecessary questions and/or data and paring down your survey to the absolute minimum. We suggest the following steps when first drafting a survey. Take a sheet of paper, and list everything that you think you may want to ask. Begin with demographic variables (e.g., gender, age, ethnicity, income, education level, marital status), and then continue on to independent and finally dependent variables. By listing variables in this order (demographic, independent, and then dependent), the data analysis will be much easier because variables will be listed in a logical order. The rule of parsimony is the idea that the researcher will "pare down" the number of questions asked to the point at which he or she has only those questions or items that are absolutely essential for the study at hand. So, begin by listing everything that you might possibly ask, and then eliminate all questions that are not absolutely essential to your study. The remaining items are those that are to be included on the survey. Another cautionary note: it is important to keep surveys as short as possible. If researchers ask too many questions, respondents run the risk of what is known as "reactivity to the test," a condition in which respondents begin answering anything just to finish (another way to think of this is to consider it "test fatigue"). To avoid test fatigue, try to use the rule of parsimony mentioned earlier.

In laying out a survey, it is important that the questionnaire is visually appealing to the eye. You want to make sure that it is free of typographical errors; use at least a twelve-point font; and if possible, avoid using colored paper with a colored ink, which makes the words difficult to read.

Survey Questions

Many researchers make some basic mistakes when developing survey questions. We outline here some of the most basic mistakes. Please don't view this list as exhaustive—there are entire textbooks devoted to the development of questionnaires and techniques for conducting survey research. Our intent here is simply to alert you to some of the most common pitfalls that researchers fall into.

The first issue deals with the collection of demographic information. Demographic information includes such things as race, gender, age, income, educational level, marital status, and other personal information. Demographic information is important and helps to define your respondents, but we caution against the overcollection of data. Asking too many demographic questions makes your survey longer and can lend it a feeling of intrusiveness. We recommend asking only those demographic questions that are necessary to your study.

The next issue is the use of ambiguous or unclear questions. These can take several forms and may include the following:

- *Vagueness of the question asked*—For example, you may be interested in your clients' use of illegal substances, and ask a question like, "Do you engage in illegal drug use?" This question lacks specificity (the phrases "engage in" and "illegal drugs" are ill defined and can mean different things to different people).
- *Difficult questions to answer*—For example, there are several issues with the question "Do you regularly place your health at risk?" It is vague (what exactly is meant by "placing your health at risk"?); it lacks a frame of reference (does "regularly" mean the same thing as routinely as in daily or does it mean on a consistent basis?).
- *Acronyms and jargon*—For example, as a social work student, you are probably very familiar with the phrase "strengths perspective," but to the average person, this is not a term they may be familiar with. At the same time, try to avoid the use of acronyms.
- *Two questions in one sentence ("double-barreled questions")*—For example, "Are you in favor of schools providing condoms and sex education to high school students?" People may be in favor of teaching sex education but not providing condoms, or vice versa.
- *Language like "never" and "always"*—For many behaviors, these responses will rarely be selected. For example, if you ask respondents to rate the number of times they can remember being praised as a child, most people will say that they "never" received praise. A more realistic response for someone who feels that he or she rarely received praise would be "rarely" or "seldom."
- *Biased language*—It is entirely possible to unintentionally manipulate the results of a survey simply by incorporating biased language. For example, a researcher may be interested in determining

the views of members of a neighborhood on registered sex offenders living in their neighborhood. One way to survey residents of
the neighborhood would be to ask them to respond to the following
question:

*Registered sex-offenders should not be allowed to live near my
children.*
Strongly agree   Agree   Neutral   Disagree   Strongly disagree

There are several things wrong with this question. First, the item
is negatively worded (i.e., "should not be"), so the researcher can't
be certain whether the respondent agrees or disagrees with this
statement. Second, the words "near my children" are vague—is the
respondent agreeing that registered sex offenders should not be
allowed to live near the researcher's children or near their own
children? A more clearly stated (and less biased statement) could
be measured by asking respondents to react to the following
statement:

"I am in favor of having registered sex offenders living in my
neighborhood."
Strongly agree   Agree   Neutral   Disagree   Strongly disagree

Perhaps you noticed in the choices that respondents were asked to rate
their opinion on a continuum. These choices, ranging from "strongly
agree" to "strongly disagree" are known as **Likert scales**. Likert scales have
been in existence since the 1930s, when a researcher (Likert) developed
this method for forced choice responses. They have proved, over the years,
to be an accurate and convenient way to measure attitudes and beliefs.
However, one note of caution, here, is the use of the "neutral" category. By
including "neutral," you run the risk of people who do not want to reveal
their opinion (especially on controversial subjects) still selecting this
option; in contrast, by not including it, you will miss those individuals who
truly do not feel one way or the other, who are, in essence, "neutral" on
the subject. The same note of caution can be made for including the category "don't know." Although some people may truly not know, by including this category, you run the risk of increasing the number of people who
select this response.

Example 8.1 shows an alumni survey, designed to collect data about past
graduates of the social work program at our university. Take a moment to
review the survey. Notice the collection of demographic information. Also
note the use of Likert scaling throughout the survey.

EXAMPLE 8.1: ALUMNI SURVEY

Alumni Survey

Year graduated from MSU _____

Gender   M   F

In the last five years, please indicate whether you have done any of these activities:

Member of NASW	Yes	No
Licensed or certified as a social worker	Yes	No
Enrolled in continuing education	Yes	No
Member of a social service board	Yes	No
Involved in a community service organization	Yes	No
Involved in a community political activity	Yes	No
Subscribe to a social work journal	Yes	No
Presented a paper at meetings or conferences	Yes	No
Published articles in social work journals and newsletters	Yes	No
Conducted research on a social work topic	Yes	No

Highest degree achieved?

BSW   MSW   Ph.D.   Other master's degree

At which location did you complete most of your classes?

MSU Morehead   MSU Ashland   MSU Prestonsburg

Alumni Survey

1. The BSW program taught relevant information.

Strongly agree	Agree	Not sure	Disagree	Strongly disagree
1	2	3	4	5

2. My undergraduate education prepared me for an entry-level position in social work.

Strongly agree	Agree	Not sure	Disagree	Strongly disagree
1	2	3	4	5

3. Morehead State University social work professors cared about their students' well-being.

Strongly agree	Agree	Not sure	Disagree	Strongly disagree
1	2	3	4	5

4. The social work program offered a great opportunity for personal growth.

Strongly agree	Agree	Not sure	Disagree	Strongly disagree
1	2	3	4	5

5. What is your highest degree attained?

BSW	MSW	MA	Ph.D.	Other

6. How well did the BSW program prepare you for graduate school?

Extremely well	Somewhat	Not very	Extremely poor
1	2	3	4

7. Overall, the Social Work Program had high academic standards.

Strongly agree	Agree	Not sure	Disagree	Strongly disagree
1	2	3	4	5

The BSW degree should be helpful in your current daily job. Please indicate the extent to which the program benefits each one of these areas.

How helpful, in your daily job would you rate information about:

8. Kowledge of social service systems?

Very useful	Somewhat useful	Neutral	Somewhat useless	Very useless
1	2	3	4	5

9. Dignity of the individual?

Very useful	Somewhat useful	Neutral	Somewhat useless	Very useless
1	2	3	4	5

10. Confidentiality?

Very useful	Somewhat useful	Neutral	Somewhat useless	Very useless
1	2	3	4	5

11. Self-determination?

Very useful	Somewhat useful	Neutral	Somewhat useless	Very useless
1	2	3	4	5

12. Person in the environment?

Very useful	Somewhat useful	Neutral	Somewhat useless	Very useless
1	2	3	4	5

13. Human development?

Very useful	Somewhat useful	Neutral	Somewhat useless	Very useless
1	2	3	4	5

14. Problem solving?

Very useful	Somewhat useful	Neutral	Somewhat useless	Very useless
1	2	3	4	5

15. Systems theory?

Very useful	Somewhat useful	Neutral	Somewhat useless	Very useless
1	2	3	4	5

16. Generalist practice?

Very useful	Somewhat useful	Neutral	Somewhat useless	Very useless
1	2	3	4	5

17. Policy?

Very useful	Somewhat useful	Neutral	Somewhat useless	Very useless
1	2	3	4	5

18. Policy as it relates to advocacy for social change?

Very useful	Somewhat useful	Neutral	Somewhat useless	Very useless
1	2	3	4	5

19. Your ability to read research?

Very useful	Somewhat useful	Neutral	Somewhat useless	Very useless
1	2	3	4	5

20. Your ability to conduct research?

Very useful	Somewhat useful	Neutral	Somewhat useless	Very useless
1	2	3	4	5

21. Your ability to supervise employees?

Very useful	Somewhat useful	Neutral	Somewhat useless	Very useless
1	2	3	4	5

How often (number of times), in your daily job, do you:

22. Use interviewing skills?

Daily	Several/Week	Once/Week	Several/Month	Couple/Month	Never
1	2	3	4	5	6

23. Counsel with individuals?

Daily	Several/Week	Once/Week	Several/Month	Couple/Month	Never
1	2	3	4	5	6

24. Counsel with groups?

Daily	Several/Week	Once/Week	Several/Month	Couple/Month	Never
1	2	3	4	5	6

25. Use problem-solving skills?

Daily	Several/Week	Once/Week	Several/Month	Couple/Month	Never
1	2	3	4	5	6

26. Provide information and referral?

Daily	Several/Week	Once/Week	Several/Month	Couple/Month	Never
1	2	3	4	5	6

27. Advocate on behalf of a client?

Daily	Several/Week	Once/Week	Several/Month	Couple/Month	Never
1	2	3	4	5	6

28. Function as an administrator of an agency?

Daily	Several/Week	Once/Week	Several/Month	Couple/Month	Never
1	2	3	4	5	6

29. Supervise employees?

Daily	Several/Week	Once/Week	Several/Month	Couple/Month	Never
1	2	3	4	5	6

30. Supervise volunteers?

Daily	Several/Week	Once/Week	Several/Month	Couple/Month	Never
1	2	3	4	5	6

31. Provide teaching and/or training?

Daily	Several/Week	Once/Week	Several/Month	Couple/Month	Never
1	2	3	4	5	6

32. Provide public speaking?

Daily	Several/Week	Once/Week	Several/Month	Couple/Month	Never
1	2	3	4	5	6

33. Organize groups?

Daily	Several/Week	Once/Week	Several/Month	Couple/Month	Never
1	2	3	4	5	6

34. Consult with other agencies?

Daily	Several/Week	Once/Week	Several/Month	Couple/Month	Never
1	2	3	4	5	6

35. Develop new programs?

Daily	Several/Week	Once/Week	Several/Month	Couple/Month	Never
1	2	3	4	5	6

36. Set treatment goals?

Daily	Several/Week	Once/Week	Several/Month	Couple/Month	Never
1	2	3	4	5	6

37. Use computer technology?

Daily	Several/Week	Once/Week	Several/Month	Couple/Month	Never
1	2	3	4	5	6

38. Deal with diversity issues?

Daily	Several/Week	Once/Week	Several/Month	Couple/Month	Never
1	2	3	4	5	6

39. The BSW program introduced me to many aspects of the social work profession.

Strongly agree	Agree	Not sure	Disagree	Strongly disagree
1	2	3	4	5

40. The program clearly showed how the history of social work and social welfare are relevant to today's issues.

Strongly agree	Agree	Not sure	Disagree	Strongly disagree
1	2	3	4	5

41. The program taught me how to work well with people from different racial and class backgrounds.

Strongly agree	Agree	Not sure	Disagree	Strongly disagree
1	2	3	4	5

42. The program taught me how to work effectively with people from different ethnic and class backgrounds.

Strongly agree	Agree	Not sure	Disagree	Strongly disagree
1	2	3	4	5

43. The program taught me how to analyze the effectiveness of interventions at one's place of employment.

Strongly agree	Agree	Not sure	Disagree	Strongly disagree
1	2	3	4	5

44. The program equipped me to understand policies and lines of authority at my job.

Strongly agree	Agree	Not sure	Disagree	Strongly disagree
1	2	3	4	5

45. I learned a great deal of practical skills in dealing with clients.

Strongly agree	Agree	Not sure	Disagree	Strongly disagree
1	2	3	4	5

46. The program had quality information on matters of sexual orientation.

Strongly agree	Agree	Not sure	Disagree	Strongly disagree
1	2	3	4	5

Pilot Testing Your Survey

Another good idea is to **pilot test** your survey. This means asking a small group of people (perhaps five or six) who have no idea what you are trying to measure to complete your survey before you give it out to the general public. Piloting provides advantages such as allowing you to make any changes or adjustments before large-scale distribution of the survey.

There are many different methods for distributing a survey. Some of the most common include telephone surveys, Internet, and face-to-face methods. Telephone surveys, mail and Internet surveys, and face-to-face interviews are the most convenient collection methods. Each has positive and negative aspects that we discuss in turn.

Administering Surveys and Expected Rates of Return

It is entirely up to researchers how to administer a survey. We discuss some of the most popular methods for distributing surveys. Each has its own advantages and disadvantages.

Telephone Surveys

Telephone surveys are relatively easy to conduct and are cost effective. One individual can call many people in a short amount of time and thus collect a large amount of data. For this reason, telephone surveys are quite popular. The downside is that telephone surveys are inherently limited to those individuals who have a telephone, who are at home when the surveyor calls, and who are willing to spend the time needed to answer questions. For this reason, people who take a telephone survey may not be representative of the group the survey is intended to describe. For example, a telephone survey was conducted on people's perceptions of the presence of police officers in the community. The person conducting the survey missed those people who either did not have a phone or were unwilling or unavailable to take the call. It could be argued that those who were willing to respond to the interviewer's questions had strong opinions concerning the presence of police in the community and wanted to be heard. For this reason, some argue that surveys have a built-in selection bias.

Mail and Internet Surveys

Another way to conduct surveys is to use mail or Internet surveys. These are popular because they are relatively simple, and if administered correctly, they can be an effective way to collect data. When you are conducting a mail or Internet survey, you should develop a brief cover letter or statement that describes the purpose of the survey, who is conducting the survey, and why it is important for respondents to fill out and return the survey. Make sure that the letter covers all ethical considerations discussed in chapter 2, and include information on the approximate amount of time it will take to complete the survey. Finally, make sure to provide a self-addressed and stamped return envelope (for surface mail) so that respondents can simply drop the completed survey in the mail. With any survey, and especially mail surveys, it is a good idea to keep in mind that people have multiple demands on their time, and anything you can do to help minimize the effort required to complete your survey will increase your response rate.

Internet surveys are gaining in popularity. They have the advantage of being relatively inexpensive to administer and the ability to reach a wide audience. One disadvantage of utilizing Internet surveys, though, is that it is almost impossible to ensure that the person who is completing the survey is who he or she says he or she is. For example, a researcher may want to survey adults who are struggling with a mental illness, but respondents to the survey can be anyone who happens to have access to the Internet and a desire to complete the questionnaire.

Interviews

Face-to-face (in-person) interviews have several advantages. For instance, the interviewer can clarify questions on the survey, thereby reducing the number of unanswered responses, which are common with mail surveys. Another advantage is that face-to-face interviews are relatively easy to administer. One individual can stand in one spot (e.g., a crowded shopping center on a weekend) and collect information from many individuals. The downside of face-to-face interviews is that they can be labor intensive, and depending on how much information is needed, a large number of people may be required to obtain a reasonable sample size.

Customer Satisfaction Surveys

One aspect of survey research that needs some special consideration is the idea of measuring customer satisfaction. As a social worker, there will be times in your career when you will be asked to measure consumers' attitudes regarding your agency's services. One of the easiest ways to do this is to construct a questionnaire. When conducting an evaluation of an agency via survey research, there are some items to keep in mind. We recommend the following:

- Pare down the number of questions to the most essential items you want to measure.
- Since most social service agencies receive some grant funding, measure items that are identified in the grant proposal as objectives.
- Focus survey items on specific goods and services.
- Consider including at least one open-ended (qualitative) question, which allows consumers to give unsolicited feedback on their impressions of the agency.

There is one important caveat to bear in mind when considering customer satisfaction surveys. Research has demonstrated that consumers consistently overrate their satisfaction with the agency they are rating. This means that they rate the agency more highly than how they truly feel about it. The reasons for this phenomenon are many and open to speculation. Perhaps it is because there is a certain aspect of social desirability—they don't want to be perceived as not being "nice." Another possibility is known as cognitive dissonance. Having spent time and energy partaking in services from an agency, consumers may be hesitant to rate themselves less than satisfied with the agency. One reason for this cognitive dissonance is that those people who respond to customer satisfaction surveys have either completed services or are still receiving services. Perhaps a more important question is to ask consumers who are no longer receiving services how satisfied they are with the agency and the services they received.

Expected Rates of Return

Like many other things in research, there are no hard-and-fast rules for survey rates of return. You, as the researcher, will have to decide what your sample size needs to be and how you will determine when you have reached an acceptable rate of return. For most researchers, a minimally acceptable rate of return is about 50 percent. So, if you want a minimum of one hundred respondents, you may need to send out at least two hundred surveys. Having participated in a great number of our own surveys, we can say that Internet and face-to-face surveys net greater rates of return than traditional mail surveys (which have the lowest rate of return).

Advantages and Disadvantages of Survey Research

Like all aspects of research, survey research has both advantages and disadvantages. Survey research has the ability to reach a large number of people with a relatively small amount of effort, which makes it a very efficient way to collect data. Along those same lines, survey research is relatively inexpensive. To that end, sociologists, marketers, businesspeople, and others who want to measure attitudes, beliefs, and behaviors have used survey research for decades. Research has proved that the investigation of illegal and socially undesirable behavior is best measured when people can feel that their answers will remain totally anonymous. One of the best ways to accomplish this is through the use of questionnaires and survey research. Survey research has the added advantage of being relatively easy to tabulate and score. With modern software such as Microsoft Excel, the Statistical Package for Social Sciences (SPSS), and other statistical programs, data tabulation, scoring, and analysis are quick and easy. Researchers can evaluate their results (including cutting and pasting reports into a word-processing program) in a matter of seconds.

The downside to survey research is that depending on the method of data collection or survey administration, there can be a limited or small response rate. With the increasing popularity of Internet-based research, response rates are less of a problem. Other issues do arise, however. For example, with Internet-based research, the researcher can never truly know who is responding to survey items. A final downside to survey research is that it provides only a brief snapshot of respondents' beliefs, attitudes, or behaviors at the time the question was asked. This is essentially a cross-sectional research design and does not really provide in-depth insight into the underlying motivation for respondents' behaviors.

Case Scenario

You are employed as a social worker in a state employment agency. Your agency has as its central mission the goal of helping people find gainful employment. It has become increasingly clear that many employers are moving away from paper applications and are using the Internet for both notifying potential employees and accepting their applications. This is true for a variety of employers, including those hiring for entry-level positions such as fast-food restaurants, warehouses, factories, and other employers. You have noticed that many of the individuals who you are assigned to work with do not possess basic computer skills, and this is keeping them from applying for work that they would otherwise be qualified for. Your supervisor has given you the task of developing a sample survey to hand out to your clients to determine their level of computer literacy; the degree to which they feel that their computer skills (or lack thereof) are precluding them from being employed; and how interested they are in developing computer literacy.

Critical-Thinking Questions

On the basis of the case scenario, answer the following questions:

1. What demographic questions, if any, will it be important to ask?

2. How will you distribute your survey? Give reasons for your choice of methods.

3. How can you be relatively sure that your results are truly representative of the population you serve and that you have obtained accurate information?

Key Points

- Surveys are a research design in which a sample of subjects is drawn from a population and studied (usually interviewed) to make inferences about the population.

- Surveys are a relatively inexpensive way to reach a large number of people quickly.

- Piloting provides advantages such as allowing you to make any changes or adjustments before you distribute a survey on a large scale.

- Telephone surveys are relatively easy to conduct and are cost effective.

- Research has demonstrated that consumers consistently overrate their satisfaction with the agency they are rating.

- For most researchers, a minimally acceptable rate of return is about 50 percent.

- Survey research has the ability to reach a large number of people with a relative small amount of effort, thus making it a very efficient way to collect data.

- One issue with Internet-based research is that researchers can never truly know who is responding to survey items.

Practice Exam

True or False

1. One advantage to survey research is the ability to reach a large number of people with relatively little expense.

2. One disadvantage of surveys is that they can be administered at only one point in time.

3. One problem that many researchers face when developing surveys is asking questions that are vague.

4. Asking too many demographic questions helps respondents feel important.

Multiple Choice

5. There are four ways of administering surveys:

   a. Face-to-face, telephone, Internet, and random selection

b. Face-to-face, telephone, Internet, and mail

c. Telephone, telegraph, Internet, and random selection

d. None of the above

6. _____ scales are forced-choice items, asking respondents to rate on a continuum.

a. Lakers

b. Lookout

c. Likert

d. None of the above

7. One of the downsides to using the Internet to survey respondents is:

a. There is no downside.

b. One should never use the Internet; it is not safe.

c. It is too expensive.

d. A researcher cannot be sure who is responding.

8. Asking two questions within one survey question is:

a. An example of using space wisely

b. An example of a double-barreled question

c. Rarely seen in survey research

d. None of the above

CHAPTER NINE

Evaluative Research Designs

CSWE Core Competencies

IN THIS CHAPTER you will find the following Council on Social Work Education (CSWE) competencies:

Educational Policy 2.1.3—Apply critical thinking to inform and communicate professional judgments

Educational Policy 2.1.6—Engage in research-informed practice and practice-informed research

Educational Policy 2.1.9—Respond to contexts that shape practice

Educational Policy 2.1.10(b)—Assessment

Educational Policy 2.1.10(d)—Evaluation

This chapter introduces some techniques for evaluating a program. While all research designs can be used to evaluate a program at some level, this chapter presents a research design that looks at process evaluations and outcome evaluations of an agency using qualitative, quantitative, and mixed-method research designs.

Social work ethics demand that we provide high-quality services to our consumers. Section 5.02(a) of the Code of Ethics of the National Association of Social Workers (2008) states: "Social workers should monitor and evaluate policies, the implementation of programs, and practice interventions." Seeking evidence of the effectiveness of existing programs is one way to determine best practices and to fulfill this goal.

In today's economy, as agencies and practitioners confront ever-tightening budgets and increased competition for shrinking funding, it is becoming increasingly necessary for programs to be able to demonstrate not only that their interventions are effective but also that they are meeting the goals and objectives that they set out to accomplish. Gone are the days when a program could simply request funding dollars with little or no thought to demonstrating effectiveness. Today, funding sources are increasingly demanding that programs be accountable for how they spend their money, how they help people, and what positive benefits result from the monies spent. Most federal grants and many state and private funding sources now require applicants to have some outside source that will conduct an independent evaluation of the outcomes of the project funded by the grant. To accomplish these tasks, a social worker needs to have at least a basic familiarity with program evaluation.

An evaluation of social service programs can be rewarding research. It is through the process of investigation and analysis that we can answer complicated questions and discover better approaches with consumers. In turn, the discovery of these better approaches can give us hope in meeting the needs of the people we serve.

Program Evaluation

Program evaluation is a research design and analysis that evaluates specific characteristics of a program within an agency. There are basically two types of program evaluations: process evaluations and outcome evaluations. Each type has a specific purpose with advantages and limitations.

Process Evaluation

A **process evaluation** is generally an internal evaluation process that is initiated in the early stages of a program. An internal evaluation is simply an evaluation that is conducted at the request or desire of the agency. A process evaluation requires the researcher to establish a **baseline**, or a beginning point in research that establishes an initial sense of how a program, group, or individual is currently functioning and allows researchers to track progress over time; changes to the baseline are then monitored over time. It utilizes a qualitative approach as it seeks new information to answer such questions as "What does our program look like?" "Is our program effective?" and "Are consumers satisfied with our services?" It also utilizes a quantitative approach through the use of a measurement instrument, such as a survey that asks, "How satisfied are you with the services you received?" to which respondents can answer on a scale from 1 ("not at all satisfied") to 5 ("very satisfied").

A process evaluation can be conducted at multiple times, and many administrators prefer to start the process evaluations early on—generally within the first ninety days of a new program's implementation. The process evaluation can then be repeated at intervals (e.g., quarterly, every six months, every nine months, yearly) to determine whether the program is accomplishing its intended goals.

For example, let us imagine for a moment that you are a social worker at a food-voucher assistance program. Your agency serves many people who speak little or no English. Your supervisor has written a grant that provides translation services for these consumers. However, rather than wait until the end of the grant period to see if your program is on target, you and your supervisor decide to conduct a process evaluation after services have been offered for ninety days. You select a day (or week) when you will interview consumers and then solicit input from several who have appointments. You ask them to spend a few minutes with you and ask them the following questions:

1. What has been your experience with the translation services?
2. What do you like best about the translation services?
3. What do you like least about the translation services?
4. How would you like to see the translation services done differently?
5. Are there any other comments you would like to make about the translation services?

Let us assume that you collected information from only three participants. You may be saying to yourself, "Given what we've learned in previous chapters, three people is a very small sample, and their answers cannot be generalized to the rest of the population." And you would be correct. You want to collect as much feedback from as many sources as possible. But remember, this is not meant to be explanatory—you are simply trying to determine how the new service is helpful and what could be done to improve services.

In general, a process evaluation has three main goals: to construct a program description, to monitor a program, and to assess the quality of services being provided. We look at each of these goals in turn.

Program Description

The first goal, **program description**, is simply an attempt to delineate the setup, routines, and consumer characteristics of a program (see example 9.1). The setup of the program includes the types of services being

EXAMPLE 9.1: SAMPLE PROGRAM DESCRIPTION

The TRUCE Program is a gang prevention program funded through the Helpful Angels and the school district. The consumer population consists of students within the school district between the ages of thirteen and nineteen who are considered at risk by the school district.

Referrals to the TRUCE Program can come from school counselors, principals, parents, teachers, and other concerned family members or professionals. Once a referral is made to the TRUCE Program, the student meets with one of the TRUCE specialists for an initial assessment and orientation into the TRUCE Program. Most students participate in the program because they have been required to do so by the school district, their parents, or the court. Students participate in the program Monday through Friday for one hour after school ends.

The three goals of the program are to help at-risk students resist gang membership, to reduce disruptive behaviors while students are at school, and to improve grades. To accomplish these goals, TRUCE specialists provide weekly one-hour groups at five sites in the service area.

The overall program objectives are the following:

1. All students will decrease disruptive behavior in the classroom by 10 percent by the end of the school year as measured by the Behavioral Checklist (to be completed by the teachers).
2. All students will increase their knowledge of how to resist peer pressure to participate in gang activity by 50 percent by the end of the school year, as evidenced by pretest and posttest scores.
3. All students will increase their grade point average by 10 percent from midterm grades to final grades, as evidenced by report cards.

To address classroom disruptions, TRUCE specialists teach classroom social competency techniques. This is done during weekly individual discussions with the student and the student's teacher.

To address how to resist pressure to join a gang, TRUCE specialists use an organized curriculum that teaches refusal skills. They do this by using experiential learning tasks, didactic lecture, and group discussion. Students participate in the curriculum for a half hour four days a week (the fifth day is reserved for meetings with the teacher).

To address student performance with class work, tutors work with students on goal setting for weekly assignments and study techniques that help them prepare for exams. Tutors are available for a half hour Monday through Friday after the student has participated in the refusal-skills training or the teacher meeting.

provided, the location of services, and the mission (i.e., the rationale for the services). Other information that you may want to gather may include the routines of the services provided, such as frequency with which services are offered, times and days services are available, and number and type of workers who offer services. Finally, you may want to measure the number of consumers you serve and their characteristics: number of consumers, sex, race, age, income level, marital status, number of children, and the like.

Remember that descriptive statistics are ways of organizing, describing, and presenting quantitative data in a manner that is concise, manageable, and understandable. They usually deal with individual variables and establish the common patterns found in each individual variable. For instance, describing a population in terms of number and percentage for sex, race, and occupation gives us a picture of some of the characteristics of the consumers served. A program description, then, provides one with an overall picture of the characteristics of the program and participants.

Program Monitoring

Program monitoring, the second goal of process evaluation, is used to examine what happens after people receive services from a program. For example, you may use program monitoring to track utilization of services over time and the effect of services on individual functioning. By monitoring how services are utilized, you can determine which services a population needs most and which services can be offered on a seasonal basis. Monitoring items may include frequency of visits, average length of each person's time in the program, number of appointments each person keeps, and number of no-shows. For instance, you find that only two consumers regularly attend a weekly support group during the spring and summer; however, during fall and winter months, there is greater attendance. On the basis of this evaluation, you offer the support group only in the fall and winter.

You will also want to determine which of the services being provided are beneficial to your service population. Let us imagine that you are a social worker who works at an agency that provides services to teen mothers. Your agency has received a grant that will be used to offer parenting classes to these young mothers. Some of the objectives outlined in the grant are that 70 percent of the mothers who participate in the parenting classes will score higher on a parenting skills posttest than on the pretest. Your job is to conduct a process evaluation at six months to determine whether the program is on track. Part of this process evaluation would be to examine the pretest and posttest scores for these mothers to see if their knowledge of parenting skills improved. Let us assume that after six months, one hundred teen mothers have completed the parenting classes. You would expect to find that at least seventy (70 percent) of them did better on the posttest than on the pretest. If this were indeed the case, you would know that the program was on track. If, however, you found that this objective was not being met, you would need to discuss with your supervisor how to proceed. Depending on how close you are to achieving the objective, it may not be cause for alarm. However, if only 50 percent did better on the posttest than the pretest, perhaps some midcourse corrections are in order.

Quality Assurance

The last goal of a process evaluation is quality assurance. Quality assurance is a means of determining the level of satisfaction of both services for consumers and programmatic issues for staff. Programs routinely ask consumers to complete a satisfaction survey as part of a termination-of-services process. Some services, such as assistance with paying an electric bill, may be a onetime event. Other services, such as group counseling or a parenting class, last weeks, months, or years. Therefore, when and how often a participant will be surveyed depends on the length of services. Also, how a consumer will be surveyed depends on the structure and funding of a program. For instance, a satisfaction survey that respondents can anonymously deposit in a box may be given to onetime consumers at the end of their appointments. Another program may have grant funding that will allow program administrators to survey consumers by mailing the satisfaction survey to everyone who has participated over the past year. One of the problems with consumer satisfaction surveys is that consumers routinely report that they are more satisfied with services than they actually feel (Ingram & Chung, 1997). However, one way to control for this is to include qualitative (open-ended) questions. For instance, you can ask, "What was the best part of your experience with this agency?" and "What was the worst part of your experience with this agency?"

To this point, our quality assurance measures have focused on the consumer. However, with process evaluations, the staff can also be included in the evaluation. Asking staff such questions as "What are we doing well?" and "What can we do to improve our services?" can provide invaluable information for shaping the direction of a new program. The following are examples of how you might utilize a process evaluation:

1. You can monitor a new or long-standing program or service and present your findings at a meeting of staff or the board of directors, or to administrators.
2. You can develop, administer, and analyze a satisfaction survey to identify strengths and areas needing improvement within your agency.
3. You can develop a program description by collecting information about the setup, routines, and consumer characteristics of a program at your agency.
4. You can develop program goals and objectives.
5. You can survey staff to look at different practice approaches being used.

Outcome Evaluation

An **outcome evaluation**, a main goal for program evaluation, is an evaluation that measures the overall effectiveness of a program—that is, it looks at the goals and objectives established by the program to answer the question "Did this program accomplish what it set out to do?" It is an external evaluation, meaning that it is requested or conducted by a regulatory or grant-funding system outside the agency. For example, a grantor might require that services at a homeless shelter be evaluated to provide evidence of whether stated objectives are being met.

Measuring Program Objectives

By nature, objectives need to be observable and measurable. A program evaluator will have a much easier time trying to evaluate the overall accomplishments of a program if the objectives are straightforward and measurable.

Let us imagine for a moment that you have been asked to assist with the outcome evaluation of a program. The program offers group counseling to female adult victims of domestic violence with the objective of increasing their self-esteem. Which of the following two objectives would you rather try to evaluate?

1. Consumers of this program will report that they are feeling better about themselves.
2. Twenty-five consumers will score at least a 40 on the Jones self-esteem instrument by the end of the ten-week program.

The second objective is much easier to evaluate because it has clear criteria (40 on the Jones instrument) with which to judge the changes; therefore, one can see the results. It is our recommendation that all program objectives be submitted to the MOST standard, which means that a **program objective** should be

- Measurable   M.O.S.T.
- Observable
- Specific
- Timelined

By creating objectives that meet the MOST standard, an evaluator can better determine whether an objective was met. Let us look at each of these items individually.

Measurable objectives allow an evaluator to collect quantitative evidence of whether a goal was met. For instance, in our previous example, an evaluator can look at consumers' Jones self-esteem pretest and posttest scores to determine whether an increase, a decrease, or no change occurred. For an objective to be observable, it must be stated in a way that enables participants to easily and correctly respond within the measurement. That is, participants can be observant of their individual behaviors, thoughts, and feelings and therefore can complete a self-esteem survey measuring those. Conversely, one cannot observe another person's self-esteem, but one can measure some behavioral indicators that research has demonstrated to be predictors of good self-esteem, such as maintaining eye contact and holding one's head up while walking.

An objective that is specific states exactly what outcome is expected for how many consumers. For instance, twenty-five consumers must score at least 40 for this objective to be considered successfully achieved.

Finally, timelined objectives give the longitudinal information for the objectives—that is, when and how often do we measure the objective? For instance, in our example, the objective will be measured after the ten-week program is completed. A similar objective might state that the objective will be measured "after every completed ten-week program for one year." In summary, program objectives that adhere to the MOST standard allow a researcher to conduct a thorough and meaningful outcome evaluation.

Writing the Report

When writing, you have to anticipate the concerns and expectations of your reading audience. The overall style and depth of what you will want to include are generally determined by the purpose of your report and the audience for whom you are writing. For example, a brief memo to your supervisor may be sufficient for reporting a description of your consumers. You may want information on the average age, total number of consumers, frequency for sex and race, and average number of visits. However, for formal reports you will need to be more detailed and include certain elements, such as objectives and their outcomes.

A report for program evaluation addresses program objectives as opposed to research hypotheses. Therefore, an outside evaluator would address the scope of the problem in the introduction, conduct a literature review to determine standards for measurements (i.e., what other outcomes have been determined for each objective), develop or choose measurements for each objective, determine an appropriate sampling size, analyze the results, and present the findings for each objective in a narrative with tables.

Example 9.2 is an outcome evaluation report for a program that provided case management services to low-income mothers in a large metropolitan city. The funding source asked for an initial report of this new program. The report consists of two sections: a consumer description model and a case management model. Objectives concerning consumer description are labeled "CD"; therefore, CD (1) is the first consumer description objective. Objectives concerning case management are labeled "CM"; therefore, CM (1) is the first case management objective.

Tables constitute an important part of a written report. A table provides a visual representation that makes information easy to read. Table 9.1 shows an agency's referral rates by type of service. This table was organized by percentage to draw attention to the highest rate of referrals. Keep in mind that any table must be accompanied by a narrative of the results.

Strengths and Weaknesses of Program Evaluation

Each type of program evaluation has both strengths and weaknesses. Some of the strengths of process evaluations are that they are relatively easy to conduct because a process evaluation is very flexible (i.e., it has no rigid structure or timeline). Therefore, a process evaluation can be conducted at any time during the fiscal year or funding cycle. In addition, there are no constricting rules as to how to conduct a process evaluation. A process evaluation can be as informal as sitting down with consumers and asking what they like and dislike, and would like to see changed about the program. In contrast, a process evaluation can be a formalized process that

EXAMPLE 9.2: OUTCOME EVALUATION REPORT

Consumer Description Model

CD(1). What percentage of pregnant infant-wellness participants initiated prenatal care in the first trimester of pregnancy?
A total of sixteen out of forty-one women (39 percent) initiated prenatal care in the first trimester of pregnancy.

CD(2). What percentage of women who received prenatal infant-wellness services gave birth to preterm infants?
Three of the twenty-five women gave birth to preterm infants (as defined by infants delivered at thirty-seven weeks or less), totaling 12 percent of the women. In the project area comparison group, 72 out of 147 (48.9 percent) women gave birth to preterm infants.

CM(1a). What percentage of clients received referrals to other social service agencies?
A total of fifty-one out of fifty-eight women (87.9 percent) were referred to other social service agencies for services. Of the remaining seven (12.1 percent), five cases were administratively closed and two were missing data.

CM(1b). Of those clients referred, what percentage received services?
Of the currently active women referred, 87.9 percent received one or more services.

CM(1c). What type of services were clients referred to?

seeks to evaluate the number of consumers served (to date), to gather demographic data about consumers, and to determine overall patterns of program usage.

Some problems that can occur with process evaluation have to do with inappropriate timing and inapplicable questions. For instance, inappropriate timing would be evaluating consumer characteristics too early in the implementation of a new program—this would provide little information. Inapplicable questions on a satisfaction survey could mean that consumers may not be able to give an adequate report of what they like and dislike or what they feel needs to change about the program. For instance, asking consumers whether they would come back again for services in the future might just measure their need for the services instead of their satisfaction.

TABLE 9.1: REFERRAL RATE BY TYPE OF SERVICE

TYPE OF SERVICE	REFERRAL RATE	NUMBER OF CLIENTS
Transportation by staff	62.7%	32
Well-baby care	37.3%	19
Emergency infant supplies	27.5%	14
Emergency assistance	27.5%	14
Housing assistance	25.5%	13
WIC	25.5%	13
Case management	25.5%	13
Child day care	21.6%	11
Emergency food	21.6%	11
Public assistance	11.8%	6
Job and/or employment training	11.8%	6
Food stamps	9.8%	5
Primary health care	9.8%	5
Translation services	7.8%	4

One of the strengths of outcome evaluation is that it is an unbiased examination of a program's objectives. By "unbiased," we mean that the program evaluator is simply examining the stated objectives to determine whether those objectives were met. Another positive aspect of outcome evaluation is that it does not try to determine what worked or did not work in the program. This is a positive aspect because the evaluator is not pressured to justify the interventions that were used—rather he or she is simply asked if the stated objectives were fulfilled.

One of the weaknesses of outcome evaluation is that it provides no indication of whether the program itself is the cause of any change in the consumer. One can never be totally sure that the change in a group, sample, or population is due to the intervention and not some outside influence.

Practical Considerations and Common Problems

Program evaluation does not have to be a daunting process, but do keep in mind some of the issues that can plague the novice evaluator. The first issue to consider is that you must be very clear about which program you are evaluating. This may seem so simple and obvious that you would think it does not need to be mentioned, but you would be surprised at how many inexperienced evaluators get bogged down in the process by not being clear about what they are evaluating. One common example is when someone attempts to evaluate an entire agency. We strongly encourage you to select one program or service within your agency to focus on. Once you have mastered the skills needed to evaluate a single program or service, you may want to move on to evaluating multiple programs simultaneously.

Once you have established which program you will evaluate, it is important to be clear with the administrator or program director as to what type of evaluation you are conducting. Some preparation questions to guide you as you start the evaluation process follow.

For process evaluations

1. How long has the program been running?
2. What would you like to see accomplished in a process evaluation?
3. How will I gain access to consumers? To staff?
4. What is the goal of this process evaluation—description, program monitoring, quality assurance, or a combination of the three?
5. How soon would you like this completed?
6. How soon would you like a written report?

For outcome evaluations

1. What are the program's objectives?
2. Are these in some written form that I can have?
3. How soon would you like this completed?
4. How soon would you like a written report?

Another common problem is that because evaluators often want a program to be effective, they take on responsibility for the success or failure of the evaluation. Similarly, the pressure to find positive results can sometimes come from the organization. Not only do individuals dislike hearing complaints about their work; a negative report can jeopardize funding. Remember that your role is that of an objective auditor and you must report all the findings. Your job is to measure and frankly report what was done against what was proposed. In other words, either the program met its stated objectives or it did not. It is not your role to speculate as to why objectives were met or not met or to soften the critique to cushion the blow to someone's ego. Stating this up front is an important protective factor for the evaluator and can increase others' confidence in the report and the evaluator, because it shows that the evaluation was ethically and objectively conducted.

Finally, it is not your responsibility to make recommendations about the findings unless the program administrator asks for these. If he or she does ask for these, recommendations can include what could be improved or done differently; these are included at the end of your report.

Case Scenario

You are a social worker employed in a large metropolitan hospital. A wealthy donor wants to donate a sizable amount of money to fund a smoking cessation program. Your supervisor has charged you with the task of developing some goals and objectives that can be implemented so that after six months the hospital can measure the success of the program to measure whether it is working.

Critical-Thinking Questions

On the basis of the case scenario, answer the following questions:

1. What would be three objectives that would measure the success of this new program? Write out your objectives, remembering to incorporate the acronym MOST.

2. From what you have learned about research methods thus far, can you be confident that the program is helping people to be successful in quitting smoking?

3. How can you know (one way or the other) that the program is achieving its desired results?

Key Points

- There are two reasons that social workers should evaluate their programs. First, section 5.02(a) of the NASW Code of Ethics (2008) demands that we "monitor and evaluate policies, the implementation of programs, and practice interventions." Second, funding sources are increasingly demanding that programs be accountable in how they spend their money, how consumers are helped, and what positive benefits result from the monies spent.

- A program evaluation is a research design and analysis that evaluates specific characteristics of a program within an agency.

- There are two types of program evaluations: process evaluations and outcome evaluations.

- A process evaluation (an internal audit) has three main goals: to construct a program description, to provide program monitoring, and to assess the quality of services being provided.

- An outcome evaluation is an external audit that measures the overall effectiveness of a program. This evaluation looks at the goals and objectives established by the program to answer the question "Did this program accomplish what it set out to do?"

Practice Exam

True or False

1. The NASW Code of Ethics mandates that social workers evaluate their practice.

2. With shrinking budgets and funding dollars available, most funding agencies have moved away from asking programs to complete program evaluations.

3. A process evaluation can be conducted multiple times over the course of a funding year.

4. One of the weaknesses of the outcome evaluation is that it provides no indication of whether the program itself is the cause of any change in the consumer.

Multiple Choice

5. Objectives should be written to meet the acronym MOST, which stands for:

   a. Measurable, objective, satisfactory, and true

   b. Meaningful, observable, sensible, and targeted

   c. Methodical, opportunistic, scientific, and tailored

   d. Methodical, observable, satisfactory, and timelined

   e. None of the above

6. There are generally two types of evaluations:

   a. Formative and outcome

   b. Outcome and developmental

   c. Developmental and timelined

   d. Observable and qualitative

   e. None of the above

7. When initially starting an outcome evaluation all of the following questions should be asked except:

   a. What are the program's objectives?

   b. Are these in some written form that I can have?

   c. How soon would you like this completed?

   d. How much of your funding comes from grant sources?

   e. None of the above—all are important questions to ask

CHAPTER TEN

Single-Subject Designs

CSWE Core Competencies

IN THIS CHAPTER you will find the following Council on Social Work Education (CSWE) competencies:

Educational Policy 2.1.3—Apply critical thinking to inform and communicate professional judgments

Educational Policy 2.1.6—Engage in research-informed practice and practice-informed research

Educational Policy 2.1.9—Respond to contexts that shape practice

Educational Policy 2.1.10(b)—Assessment

Educational Policy 2.1.10(d)—Evaluation

This chapter discusses single-subject designs and some of the techniques for conducting this type of research. In addition, this chapter provides a discussion of how to interpret your results in a single-subject-design study and explores some of the limitations of this type of research.

What Is a Single-Subject Design?

The single-subject design has many names and may be referred to as small-*n* research design, idiographic design, single-case experimental design, and interrupted time-series research design. Although it can be used to evaluate families and groups of more than one person, the single-subject design is a quantitative method of research that is generally used for evaluating an individual's progress over time. Specifically, the single-subject design is a tool that measures whether a relationship exists between an intervention and a specific outcome. For instance, measuring a person's depression over time would give an indication as to whether antidepressant therapy is working. Single-subject designs use the logic of time-series designs (you may want to refer back to chapter 7 to refresh your memory). However, rather than using a large group of subjects, the single-subject design measures the changes that occur in an individual.

The single-subject design emerged as a practice tool for evaluating individual progress in the late 1960s and early 1970s. It was partly a reaction to the constrictions of the group research design and partly a result of the works of behavioral psychologists such as B. F. Skinner. Skinner was concerned with behavior modification and believed that rewards and reinforcers could be used to shape or change behaviors. For example, if an instructor wants to promote class participation, then he or she would need to find something that the class would consider desirable (a reward or reinforcer). If the instructor were to give out chocolate bars every time someone in the class asked a question or volunteered an answer, class participation would probably be very high. Reinforcing a desired behavior is one underlying concept behind behavioral modification.

Elements of Single-Subject-Design Research

There are basic elements to all single-subject-design studies. These are selecting the target outcome, selecting the intervention, selecting the measurement tool, collecting baseline data, collecting intervention data, and conducting the analysis (compiling the results).

Selecting the Target Outcome

For the single-subject design to be successful, the social worker must first help the participant determine the behavior or feelings to be changed. For instance, the participant may want to improve his or her parenting skills (behavior) or self-esteem (feeling). It is crucial that the social worker and the participant be able to agree on the **target outcome**, or the goal of the intervention (i.e., the way the participant will act or feel in the future). This is similar to defining and specifying your variables in a quantitative experiment.

You will find that some variables are very easy to define. For example, if a consumer comes to you and says she wants help with her abuse of alcohol or other drugs, then the variable might be defined as the number of times the person drinks or uses any mind-altering chemicals each day. But not all variables are so easily defined. What if a consumer comes to you and asks for help with his low self-esteem? This concept is abstract, subjective, and impossible to observe directly; therefore, it is necessary to find a way to measure this variable. As we discussed in chapter 4, one way to measure a construct is to use a standardized measure. For instance, you could select the Self-Esteem Rating Scale. You may then say that the target outcome, to increase self-esteem by the end of the intervention, will be determined by the scores on the Self-Esteem Rating Scale.

Selecting the Intervention

An intervention is the technique used to facilitate a change in research. As in all other quantitative research, in a single-subject research design it is important to select an intervention on the basis of a literature review. You, as the researcher, would review the literature and select the intervention that is most appropriate for your research participant. This means that you do not just guess at the best intervention or do what others are doing; rather, you read empirical studies and find the intervention that has proved to be a best-practice approach. Chances are that you will find a variety of interventions for any particular problem. Your task is to select one that fits your participant. For example, if the target outcome is the alleviation of depression, you may conduct a literature review that suggests a variety of methods for treating depression, including exercise, cognitive-behavioral therapy, and medication. However, if your participant is physically challenged, exercise may not be the most appropriate intervention. As another example, let us say that your participant is a thirteen-year-old female with poor self-esteem. Perhaps for this individual you select daily affirmations for the intervention. This intervention requires the participant to look in the mirror each day for five minutes and repeat a series of positive affirmations (e.g., "I am beautiful," "I am a good person").

Selecting the Measure

A measure can be as simple as having participants document every time they smoke a cigarette and bring their numbers each week to a quit-smoking support group. Standardized measures are often used to collect data in single-subject research because they are convenient and have established reliability and validity. Fischer and Corcoran (2007) present hundreds of different measures in their two volumes of compiled measurement scales for adults, couples, families, and children. For example, you might choose to measure participants' depression by using the Depression Self-Rating Scale. This is an eighteen-item measure that uses simplified language, short statements, and limited response categories, all of which allow the participant to complete the questionnaire quickly. Examples of these items are "I feel like crying" and "I feel very lonely." A response can be "most of the time," "sometimes," or "never."

Collecting Baseline Data

It is important to remember that no intervention occurs during the baseline phase. The baseline is used to establish a reference point to which any targeted change in the individual following the intervention is compared. During the baseline phase, it is important to collect information over a period of time. It is suggested that you have a minimum of three observations, for instance, three days or events. This allows you to average out the behavior and helps to guard against anomalies. For example, let us assume that you are measuring the baseline for depression. You may ask your participant to complete a standardized depression inventory. If you have her complete the scale only one time, you cannot be sure that her answers are indicative of a particularly good day (with less depression) or an especially bad day (with higher levels of depression). But if you ask her to complete the same scale over a week, filling out the scale each night before bedtime, for instance, you can assume that an average of the scores for the seven days is fairly representative of the baseline level of depression.

Collecting Intervention Data

Once the target outcome has been agreed on, the appropriate intervention has been selected, a method for measuring the target outcome has been chosen, and the baseline data have been collected, you must then collect the intervention data. In our example, you would ask the participant to start the intervention (e.g., exercise, cognitive-behavioral counseling, medication) while continuing to complete the depression scale each night for eight weeks. If her depression decreases over the eight weeks, it would be logical to conclude that the intervention worked. As we discussed in chapter 7, it can be tempting to say that there is a causal relationship, in other words, that cognitive-behavioral counseling caused her depression to decrease. However, we cannot prove that the intervention alone caused the change—the difference in the behavior may also be due to some outside influence totally separate from anything in the intervention. That is, people sometimes get better because they mature or because their environment changes (e.g., there may be a change in marital status or employment status).

Reporting Results

There are two ways to report the results of a single-subject design. The first and simplest way is to simply graph the results and examine the graph to determine whether a change has occurred over time. Figure 10.1 shows the results of a single-subject design that the social worker has charted using Microsoft Excel. The score is the overall weekly mean score, where a score of 6 indicates a high level of depression and a score of 0 indicates no depression. A cursory glance at the figure reveals that the depression decreased between the baseline phase (four weeks) and the intervention phase (eight weeks) of the research. This reviewing of charted data is known as eyeballing data, which simply means scanning the results to look for obvious differences between the baseline and intervention phases. But let us assume for a moment that the change in level of depression is not so obviously clear. Figure 10.2 represents a participant's scores where the difference between the baseline and intervention phases is relatively minor (and thus presents a challenge when we inspect the graph to determine whether a significant change occurred). To determine whether this smaller change can be considered important, we can simply calculate the average scores and report that there was no difference. Or we can utilize a computer-generated statistical analysis of the data to determine whether our intervention was effective.

FIGURE 10.1: SINGLE-SUBJECT DESIGN: SUCCESSFUL DEPRESSION INTERVENTION

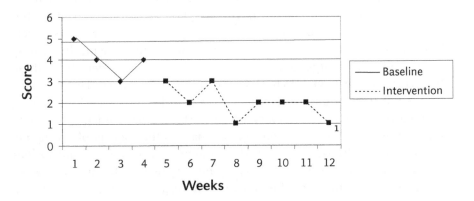

FIGURE 10.2: SINGLE-SUBJECT DESIGN: UNSUCCESSFUL DEPRESSION INTERVENTION

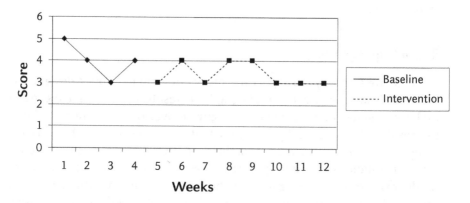

Types of Single-Subject Designs

The designs that we discuss here are all based on a basic AB design, where A always stands for the baseline score, and B always represents the scores during the intervention. The ABA design expands on this by adding an additional baseline, the ABAB design repeats the baseline and intervention, and the ABC design introduces a new intervention.

The AB Design

The AB design is the most common and least complicated of the measurement designs because there is one baseline measure and one intervention. The following example AB design is used to reduce acting-out behaviors in the classroom.

John is a social work student doing a field experience at an elementary school's resource center on Tuesdays through Fridays. He received a referral for a seven-year-old boy who has been acting out for the past week. The teacher would like for the student to work on reducing his acting-out behaviors (the target outcome). The teacher has been identifying these behaviors on a behavioral checklist for the past four days. This checklist allows the user to place check marks next to behaviors such as talking without permission; hitting, kicking, or pushing other students; and cursing; in this way, the teacher has operationalized the concept of acting out. As you can see in example 10.1, the baseline scores averaged out to four incidences a day over the four days. John conducts a literature review of effective interventions for child-related behavioral problems. John's chosen

---

EXAMPLE 10.1: AB DESIGN RESULTS

ELEMENT	RESULTS
Target outcome	Decrease in acting out behaviors in the classroom.
Intervention	Play and listen for a half hour each Tuesday through Friday
Measurement tool	Behavioral checklist
Baseline data (A)	5, 4, 3, 4 (4 days)
Intervention data (B)	3, 2, 3, 1, 2, 2, 2, 1 (eight days)
Results	Mean scores: A = 4, B = 2 (decrease in scores by 50%)

---

intervention is to meet with the student for a half hour every Tuesday through Friday for two weeks for free play. Together they will color or play a game of the student's choice (e.g., card games, board games), during which time the student can talk about anything that is on his mind, or they can forgo the game and simply talk. During these visits, the student starts talking to John about his parents' divorce and how it has made him sad and angry. John normalizes the child's feelings (i.e., tells the child that what he is feeling is normal) and encourages the child to talk with his parents and the teacher when he feels sad or angry. The teacher continues to chart acting-out behaviors during the two weeks that John provides the intervention. The intervention scores average out to be two incidences per day, a decrease of 50 percent.

While simple to use, this design has limitations. For instance, you do not know how long the effect of the intervention will last, and it is limited to measuring only one intervention. The following designs address each of these issues.

The ABA Design

If you wanted to be more certain that it was the intervention that was responsible for the change (and not some outside influence), then a slightly more sophisticated design like the ABA design would be appropriate. Here, the second A represents the withdrawal of the intervention and the return to baseline. In other words, you would continue to measure the participant after the completion of the intervention. For instance, the child who has been acting out completes the two-week intervention, but the teacher continues to measure any acting-out behaviors, using the behavioral checklist to see whether the effect of the intervention continues after the intervention ceases.

Critics of this method state that you can never truly return to a baseline once an intervention has been introduced. In other words, the child has been changed by the intervention and therefore will not have the same scores as before the intervention, even if the acting out increases. However, this method can be used to monitor how long the effect of the intervention lasts. In other words, once the student has stopped spending time playing and talking to John, how long will the effect last before the acting-out behaviors return (and possibly worsen)? By monitoring the behaviors after the intervention stops, we can know when to reintroduce the intervention or another intervention.

The ABAB Design

The ABAB design is slightly more sophisticated than the ABA design. In the ABAB design you begin with the baseline, introduce the intervention, withdraw the intervention and return to baseline, and then reintroduce the intervention. As in the previous example, if acting-out behaviors are monitored after the intervention has ceased and we observe an increase in acting-out behaviors, we can reintroduce the visits with John and monitor the effect over time. One would expect to find a decrease in acting-out behaviors after the reintroduction of the intervention. If this were the case, it would be safe to assume that the intervention was working again. An issue to keep in mind is that while one intervention might work for short periods of time, this design does not allow for different or multiple interventions that may have more lasting effects. In this scenario, the child could become dependent on John's intervention. This is why John advised the child to also talk to his parents and teacher, which could be another intervention that could be measured.

The ABC Design

Up to this point, we have been discussing the use of one intervention. You may be wondering, "What about some complicated target outcomes that require multiple interventions, such as depression?" A review of the literature on depression shows that the most effective treatment is a combination of cognitive-behavioral treatment and medication. For a target outcome that requires more than one intervention, it is recommended that you use an ABC design. An ABC design works the same way as an AB design except that it utilizes multiple interventions (introduced in sequence). Again, using our example of depression, you would measure the baseline phase, then you would introduce the first intervention (cognitive-behavioral counseling) and measure it over eight weeks, and then in the weeks that follow you would introduce the second intervention (antidepressants) while continuing the measurement. This design may also be used when one intervention alone is not yielding the results we anticipate. In other words, we start out with an AB design, but the level of depression does not decrease as much as was hoped with cognitive behavioral counseling. Therefore, a more intrusive intervention (medication) is introduced to determine whether the combination of the interventions will provide relief. A limitation of this design is that you do not know for sure how much the first intervention is creating the change after the second intervention is introduced. In other words, would the change have occurred anyway with more time?

Strengths and Limitations of Single-Subject Designs

One of the strengths of single-subject designs has already been discussed: by measuring the participant's progress toward the target outcome (i.e., the variable), you can determine whether an intervention is successful. However, there is another way to use single-subject research designs. The results of the intervention can be shared with the participant to reinforce progress and treatment decisions. That is, the results themselves become an intervention. For example, the participant with depression has a very bad day during the sixth week of treatment and feels that she is making no progress and wants to quit the intervention. By reviewing the results of figure 10.1 with the participant, you can point out her overall progress. This is similar to what individuals do when they are dieting. By weighing themselves weekly and seeing a measurable drop in weight, they reinforce their desire to continue the diet, even when they feel discouraged because they did not lose weight one week. Conversely, if a participant is not progressing as expected, sharing the results may support a decision to introduce a different or more intrusive intervention, such as medication or hospitalization.

Despite the benefits it offers, the single-subject design is limited by the small sample size it uses. This precludes the results from being generalized to others. While this has obvious application for the participant, it does not add to the general knowledge of the public. Also, without a control group, one cannot tell whether a research participant would naturally improve without the intervention.

However, the single-subject design is still a very useful tool for practitioners who want evidence-based ways to evaluate their practice. The single-subject design, like all quantitative research, is driven by theory and guided by research, and it is a useful tool for evaluating whether an individual is making progress.

Case Scenario

You are a caseworker in a community mental health facility. Your client is a twenty-one-year-old female who reports that she constantly feels that she is worthless. She has had a series of dysfunctional relationships with men. She feels that she does not deserve to find someone who will treat her decently. She has also had a number of health problems that cause her to feel bad about herself. These health problems have caused her to drop out of school, and she has been unable to hold a job. The subject frequently has self-defeating thoughts. Your task is to work with your client to devise a single-subject design.

Critical-Thinking Questions

On the basis of the case scenario outlined here, answer the following questions:

1. What keywords would you use in a literature review to design an intervention for your client?

2. What type of single-subject design would you implement? Give your reasons for choosing this particular design.

3. What would be the target behavior in which you would try to intervene?

4. How would you operationalize the target behavior?

5. What would be the number of baseline observations?

6. What would be the number of observations (post-intervention)?

Key Points

- A single-subject research design is a method for evaluating individual progress over time.

- The basic elements of all single-subject design research are selecting the target outcome, selecting the intervention, selecting the measurement tool, collecting baseline data, collecting intervention data, and conducting the analysis (compiling the results).

- There are four types of single-subject research designs: AB (one baseline and one intervention), ABA (which adds an additional baseline), ABAB (which repeats the baseline and intervention), and ABC (which introduces a new intervention).

Practice Exam

True or False

1. A single-subject research design is a method for evaluating individual progress over the course of several years.

2. There are four types of single-subject research designs: AB, ABA, ABAB, and ABC.

3. Single-subject designs are known by many names; one of them is small-*n* research.

Multiple Choice

4. The minimum number of observations during the baseline phase is:

   a. One

   b. Two

   c. Three

   d. Four

   e. None of the above

5. One of the most important parts of single-subject-design research is:

   a. Establishing the target behavior

   b. Establishing the number of baseline observations

   c. Establishing how you will ensure that the client is being truthful

   d. Establishing how you will measure the outcome

   e. None of the above

6. Researchers use which of the following to select interventions for a single-subject design:

   a. A literature review

   b. Practice wisdom

   c. The advice of other clinicians

   d. All of the above

   e. None of the above

7. Because of the following, it is difficult to generalize the results of a single-subject design to others:

   a. The small amount of data collected

   b. The small sample size

   c. The possibility that the client is not being truthful

   d. All of the above

   e. None of the above

8. Single-subject designs were partly the result of the work of:

   a. B. F. Skinner

   b. Sigmund Freud

   c. James Watson

   d. Carl Rogers

   e. None of the above

CHAPTER ELEVEN

Introduction to Descriptive Statistics

CSWE Core Competencies

IN THIS CHAPTER you will find the following Council on Social Work Education (CSWE) competencies:

Educational Policy 2.1.3—Apply critical thinking to inform and communicate professional judgments

Educational Policy 2.1.6—Engage in research-informed practice and practice-informed research

Educational Policy 2.1.9—Respond to contexts that shape practice

Educational Policy 2.1.10(b)—Assessment

Once you have conducted a literature review, stated your research question, identified your variables, selected a research method, and determined how to collect your sample, you will need to decide how your data will be analyzed. Remember that quantitative research allows us to describe variables and to explore relationships between variables. Data that are collected can be described, and the results of quantitative data are presented in numerical form in tables and graphs. In this chapter we explore how to describe the numerical data we collect for individual variables, and in chapter 12 we discuss analyses that examine associations between variables.

What Is Data Analysis?

Quantitative data analysis is defined as the process of utilizing a variety of statistical procedures to analyze numerical data. Data analysis is usually

conducted in steps—first the descriptive analysis of the individual variables is conducted, and then inferential statistics are used to analyze the
associations between variables. Data analysis involves counting responses
and using other statistical procedures to discover the identifying characteristics of individual variables in a sample and the relationships between two
or more variables in the sample. The type of analysis you use depends on
the level of your variables and the research method you choose.

The First Step of Data Analysis

There are two steps to analyzing numerical data: using descriptive statistics and then inferential statistics (discussed in chapter 12). **Descriptive
statistics** are ways of organizing, describing, and presenting quantitative
(numerical) data in a manner that is concise, manageable, and understandable. They usually deal with each variable individually and establish the
common patterns found in each individual variable. Describing a sample
in terms of the individual variables (e.g., sex, race, occupation) through
measures such as totals and percentages gives us a picture of some of
the characteristics of a sample. Descriptive analysis often is helpful for
understanding the extent of an event or occurrence, such as the number of
rapes on a college campus or the typical salary of child-welfare workers.
This method is used with both quantitative and qualitative methods. And
while numerical descriptions of the sample and/or the common responses
can be used in both methods of research, they are not always used in
qualitative methods, but they *must* be used in quantitative methods.

Table 11.1 shows results from a study conducted on test cheating on
a college campus. This study draws on the literature by using fourteen
independent variables to explain the cheating habits of 118 students in a
central Appalachian university (the model includes seven demographic factors as well as interpretations of variables related to professors and students). The table reports the results of the five descriptive variables
collected for the study. To assess these variables, students were asked to
read the prompt: "In the last academic year, how often have you engaged
in the following actions?" Seven ways to cheat were listed beneath the
question. Students were asked to use a four-point frequency scale to
respond to each variable. The response "never" was coded as 1, "once" as
2, "two to ten times" as 3, and "more than 10 times" as 4.

Overall, the results show that the majority of the students in the sample
at least occasionally practice cheating. Most students have tried all but one
of the actions listed. The majority abstained only from the riskier act of

Table 11.1: Descriptive Statistics for Test Cheating

ITEM	NEVER	ONCE	2–10 TIMES	10 OR MORE TIMES	MEAN
Copying from another student during an exam without his or her knowledge	37%	21%	40%	2%	2.059
Copying from another student during an exam with his or her knowledge	40%	23%	35%	2%	1.975
Using unpermit-ted notes during an exam	66%	18%	15%	1%	1.508
Getting questions or answers from someone who has already taken the test	24%	15%	50%	11%	2.483
Helping someone else cheat on a test	42%	17%	37%	3%	2.017
Sharing notes from a take-home exam	11%	11%	70%	8%	2.746
Making answer sheet available to enable another student to see the answer	43%	20%	33%	4%	1.983

Source: Robinson, E., Ambergey, R., Swank, E., & Faulkner, C. (2004). Test cheating in a rural college: Studying the importance of individual and situational factors. *College Student Journal, 38*(3), 380–395.

sneaking cheat sheets into the classroom (66 percent said they never did), whereas between 57 percent and 89 percent of students admitted to other cheating techniques. This means that about three out of five students have copied from other students' exams or made their tests available to other students. Moreover, three out of four students have received test questions from someone who has completed the test, and an overwhelming nine out of ten students have improperly collaborated on a take-home exam.

Descriptive Analysis

Descriptive statistics help us to make sense of a large amount of data by finding both what is common or typical for a variable and what exceptions exist for a variable. Suppose for a moment that you have conducted a study that involves one hundred participants and you asked them to complete a survey that consisted of twenty questions. This would result in two thousand answers—a large amount of material for anyone to read through and attempt to understand. Descriptive statistics allow us to **aggregate** data (i.e., to compile information in a concise, manageable, and understandable manner) so that the data can be examined relatively quickly. Chances are that you have used descriptive statistics for much of your life without knowing it. For instance, most people can describe what their average weight is and within what range their weight generally fluctuates. By calculating the average (also known as the mean) and the range of the variable (weight), we are using one type of descriptive statistics called univariate analysis. **Univariate analysis** involves the examination across cases of one variable at a time. There are three major characteristics of a single variable that we tend to look at: distribution, central tendencies, and dispersion.

Measures of Distribution

Distribution of data is a summary of the frequency of individual values or ranges of values for a variable. The simplest distribution would list every value of a variable and the number of people who had each value. **Frequency**, as the word implies, is the number of times that a response occurs. For example, we might discuss the frequency of absences for members of a class (the number of students who failed to attend class today). A frequency can be reported as a total (two out of twenty students were absent today) and as a percentage (10 percent of the twenty students were absent today).

We can also group responses so that we can report the information in more manageable terms. For instance, we might group the annual income of the families of incoming freshmen into five categories, as in table 11.2, rather than reporting a list of the one hundred responses.

TABLE 11.2: ANNUAL INCOME OF FAMILIES OF INCOMING FRESHMEN

FREQUENCY	INCOME	PERCENTAGE
50	Less than $25,000	50
20	$25,001–$50,000	20
15	$50,001–$75,000	15
10	$75,001–$100,000	10
5	More than $100,000	5

Measures of Central Tendency

Measures of central tendency are a statistic (number) that is used to represent a set of responses for a variable. A **central tendency** is an estimate of the center of a distribution of values. You can think of central tendencies as the means to determine what is most typical, common, and routine. There are three major types of estimates of central tendency— mean, median, and mode—of which the mean is the most-often-used measure of central tendency.

A **mean** is a statistical average. You can use a mean for any variable that is collected through interval-level or ratio-level responses (e.g., weight, miles driving, grade point average, age). The mean is a precise way to detect what is typical because it calculates the middle score by taking all scores into account. If you wanted to find the typical or average age of people in your class, you could simply add the ages of each person together and divide the sum by the number of people in your class.

The second measure of central tendency is the **median**. The median is simply the midpoint of a set of numbers. To get an accurate median, you must first order the data from low to high, and then find the number that falls in the middle. For instance, if you have a set of numbers from 1 to 5, the median would be 3, because 3 falls directly in the middle, with two numbers below it (1 and 2) and two numbers above it (4 and 5). However, if your numbers ranged from 1 to 4, then the median would be 2.5 (the midpoint between 1 and 4).

The final measure of central tendency is the **mode**. The mode is the most frequently occurring response found for a variable. Let us assume for a moment that in seeking the mean for your classmates' ages, the number 21 kept occurring more than any other number. Then 21 would be the mode, or the most frequently occurring number in the variable of age.

Modes are most commonly reported when the researcher has used a nominal measure of a variable, such as the number of Catholics, Protestants, and Muslims in a study.

Because measures of central tendency attempt to represent how data are grouped around what is average for a variable, it is highly probable that you use these methods without realizing it. For example, if you have ever paid attention to your grade point average, you are examining a measure of central tendency (the mean of your class grades).

You need to make sure that when choosing a statistical measure, you are using the appropriate level of measurement. For example, it would not make sense to report the average for a nominal- or ordinal-level variable (e.g., reporting the average sex for a group of people would be impossible). A second important point is that a statistical mean is very sensitive to outliers. An **outlier** is an anomaly or result that is far different from most of the results for the group. An outlier is a number or variable that has extreme values that can skew the overall results (especially in a statistical average). For example, let us imagine for a moment that you want to measure the mean income of consumers in your agency. Most of the consumers your agency serves are poor (as measured by the federal poverty guidelines). However, you have one consumer whose annual income is greater than $100,000. This one person would be considered an outlier, and including his or her income would skew the overall mean income and make it appear greater than what is actually true. The question arises as to what to do about outliers: Do you simply ignore them? Do you throw them out? There is no one answer. One solution may be to report the information both ways. For example, you may report that the average income of the consumers in your agency is $25,201; however, there is one consumer who has an income of more than $100,000. When this income is removed from the analysis, the average income is $14,287.

In summary, central tendency statistics report how much our data are alike or similar. In other words, how much do the subjects reflect similar characteristics, views, or beliefs? For example, let us say you are trying to decide whether to take a particular elective class. You ask twenty students who have taken the class previously to rate the class on a scale from 1 (didn't like it very much) to 10 (liked it a lot). Seven students give the class a 10, eight students give the class a 9, and five students give the class an 8. The mean of the responses is 9.1 (total score of 182 divided by twenty responses). You might conclude that, on the basis of the students you surveyed, students who have taken the class typically liked the class very much. In fact, the mode was 9 (eight students) and the median was also 9 (midpoint between 8 and 10).

Measures of Dispersion

A **measure of dispersion** shows how dissimilar or different the data are, and it is reported by how the scores are arranged (fall) around the mean. Measures of dispersion, also referred to as measures of variability, report the overall spread of scores from the mean. Do responses stay close to the mean or do they fall away from what is typical? Put another way, how close do the scores cluster near the typical answer? An example of a distribution with a small dispersion could be the results you obtain from asking everyone in your class what their desired grade is (assuming that everyone wants an A and no one wants to fail). The topic of legal abortion can create a wide dispersion, as many people hold opposing views. Measures of dispersion are used only for studies with interval- or ratio-level data.

The simplest measure of dispersion is range. **Range** is the overall spread or variability of a variable; it tells us the difference between the lowest (minimum) and highest (maximum) values (responses) for a variable. For example, if the ages of the students in your class cover a span from eighteen years old to seventy-three years old, you would say that the range is 55 (the difference between 18 and 73), and that the minimum is 18 and the maximum is 73. A wide range of scores would indicate that responses are more dissimilar to the mean than a narrow range of scores would be. Ranges are easy to calculate, but they tell the reader very little information. For instance, we do not know where the ages of the respondents fall in the 18–73 age continuum.

Variance is a statistical measure used to examine the spread of scores in a distribution. The larger the variance, the farther the scores are from the mean; the smaller the variance, the closer the scores are to the mean. That is, if the scores vary a lot from one another (have a large variance), we can assume that the responses vary a lot from the typical response (they are dissimilar from the mean). If the scores do not vary a lot (have a small variance), we can assume that the responses are more typical of the mean.

Figure 11.1 is a **histogram** (a vertical block graph used in statistics to visually present interval- or ratio-level data) that shows a distribution of scores that are closely clumped around the mean. This type of distribution is called **leptokurtosis**. Leptokurtosis is the shape of a distribution of scores that is tall and narrow because the majority of scores closely resemble the mean. Figure 11.1 presents the frequency of Alcoholics Anonymous meetings per month for 406 recovering addicts. The mean number of meetings was 15.5, and the range was 17, with a minimum of 8 and a maximum of 25. Looking at the graph, you can see that most respondents reported a

FIGURE 11.1: HISTOGRAM WITH LEPTOKURTOSIS

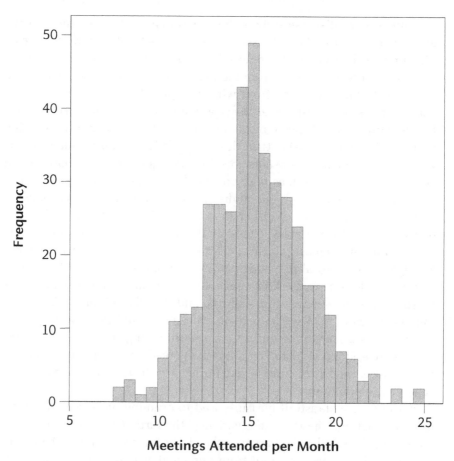

similar number of meetings (13–17), which is very close to the mean (15.5). Very few of the scores fall away from the mean (fewer than 13 or more than 17). This causes the distribution to be tall and narrow, or leptokurtic.

Figure 11.2 is a histogram that shows how a distribution looks if the scores are dissimilar from the mean. This type of distribution is called **platykurtosis**. Platykurtosis is the shape of a distribution of scores that is flat and wide because the majority of scores differ from the mean. This graph is displaying the month of birth of 1,487 respondents. As you can see, the answers in this population are dissimilar. Therefore, the distribution is spread wide and flat.

Finally, we will look at the standard deviation. A **standard deviation** is a measure of dispersion that is calculated by taking the square root of variance. It is the most commonly used measure of dispersion. We make

FIGURE 11.2: HISTOGRAM WITH PLATYKURTOSIS

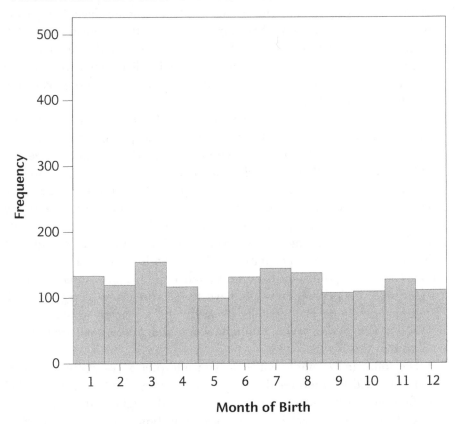

two assumptions when looking at standard deviation—first, that we are dealing with interval-level or ratio-level variables, and second, that the data are normally distributed.

A **normal distribution** of data is the symmetrical distribution of scores around the mean, with the most scores clustered around the mean and tapering off on both sides. Normally distributed data resemble a bell-shaped curve, where the mean is zero. If we folded a bell-shaped curve in half, one half would perfectly match the other. Therefore, a bell-shaped curve is the distribution of scores that are symmetrically spread around the mean so that each side of the mean resembles the other. If we assume that our data are normally distributed on the basis of probability distribution theory (the theory that data are equally distributed on both sides of the mean), then we can make other assumptions. For example, we can be more confident that our sample adequately reflects the population from which it was drawn. For instance, we can assume that 68.26 percent of any population will fall within one standard deviation of the mean. We can assume that 95.44 percent will fall within two standard deviations of the mean. And we can assume that 99.74 percent of the population will fall within three standard deviations of the mean. The more the data fall symmetrically around the mean, the more normally distributed we say they are. The less symmetrical the data are from the mean, the more likely it is that the result is out of the norm.

One of the easiest ways to explain this is with IQ tests. It is known that if IQ tests were administered to a large group of people (for example, 1,000 people), 68.26 percent would score within one standard deviation. Average IQ is 100 points (with a standard deviation of ± 15 points). Therefore, we can be confident that 682.6 people (68.26 percent) would score 100 ± 15 points (one standard deviation), or between 85 and 115 points. We can be confident that 954.4 people (95.44 percent) would score 100 ± 30 points (two standard deviations), or between 70 and 130. We can be confident that 997.4 people (99.74 percent) would score within three standard deviations (100 ± 45 points), or between 55 and 145. This means that less than 1 percent of the population would have an IQ score lower than 55 (considered moderately developmentally delayed), and 1 percent would have an IQ above 145 (genius level). Common sense and our own experience also tell us that this is true.

The following example will help you interpret a descriptive analysis: You are asked to interpret the results of a survey conducted with child-welfare employees in one hundred agencies throughout the state (table 11.3). In the top row are four variables (education level in years, current salary, months since hire, and minority classification). The first column shows the type of descriptive statistics that were measured (mean; median; mode; variance; standard deviation; and range, with minimum and maximum). The number of people who responded (n) for each variable, except current salary, is 474; the number of people who responded for current salary is 473. Keep in mind that some individuals may choose not to answer one or more questions, which would make the n different for that variable. Under the n are the measures of central tendency (mean, median, and mode), then the measures of dispersion (range, variance, and standard deviation).

Let's examine three variables in table 11.3, starting on the right and working left. Minority classification is coded (i.e., a number is assigned to represent an answer). The code is 0 = "No, not a minority" and 1 = "Yes, a minority." As you can see, this variable provides us with minimal

TABLE 11.3: DESCRIPTIVE STATISTICS OF CHILD WELFARE EMPLOYEES

	YEARS OF EDUCATION (n = 474)	CURRENT SALARY (n = 473)	MONTHS SINCE HIRE (n = 474)	MINORITY CLASSIFI- CATION (n = 474)
Mean	16.49	$34,419.57	81.11	.22
Median	16.00	$28,875.00	81.00	.00
Mode	16.00	$30,750.00	81	0
Variance	4.322	—	101.223	.172
SD	2.885	$17,075.66	10.061	.414
Range	6	$119,250.00	35	1
Minimum	12	$15,750.00	63	0
Maximum	18	$135,000.00	98	1

information because it is nominal. Therefore, we cannot interpret this variable using measures of dispersion. We can, however, use one central tendency by reporting the mode for this variable (the most frequently reported response is "No, not a minority"). This is still very limited information that does not tell us how many reported minority status as opposed to nonminority status.

The months-since-hire variable shows the same number (or value) for mean, median, and mode. This means that the average, the midpoint, and the most frequently occurring value is 81—that is, eighty-one months (almost seven years) employed in child welfare. The variance for these scores is 101.223. Variance tells us how closely the numbers are distributed in relation to the mean. Since the mean is 81 and the variance is 101, we might expect the scores to be fairly equally distributed around the mean like a normal bell-shaped curve—not too close and not too far away (see figure 11.3). If the variance were 85, we would expect the scores to be closer to the mean (creating a tall and narrow graph), and if the variance were 130, we would expect the scores to spread farther from the mean (creating a shorter but wider graph). The standard deviation is 10.061 or, rounded, 10 (1 SD = 10). The range is 35, with a minimum of 63 and a maximum of 98 months.

Now we can calculate the following: What is the number of months since hire for 68.26 percent of the employees? To do this, we subtract 1 SD

FIGURE 11.3: HISTOGRAM WITH BELL-SHAPED CURVE, NORMAL DISTRIBUTION

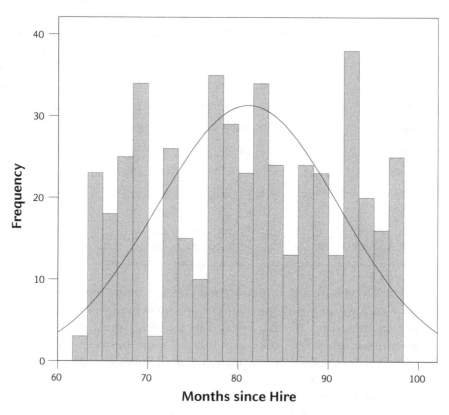

(10) from the mean (81), which equals 71. Then we add 1 SD (10) to the mean (81), which gives us 91. This gives us our spread on both sides of the mean. Thus, it has been between seventy-one and ninety-one months since 68.26 percent of employees were hired.

Keep in mind that we *assume* a normal distribution, but in actuality, a distribution may be skewed (meaning that there are more responses on the left or right side of the mean). When plotted on a graph, a **skewed distribution** of scores produces an asymmetrical curve. Distributions skewed to the left are said to be negatively skewed, and those skewed to the right are positively skewed. Figure 11.4 is a visual representation of the variable current salary that contains a distribution of the 473 responses ($n = 473$). The mean would be at the top of the curve. As you can see, the majority of responses are at or below the mean average salary of $34,419 (i.e., the most responses are in the $20,000–$35,000 range), whereas fewer responses fall

FIGURE 11.4: HISTOGRAM WITH BELL-SHAPED CURVE

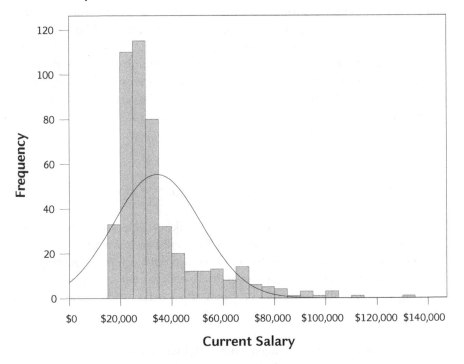

to the right and farther away from the mean (i.e., there are fewer responses as the salary increases past $35,000).

Strengths and Limitations of Descriptive Statistics

Descriptive statistics are necessary and valuable. They can provide an overview of general patterns of demographic variables such as sex, age, income, race, and marital status. Descriptive statistics help to organize the data and present information in an understandable form. It is advisable always to include descriptive statistics at the beginning of your results section. One of the major limitations of descriptive statistics, however, is that they offer no insight into the relationships among variables. That is, they fail to explore associations and explanatory issues concerning how variables are connected and whether the results can be generalized outside the sample.

Let us imagine for a moment that you are a case manager working with parents who physically abuse their children. You are interested in investigating the relationship between three independent variables: a ratio-level variable for income, a nominal-level variable for parenting status (single-parent versus two-parent households), and another ratio-level variable for number of children in the home. Your dependent variable (ordinal-level variable) is the type of abuse inflicted on the child. Although descriptive statistics can tell you the average income of your consumers, they offer no insight into the relationship between household income and type of abuse. To examine that relationship, we need a more sophisticated statistical approach. In other words, to examine the relationship between independent and dependent variables, we turn to inferential statistics. Inferential statistics are discussed in the next chapter.

Case Scenario

You are an undergraduate student who is taking a class in research methods. Your instructor has given you the following assignment:

As a faculty, we are interested in knowing more about the demographic makeup of our social work students. Your assignment is to gather the following demographic information about the social work students in our university:

1. What is the average age of the social work students?
2. How many are male? How many are female?
3. What are the percentages of the various ethnicities?
4. How many of the social work students are married and/or living as married?
5. How many are employed?

Critical-Thinking Questions

On the basis of the case scenario, answer the following questions:

1. How would you go about gathering the information?

2. Would you try to gather information from all the students or simply use a representative sample? Give reasons for your answer.

3. How can you feel confident about your results (given your research methods)?

4. What are the limitations of your findings?

Key Points

- Data analysis is the process of using a variety of statistical procedures to analyze data.

- Data analysis is usually conducted in two steps—first the descriptive analysis of the individual variables is conducted, and then inferential statistics are used to analyze the associations between variables.

- Descriptive statistics are ways of organizing, describing, and presenting quantitative data in a manner that is concise, manageable, and understandable.

- Inferential statistics are statistical procedures that are used to examine associations about a population on the basis of the results found in a sample.

- The five commonly used types of descriptive statistics are the mean, median, mode, range, and frequency.

- Measures of central tendency are statistical measures that report how much the data are alike or similar. The mean (average of the scores), median (midpoint of the scores), and mode (most frequently occurring score) are all measures of central tendency.

- Measures of dispersion, also known as measures of variability, are statistical measures that reflect dissimilarities in our sample.

- Three types of measures of dispersion are range (the overall spread or variability from the minimum score to the maximum score), variance (the spread of scores in a distribution of scores), and standard deviation (the square root of variance and most commonly used measure of dispersion).

- Normal distribution of data is an assumption used in statistical procedures that scores are probably distributed equally around the mean. Normally distributed data resemble a bell-shaped curve.

Practice Exam

True or False

1. One of the limitations of descriptive statistics is that they allow us only to examine the characteristics of one variable at a time (not the relationships between variables).

2. There are five types of descriptive statistics: mean, median, mode, frequency, and average.

3. Descriptive statistics are ways of organizing, describing, and presenting quantitative data in a manner that is concise, manageable, and understandable.

4. Measures of dispersion, also known as measures of variability, are statistical measures that reflect dissimilarities in our sample.

Multiple Choice

5. Normally distributed data resemble:

    a. An oval

    b. A bell-shaped curve

    c. A circle

    d. A triangle

    e. None of the above

6. Which of the following are measures of central tendency:

    a. Mean, median, and range

    b. Mode, range, and frequency

    c. Frequency, standard deviation, and nonstandard deviation

    d. Mean, median, and mode

    e. None of the above

7. In a normal distribution, how many would score within two standard deviations:

    a. 68 percent

    b. 75 percent

    c. 80 percent

    d. 90 percent

    e. None of the above

8. Data analysis is usually conducted in two steps. These two steps are:

a. Conduct the literature review and write the report

b. Complete first the descriptive statistics and then the inferential statistics

c. Interview the respondents and then conduct the literature review

d. Complete the literature review and then the inferential statistics

e. None of the above

CHAPTER TWELVE

Introduction to Inferential Statistics

CSWE Core Competencies

IN THIS CHAPTER you will find the following Council on Social Work Education (CSWE) competencies:

Educational Policy 2.1.3—Apply critical thinking to inform and communicate professional judgments

Educational Policy 2.1.6—Engage in research-informed practice and practice-informed research

Educational Policy 2.1.9—Respond to contexts that shape practice

Educational Policy 2.1.10(b)—Assessment

This chapter introduces the use of inferential statistics. Keep in mind that one chapter is insufficient to cover this topic adequately, and the purpose of including an introduction to inferential statistics is to provide a basic overview for you to consider in developing your research proposal and interpreting statistical outputs in studies that you review. Therefore, we define inferential statistics here and explain how they are used to test hypotheses. We also examine how to measure associations between variables and discuss significance values, which allows us to determine whether two variables or two groups are statistically important (significant) to the study. This chapter also examines two distinct types of inferential statistics—parametric and nonparametric statistics—and provides a description of several of the more common procedures used within these categories.

What Are Inferential Statistics?

Inferential statistics examine associations between variables and use significance tests and other measures to make inferences about the collected quantitative data. For instance, we can look at whether gender and education have a relationship with occupation. That is, in a sample, do more women tend to work in certain occupations and more men in other occupations? Similarly, is there a relationship between a person's occupation and his or her level of education? Inferential statistics are also used to assess how likely it is that group differences or correlations between the variables in the sample exist in the population.

Any quantitative study can be designed to use inferential statistics, but no qualitative studies can use inferential statistics, and many qualitative studies do not describe the sample in numerical terms (i.e., they do not use descriptive statistics). These studies examine not how often the participants have had a common experience but rather the experience itself and how participants are living it. In addition, the issue may not be how many individuals are in a sample because the sample may be only one individual. In these exploratory studies, the descriptions are related in words, not numbers.

Four Types of Correlation

A **measure of association** is any of several statistical procedures that allow you to measure the correlation between variables. In simplified terms, this concept deals with the degree of association between variables. Inferential statistics tell the reader how much the change in the dependent variable is related to the change in the independent variable (in our example, how much sex influences the career choice of workers). There are four types of correlations that can exist between variables: no correlation, a positive correlation, a negative correlation, and a curvilinear correlation. Although the four types of relationships that can exist might sound complicated, both the articles that you examine in your literature review and the statistical program that you use in your own study analysis will tell you the direction of the relationship.

No Correlation

The first type of relationship is **no correlation** between the two variables—they are simply not related (one variable does not influence the other). For example, let's assume that high school students are taking a class to learn refusal skills that they can use when their friends encourage them to use drugs. After the class, researchers can try to determine whether the class had any effects on students' use of drugs. A no-relationship situation would mean that roughly the same proportion of students do and do not use drugs before and after the class—the two variables are not related. Another way of stating this is that the class had no relationship with (or effect on) students' drug use.

Positive Correlation

A second way that two variables can be related is by way of a positive correlation. A **positive correlation** occurs when the dependent variable increases as the independent variable increases. For example, when studying the drug use of high school students, a researcher might ask about their parents' drug use or whether their friends use illegal substances. If the researcher finds that students who smoke marijuana are more likely to have family members who use drugs, and if students who smoke marijuana regularly also hang out with other users, then the researcher has found positive correlations.

Negative Correlation

The third relationship is known as a negative correlation. A **negative correlation** (also called an inverse relationship) means that as one variable increases, the other decreases. For example, research shows that the cost of drugs is related to drug use. An inverse relationship is demonstrated when the cost of drugs increases as the amount of drug use decreases.

Curvilinear Correlation

The last type of relationship is known as a **curvilinear correlation**. This type of relationship can start off as either a positive relationship or a negative relationship, and then it begins to curve. For instance, it is very possible that test anxiety drops commensurate to the amount of time spent studying but at some point begins to level off (i.e., not drop any further). There is probably a point at which anxiety will still be present regardless of how much time one spends studying. In fact, anxiety may even start increasing again as the time of the actual test approaches. This is a curvilinear relationship.

Determining the Strength of the Correlation

Because this book is directed toward students in their first research course, we focus on how statistical calculations (i.e., outputs) help researchers examine the strength of the relationships between independent and dependent variables.

The strength of the relationship (or how well the variables fit with each other) is represented by a number between -1 and $+1$. This number indicates whether the correlation between the variables is nonexistent, weak, moderate, or strong. Most correlation analyses report a raw value for a relationship between two variables on a scale that ranges from 0 to 1. This means that the results will tell you how much the variables relate to each other. A correlation value of 0 tells you that there is absolutely no relationship whatsoever between the two variables. The stronger the relationship between two variables, the closer the analysis findings will be to the number 1. So, a correlation analysis can yield a value from 0 (meaning that the two variables are not correlated) to 1 (meaning that they are perfectly correlated). Therefore, a relationship of .5 is a moderately strong, positive relationship. For a negative relationship, the same is true, except that numbers range from -1 to 0. The negative sign implies an inverse relationship. Therefore, a relationship of -.5 (as represented in figure 12.1) is a moderately strong inverse or negative relationship. A common error that students make is to assign value to the negative sign—in other words, to assume that a negative value yields poor results.

Probability Values and Confidence Intervals

The **probability value**, or p value, is a report of whether the strength of a relationship is statistically significant or whether it could have occurred by chance. Most researchers set the level for statistical significance at .05 or smaller, which means that there is less than a one-in-twenty chance that the results are due to sampling error. You will see this significance level shown as $p < .05$, where the p represents probability, the symbol $<$ means "less than," and .05 represents the level of statistical significance. Thus

FIGURE 12.1: NEGATIVE CORRELATION

Perfectly Correlated   **No Correlation**

| -1 | $-.9$ | $-.8$ | $-.7$ | $-.6$ | $-.5$ | $-.4$ | $-.3$ | $-.2$ | $-.1$ | 0 |

whenever you see a probability level such as $p < .05$, $p < .01$, or $p < .001$ in a table, you know that the relationship is strong enough to be considered statistically significant. This means that the prediction of the relationship (the hypothesis) was correct and that the relationship between the two variables was so powerful that it could not be considered a fluke.

A **confidence interval** tells us how certain we can be that our sample is reflective of the population from which it was drawn. As a common rule, most researchers establish a confidence interval of 95 percent. This means that they want to be 95 percent certain that the findings from the analysis are not in error. The confidence interval is determined at the time that the analysis is conducted.

Imagine that you recruited fifty volunteers and measured the amount of time they spent studying for their midterm exam. You recorded this and then asked them to report their numerical grade on the midterm. You could then complete a statistical analysis to determine whether a relationship exists between amount of time spent studying and test grades. What if the results showed that the two variables were positively associated at a correlation of .49 and a p value of less than .05 ($p < .05$)? We then could determine that there is indeed a relationship between amount of time spent studying and exam grades, and that it is not likely that it occurred by chance.

Parametric Statistics

The first of the two types of inferential statistics, **parametric statistics**, is based on a set of assumptions or rules that must be met: that your data are normally distributed, that the dependent variable is measured at an interval or ratio level, and that you have a sample size of at least fifty. If the collected data do not meet all these conditions, then you should not use parametric statistics. Some of the most common parametric procedures are Pearson's r, multiple regression (sometimes referred to as linear regression), t-tests, and analysis of variance (ANOVA).

Pearson's r

One of the most common measures of association is known as Pearson's product moment correlation (Pearson's r). **Pearson's r** seeks to determine whether a relationship exists between two variables (one independent variable and one dependent variable) and the direction of the relationship. It also shows the degree to which the variables are related and the probability that the relationship occurred by chance. This analysis assumes that both the independent and dependent variables are measured at the interval or ratio level. An example of this might be amount of education attained and salary. To determine whether these two variables affect each other, Pearson's r is used. Pearson's r is a type of **bivariate analysis** (also called simple regression), or an analysis that examines the relationship between one independent and one dependent variable. There are several other bivariate associations, including eta, gamma, lambda, Kendall's tau, and Spearman's rho. However, the Pearson's correlation is so commonly used that it is commonly associated with the word *correlation.*

Imagine for a moment, that you are a caseworker working with first-generation college students. Research has demonstrated that there is a correlation between the two variables: father's highest year of school completed and a child's highest year of education. In other words, the more education that a parent has, the more education a child is likely to obtain. To test this out, you might ask your students to provide information about the highest grade level their fathers had completed in school. Then, you might also ask about the amount of education your client has obtained. Table 12.1 shows a correlation procedure that you run, utilizing the **Statistical Package for Social Sciences (SPSS)**, a statistical program that social science researchers commonly use to analyze research data. The table shows that there is a positive relationship (.263) between the two variables of a father's highest year of school completed (highest year of school completed, father) and the respondents' highest degree of school completed (highest year of school completed). The N represents the sample size (1,510 respondents). Note that here there are two different numbers for N (sample size). This is because 1,510 respondents reported their highest year of

TABLE 12.1: CORRELATIONS

		HIGHEST YEAR OF SCHOOL COMPLETED	HIGHEST YEAR SCHOOL COMPLETED, FATHER
Highest year of school completed	Pearson correlation	1	.263*
	Sig. (2-tailed)		.000
	N	1,510	1,065
Highest year school completed, father	Pearson correlation	.263*	1
	Sig. (2-tailed)	.000	
	N	1,065	1,069

*Correlation is significant at the .001 level (2-tailed).

school completed, and only 1,065 subjects reported their father's highest year of education. *Sig.* represents significance score, which is .000, and the significance level in this case was set at = .01. In inferential statistics, a two-tailed test of significance divides the two tails of the distribution in either direction from the expected value. It is clear that the relationship has a significantly positive correlation. This would be noted as $r = .263$, $p < .05$. Therefore, there is a correlation between the amount of education of one's father and the education level attained by children.

Rarely will you find research studies in which the researchers have used only one independent and one dependent variable. It is clear that nothing is influenced by only one variable. That is, a person's salary is not influenced entirely by his or her educational level, and a person's feelings about spanking are not purely determined by the age at which he or she married. For instance, we can assume that a person's salary is also influenced by a slew of other factors, such as discrimination against women and minority racial groups, the geography of where one lives, and availability of transportation. Much more common is the inclusion of multiple independent variables (and it is not uncommon for studies to have multiple dependent variables).

Multiple Regression

Multiple regression (or linear regression) is a statistical procedure that measures the correlation between an independent variable and the dependent variable while holding other independent variables constant. Another way of saying this is that it determines the impact of one independent variable on the dependent variable while removing the influence of other independent variables. While multiple regression is important for many reasons, one of the most important reasons is that it is a statistical way to deal with issues of confounding variables, because a researcher can place an endless amount of independent and control variables into the statistical model for a multiple regression.

Let us return for a moment to our study about fathers' educational level. Table 12.1 showed that there is a positive relationship between the two variables but that they are not perfectly correlated. In fact, the strength of the correlation is only .263, which is a weak to moderate relationship. We can say with confidence that there is a relationhip between the highest level of education that a parent has obtained and educational attainment in children. Another way to state this is to say that a parent's educational level is a predictor of the amount of education that a child will obtain. How can we determine the strength of the relationship more precisely? One way is to control for other variables. A researcher may want to hold constant certain variables in the study. In this example, it was discovered in the literature review that education level obtained by the parent had an impact on the level of education obtained by children. In fact, researchers found that the higher the educational level of parents, the more likely that children would go on to pursue college and advanced degrees.

Let's use another example where we have collected more than one independent variable. If we were to suggest that there is a relationship between amount of education and income, you might agree. On the surface, that would make sense. We could even perform bivariate analysis to test whether this hypothesis is true (see table 12.2).

From the results in table 12.2, we can see that there is a positive relationship (.342) between education (EDUC) and respondent's income (RINCOM91). This would be noted as $r = .342$, $p < .05$. However, you may be thinking, "Yes, that makes sense, but there is more to predicting income than just education level." And you would be right. For example, we know that men, on the whole, earn more income than women. And we know that, for the most part, whites are paid more than people of color. So we might run a second analysis that would look at the role of education after controlling for the variables of sex and race. In short, we would run multiple regression (see table 12.3).

You may notice that SPSS gives you a different table for multiple regression than for a simple bivariate analysis. Even though much more information is presented for multiple regression, it is still possible to learn to interpret the results without having to understand all the underlying theory. In the table, you want to pay attention to the standardized **coefficients**

TABLE 12.2: CORRELATIONS BETWEEN EDUCATIONAL LEVEL AND INCOME

		HIGHEST YEAR OF SCHOOL COMPLETED	RESPONDENT'S INCOME
Highest year of school completed	Pearson correlation	1	.342*
	Sig. (2-tailed)		.000
	N	1,496	991
Respondent's income	Pearson correlation	.342*	1
	Sig. (2-tailed)	.000	
	N	991	1,496

*Correlation is significant at the .001 level.

TABLE 12.3: COEFFICIENTS FOR EDUCATIONAL LEVEL AND INCOME, CONTROLLING FOR SEX AND RACE (DEPENDENT VARIABLE = TOTAL FAMILY INCOME)

MODEL		UNSTANDARDIZED COEFFICIENTS		STANDARDIZED COEFFICIENTS		
		B	Std. Error	BETA	t	SIG.
1	(Constant)	7.158	.778		9.202	.000
	Highest year of school completed	.756	.042	.429	18.059	.000
	Respondent's sex	− 1.075	.260	− .098	− 4.141	.000
	Respondent's race	− .551	.253	− .052	− 2.175	.030

(known as the beta or beta weight). You use the same methods to interpret the beta as for the correlation in the bivariate analysis. This means that you look for beta weight to determine the strength of the relationship. The significance level (sig.) is reported the same as in bivariate analysis. You would look for a significance of less than of .05. In table 12.3, we see that education is the strongest predictor of (i.e., has the strongest relationship with) the dependent variable of income because it has the largest beta and a significance level of less than .05 when sex and race are controlled for. This is noted as beta = .429, $p < .05$. While sex and race are both significant ($p < .05$), they are weak relationships at .098 and .052 respectively, as shown in the output.

t-Tests

A ***t*-test** is a statistical procedure that tests the means of two groups to determine whether they are statistically different. There are two common types of *t*-tests—independent and paired samples (also known as dependent-samples *t*-tests). We examine each individually.

The **independent-samples *t*-test** is utilized when a researcher needs to compare two groups to see whether the independent variable has an effect on the dependent variable. For example, let's assume that you want to measure the difference between a group of males and a group of females and their beliefs about teaching sex education in schools. The hypothesis might be that women and men have different beliefs about teaching sex education in schools. The independent-samples *t*-test would be appropriate for this analysis. After we survey a group of males and a group of females, we would compare their answers. From tables 12.4 and 12.5, we can conclude that there is no difference in people's attitudes about sex education on the basis of their sex. Table 12.4 presents both a *t*-score and a significance score. The significance should be .05 or smaller, which is not the case in this example. Instead, the researcher would have to accept the null hypothesis and look for other independent variables that might sway opinions about teaching sex education in schools.

We might also want to compare a client against him- or herself over time. Perhaps we are interested in administering a pretest to a group of participants and then providing some form of intervention. At the end of the intervention we want to administer a posttest and then compare the pretest scores to the posttest scores to determine whether the participants' situations improved, remained the same, or became worse after the intervention. For this analysis we would use a paired-samples *t*-test. A **paired-samples *t*-test** (also known as dependent-samples *t*-test) can be defined as a test of significance of the differences between two different sets of scores for the same respondents.

For example, let's assume that you are a drug abuse counselor whose job it is to teach middle school students about the spread of the HIV virus. You administer a pretest designed to test their knowledge about HIV and then you present them with some factual information. At the end of the

TABLE 12.4: INDEPENDENT SAMPLES *T*-TEST

	t-TEST FOR EQUALITY OF MEANS	
	t	SIG. (2-TAILED)
Sex education in public schools	− .458	.647

TABLE 12.5: INDEPENDENT SAMPLES *T*-TEST: COMPARING SEX AND ATTITUDES TOWARD TEACHING SEX EDUCATION IN SCHOOLS

	RESPONDENT'S SEX	N	MEAN
Sex education in public schools	Male	444	1.15
	Female	540	1.16

presentation, you administer the same test as a posttest to see whether their scores changed. It would be a simple matter, then, to measure the pretest results against the posttest results using a paired samples t-test. The results would report a t-value, which refers to the standard deviation. In general, you want to look for a t-value of three standard deviations or greater. In this case, the t-value is 26.473, and its significance level is well below .05 ($p < .000$). This finding would be noted as $t = 26.473, p < .05$. You would probably be excited to conclude that the intervention was a success. Again, we must caution that this is a simplified discussion of interpreting t-test results. To fully understand how to interpret a t-test, you must consider such things as sample size and something called degrees of freedom (df). We use this example only to give you a rough idea of how you can use a t-test in the research process.

Analysis of Variance

Analysis of variance (ANOVA) is a parametric statistical procedure that allows us to examine the difference between the mean scores of two or more groups simultaneously. This is an extension of the independent t-test in that the t-test is limited to only two groups. An ANOVA examines and compares the means within each group and then compares those to the means of other groups to see whether there is a significant difference. To use ANOVA, you must have an interval- or ratio-level dependent variable.

ANOVA is useful for comparing several measurements between two groups (treatment and nontreatment). To illustrate how to use ANOVA, we walk you through a simple example of a research design that used ANOVA in the analysis of the data.

First, you conduct a literature review, which shows that participating in low-elements challenge courses increases group cohesion (i.e., satisfaction) and individual self-esteem. Low-elements challenge courses are a series of sequenced events in which group members have to work together to solve problems.

You formulate the research question "Can participating in low-element challenges also increase group satisfaction and individual self-esteem in families?" and develop two hypotheses: (1) families participating in a low-elements challenge course will report a significant increase in family satisfaction after the intervention compared to the nontreatment group, and (2) individuals participating in a low-elements challenge course will report a significant increase in self-esteem after the intervention compared to the nontreatment group.

You select two measurement surveys to measure family satisfaction: the Self-Report Family Instrument (SRF) and the Kansas Family Life Satisfaction Scale (KFL). You select the Rosenberg Self-Esteem Scale (RSE) to measure individual self-esteem.

Your sample is a convenience sample. Families agree either to participate in the treatment group or to simply complete the surveys (nontreatment group). The treatment group receives the low-elements challenge-course intervention, and participants are asked to complete the two surveys that measure family satisfaction and one survey that measures self-esteem. The nontreatment group simply completes the three surveys without receiving the intervention.

To analyze the data, you use ANOVA to compare the three measures between the two groups, and you report the results in an SPSS output table. In table 12.6 there are three dependent variables: the results of the SRF, the KFL, and the RSE. Notice, first of all, that among other things, SPSS reports an F value. The F value and the significance score are interpreted together. As a general rule, when interpreting the F value, you want the number to be greater than 2, but the important statistic is the significance value, which should be .05 or smaller. A quick glance at the table reveals that all the F values are well above 2 and the significance levels are all .05 or smaller. These results would be noted as $F = 22.77$, $p < .05$ for the SRF; $F = 59.37$, $p < .05$ for the KFL; and $F = 58.91$, $p < .05$ for the RSE. Without going into too much detail about the interpretation of results, we can infer from these results that the results of the treatment

TABLE 12.6: ANOVA COMPARISON BETWEEN TREATMENT GROUP AND NONTREATMENT GROUP

		df	F	SIG.
SRF	Between groups	1	22.776	.000
	Within groups	62		
	Total	63		
KFL	Between groups	1	59.375	.000
	Within groups	62		
	Total	63		
RSE	Between groups	1	58.9176	.000
	Within groups	62		
	Total	63		

group were inherently different from those of the comparison group for all three measures. In short, the treatment group showed a significant increase in family satisfaction and self-esteem after the intervention compared to the nontreatment group.

Nonparametric Statistics

Nonparametric statistics are used when the data depart from the criteria established for parametric statistics. For instance, you might have a small sample size and so do not meet the assumption of a normal distribution, or you may have a nominal- or ordinal-level dependent variable. For analyzing this type of data, you would use nonparametric statistics.

There are actually several different types of nonparametric statistics. To explore each and every one of them is far beyond the scope of this text; therefore, we present the most commonly used of the nonparametric statistics, the cross-tabs analysis. Cross-tabs is a procedure that forms two-way tables and provides a variety of tests and measures of association for these tables. The structure of the table and whether categories are ordered determine what test or measure to use.

Chi-square is a nonparametric statistical procedure that is commonly used when a researcher has a small sample size and a dependent variable that is nominal or ordinal level to determine whether there is truly a difference in groups. An example of such a situation is when a researcher seeks to determine whether people of different races are drawn to different sorts of religions (e.g., Catholicism, Protestantism, Judaism, Islam, Buddhism). Chi-square is represented as χ^2 in the documentation of results. Therefore, when reading a study, you know that the symbol χ^2 means that the authors are reporting the significance of a finding for which they used chi-square. The chi-square statistic predicts what would have happened in a normally distributed set of data and then compares what really happened to determine whether the two are significantly different. Chi-square is easier to interpret than other statistics—you simply compare the expected frequencies (what the statistical program projects would have occurred) against what was actually observed (from the data collected).

For example, respondents in a study were asked whether they favor or oppose laws that require gun owners to hold permits (see tables 12.7–12.9). The hypothesis is that there would be a significant difference between women's and men's opinions concerning gun laws.

TABLE 12.7: CROSS-TABS ANALYSIS: OBSERVED AND EXPECTED SCORES

	OBSERVED N	EXPECTED N	RESIDUAL
1 Favor	811	492.0	319.0
2 Oppose	173	492.0	−319.0
Total	984		

TABLE 12.8: CROSS-TABS ANALYSIS: SEX AND OPINION ON GUN PERMIT LAWS

		FAVOR OR OPPOSE GUN PERMITS		
		FAVOR	OPPOSE	TOTAL
Respondent's sex	Male	314	111	425
	Female	497	62	559
Total		811	173	984

TABLE 12.9: CROSS-TABS ANALYSIS: SIGNIFICANCE RESULTS

	SEX	GUNLAW
Chi-Square[a,b]	31.683	413.663
df	1	1
Asymp. sig.	.000	.000

a. Zero cells (.0 percent) have expected frequencies less than 5. The minimum expected cell frequency is 750.0.
b. Zero cells (.0 percent) have expected frequencies less than 5. The minimum expected cell frequency is 492.0.

In table 12.7, it was expected that 492 (half of those responding) would favor laws requiring gun permits and that the other half would oppose these laws. However, what was observed in this sample was that 811 of all respondents favored gun permit laws and 173 of all respondents opposed them. Table 12.8 shows us that females significantly favored gun-permit laws (497) over males (314). In table 12.9, the chi-square significance (asymp. sig.) shows that the findings were significant (.000) for both the gun-permit-law variable and the sex variable. The chi-square value (31.683) would be reported in the following manner: $\chi^2 = 31.68$, $p < .05$.

Strengths and Limitations of Inferential Statistics

Inferential statistics are both necessary and valuable. They provide a level of sophistication that goes well beyond anything that is possible when one is describing individual variables. For instance, simple regression can help us determine the strength of a relationship between variables, and an independent-samples t-test can help us to know whether one group is statistically different from another. Let's say that you want to know if one group (who studied twice as much as another group for an entire semester) did better than the other group on a final exam. Inferential statistics can help you know whether the difference occurred because the first group studied more or is simply a result of chance.

There are limitations with statistics, just as there are limitations with anything. Statistics, especially inferential statistics, deal with probability. Although we can establish confidence levels as high as one in a thousand if we so desire, no statistical significance can be absolutely infallible (i.e., absolutely certain that the results did not happen by chance). A second limitation is the issue of causality. We have stated several times in this text that correlation does not imply causation. This bears repeating. However, keeping those things in mind, we can still gain much useful information from inferential statistics.

Which Statistical Program Is Right for Me?

As it becomes increasingly necessary for social workers to learn some basic techniques for evaluating their own practice, many have begun to use statistical programs in their workplaces and private practices. Some of the most popular statistical programs on the market today are SPSS, SAS, and MicroCase. The question arises, then, which statistical package is the best for you? The answer to that question depends on several things. First, do you (or your agency) have a particular statistical program already, or are you already familiar with one statistical program? If you are currently using one program and you are familiar with that program, it is often easier to purchase upgrades than to switch to another program. Second, how much are you going to use a statistical program? Many people use Microsoft Excel for all their statistical needs. The advantages to this are that the program is already installed on most office and home computers and there is no need to purchase a new program. The downside is that there can be a steep learning curve before new users can create the formulas for statistical analysis with Excel. Finally, how much do you want to spend? Some statistical programs can be quite expensive (running into the thousands of dollars for multiple-site installations). These are questions to consider as you decide which program is best for your needs.

Case Scenario

You are a case manager employed in a long-term residential facility for adolescents. You have noticed that a significant number of the teens assigned to your caseload have problems with alcohol and other drugs. You begin to discuss this with your colleagues, and many of them state that they have noticed a similar phenomenon. As you begin to explore this and look for antecedents, you notice that most of the clients in your caseload who have trouble with alcohol and other drugs are victims of child maltreatment. You decide to investigate the relationship between child maltreatment (independent variable) and substance abuse (dependent variable). To research this, you decide to look at closed case records. This method of investigation is known as **data abstraction**. Data abstraction is the method of taking information from records that have been closed to investigate relationships between variables.

Critical-Thinking Questions

On the basis of the case scenario, answer the following questions:

1. Are there ethical issues with investigating closed case records? If yes, what are the ethical concerns?

2. What would be an acceptable sample size? How did you arrive at that number?

3. How would you measure the dependent variable in this study? What level of measurement would you use?

Key Points

· There are two types of inferential statistics—parametric and nonparametric.

- Parametric statistics have a set of assumptions or rules that must be met: that your data are normally distributed, that the dependent variable is measured at an interval or ratio level, and that you have a sample size of at least fifty.

- Nonparametric statistics are used when the data depart from the criteria established for parametric statistics.

- The probability value (*p* value) is used to determine whether the strength of the relationship is statistically significant or whether it could have occurred by chance.

- Multiple regression measures the impact of a dependent variable and an independent variable on each other while removing the impact of the other variables in the study.

- A *t*-test is a statistical procedure that compares the means of two groups to determine whether they are significantly different.

- Analysis of variance (ANOVA) is a statistical procedure that allows us to compare the mean scores of two or more groups simultaneously.

- Cross-tabs is a nonparametric statistical procedure commonly used when a researcher has a small sample size and a dependent variable that is nominal or ordinal to determine whether there is a significant difference between groups.

Practice Exam

True or False

1. Statistical procedures are categorized as descriptive and inferential.

2. Inferential statistics allow us to draw conclusions about the relationships between variables.

3. One of the assumptions of nonparametric statistics is that data are normally distributed.

4. One of the most common nonparametric statistical procedures is known as chi-square.

5. A *t*-test is a statistical procedure that compares the means of two groups to determine whether they are significantly different.

Multiple Choice

6. There are four ways that data can be correlated in a simple regression:

   a. No relationship, positive relationship, negative or inverse relationship, and curvilinear relationship

   b. No relationship, positive relationship, negative or inverse relationship, and logical positive relationship

   c. Positive relationship, negative relationship, inverse relationship, and inverse relationship

   d. No relationship, unclear relationship, distant relationship, and fragmented relationship

   e. None of the above

7. Analysis of variance (ANOVA) allows us:

   a. To measure how strongly two variables are correlated

   b. To decide whether a statistical procedure is statistically significant

   c. To compare the mean scores of two or more groups simultaneously

   d. To compare scores of nominal-level dependent variables

   e. None of the above

8. When we are employing parametric statistics, we need to:

   a. Make sure our data are normally distributed

   b. Make sure we have a sample size of at least fifty

   c. Make sure that our dependent variable is measured at an interval or ratio level

   d. All of the above

   e. None of the above

CHAPTER THIRTEEN

Practicing Your Research Skills

CSWE Competencies

IN THIS CHAPTER you will find the following Council on Social Work Education (CSWE) competencies:

Educational Policy 2.1.2—Apply social work ethical principles to guide professional practice

Educational Policy 2.1.3—Apply critical thinking to inform and communicate professional judgments

Educational Policy 2.1.6—Engage in research-informed practice and practice-informed research

Educational Policy 2.1.9—Respond to contexts that shape practice

Educational Policy 2.1.10(b)—Assessment

Educational Policy 2.1.10 (d)—Evaluation

Example Research Proposal

The following is a sample research proposal. In reviewing the proposal, see if you can identify the following elements: research question, independent variable(s), and dependent variable. What level were these variables measured at? Pay attention to how the author constructed the literature review and how the methods section was written.

- -

Symptoms of Posttraumatic Stress Disorder and the Effects of Intimate Partner Violence

Student Name Here

University Name Here

Class Title, Section, and Name Here

- -

Abstract

The purpose of this article is to investigate the relationship between intimate partner violence and posttraumatic stress disorder (PTSD). The purpose of this study is to find out whether those who have experienced intimate partner violence do have symptoms of posttraumatic stress disorder. This in turn can help health-care professionals properly evaluate those clients who have experienced intimate partner violence.

- -

Introduction

A wide array of symptoms have been associated with the experience of sexual and physical abuse, including depression, increased fears, sexual problems, anxiety, guilt, nightmares, sleep difficulties, nervousness, tendency toward revictimization, phobias, substance abuse, exaggerated startle response, and aggression. It has been suggested that posttraumatic stress disorder (PTSD) overlaps these common symptoms in victims. PTSD is characterized by a reexperiencing of a trauma, numbing, avoidance of events associated with a trauma, and hyperalertness or exaggerated startle response (Wijma, 2000). According to the National Center for PTSD (2008), PTSD is an anxiety disorder that can occur after one has been through a traumatic event, including sexual or physical abuse. PTSD symptoms can disappear over time, but about one in three people with PTSD may continue to experience some symptoms.

The purpose of this study is to examine the relative effects of intimate partner violence (IPV) and the outcome of PTSD. The findings of previous research show that there is a strong correlation of those who have experienced IPV and symptoms of PTSD. The hypothesis that PTSD symptoms are related to IPV was tested in this study using two scales, a ten-item scale that assesses battering and a seventeen-item scale that assesses symptoms of posttraumatic stress disorder. The purpose of this study is for mental health and social service professionals to obtain a better understanding of the adverse health outcomes that can occur to those who have experienced a traumatic event such as battering. This in turn will provide professionals with the knowledge and experience they need to assist their clients in linking them with the right resources.

Literature Review

A substantial body of research supports the notion that victims of intimate partner violence experience symptoms of posttraumatic stress disorder (Barker-Collo, 2000; Dutton, 2006; Laffaye, Kennedy, & Stein, 2003; Lang, Kennedy, & Stein, 2002; Perez, 2008; Wijma, 2000; Woods, 2005). Although few of these studies focus solely on posttraumatic stress disorder, PTSD is included among the outcomes resulting from intimate partner violence. Negative mental health outcomes are significantly evident in the research listed earlier, with a positive correlation between the outcome of intimate partner violence and mental health outcomes that adversely affect those who have participated in the research studies. Only on one occasion was posttraumatic stress disorder not related to physical violence, but a positive correlation was found between sexual violence and posttraumatic stress disorder (Bennice, 2003).

Most studies commonly define intimate partner violence as physical, sexual, and emotional or psychological abuse or violence perpetrated by intimate partners or acquaintances, including persons who are current or former spouses, cohabiting partners, boyfriends or girlfriends, and dating partners. It includes abuse in the context of same-sex as well as heterosexual intimate relationships (Carlson, 2008). However, studies show that women are more commonly victims of intimate partner violence, and according to the National Violence against Women Survey, women are most likely victimized by people whom they know (Browne & Williams, 1993; Tjaden & Thoennes, 2000).

Studies have also included sexual abuse, including rape, as intimate partner violence. Although all fifty states now recognize wife rape as a crime, some form of exemption still remains for husbands in more than half of the states, and as a consequence, married women may hesitate to question forced sex because they believe that they have no right to refuse sexual advances made by their husbands (Bennice, 2003).

The most common tool for assessing posttraumatic stress disorder is the PTSD Symptom Scale (PSS), a seventeen-item self-report scale based on the

Diagnostic and Statistical Manual, 3rd edition, revised (DSM-III-R), PTSD criteria, including reexperiencing, avoidance, and arousal symptom clusters. According to Bennice (2003), the 0–3 response scale captures the frequency of each symptom over the previous two weeks. The PSS was found to have satisfactory internal consistency, high test-retest reliability, and good concurrent and convergent validity with rape victims (Bennice, 2003).

None of the literature has agreed on a scale to measure violence, although some used the Supplemented Conflict Tactics Scale, a nineteen-item measure that assesses ways of responding to conflict among couples. This scale, however, is also outdated in relation to the newest edition of the DSM. The scale is said to measure physical and sexual violence, but the variables are measured in nominal form, which makes them mutually exclusive, and so also creates a question of the methodological validity. Other literature focused mainly on sexual abuse, using the Sexual Experiences Survey, which assesses the type and severity of sexual victimization (Barker-Collo, 2000; Bennice, 2003; Wijma, 2000). Its internal consistencies are also questionable since the variables are also nominal.

In summary, there was no consistent scale used in the literature to measure the amount of violence. Although many of the outcomes correlated PTSD with intimate partner violence—some of which included sexual violence in the definition of intimate partner violence—others focused on other mental health outcomes, including PTSD.

It is not as common for intimate partner violence to be perpetrated on males, although some literature exists on the subject (Browne & Williams, 1993; Tjaden & Thoennes, 2000). The literature focused mainly on female subjects, given the convenience of domestic violence shelters and gynecological physician's offices providing access to subjects who were willing to participate in the studies (Barker-Collo, 2000; Dutton, 2006; Laffaye et al., 2003; Lang et al., 2002; Perez, 2008; Wijma, 2000; Woods, 2005). Most studies also focused on a smaller sample size, most likely because of the use of convenience sampling (Barker-Collo, 2000; Bennice, 2003; Woods, 2005).

In conclusion, the literature that relates PTSD and intimate partner violence consistently agrees that the symptoms of posttraumatic stress are in fact related to people who have experienced intimate partner physical violence, and more so in those who have experienced intimate partner sexual violence. The correlations between the two are significantly positive in relation to each other, although the variables in each slightly differ in studies. No research has specifically stated that PTSD is in fact caused by intimate partner violence, and none has directly focused on just intimate partner violence and posttraumatic stress disorder.

Methods

Women who have experienced IPV are more likely to have symptoms of PTSD than those who have not experienced IPV. The variables in this study are intimate partner violence and posttraumatic stress disorder, with IPV being the independent variable and PTSD being the dependent variable. These variables are measured using interval-level scales that other researchers have used. Demographic variables included in the study are participant gender, age, race, education level, and socioeconomic status.

Respondents

The researcher will use voluntary participants from domestic violence shelters in eastern Kentucky and a comparison group of Morehead State University (MSU) students. The sampling will be a convenience sample, including individuals who have experienced intimate partner violence before going to a shelter. However, the issue of diversity arises, as the sample encompasses only a small portion of domestic violence victims, mainly women, with Morehead State University students as a comparison. The comparison sample is a convenience sample of students who attend Morehead State University. Each resident of the shelter and each student will be invited to volunteer to fill out a survey that encompasses the PTSD symptom scale along with the Women's Experience Battering Scale (WEB).

Instrumentation

The WEB assesses whether there have been episodes of battering or partner violence, and the PTSD scale assesses the symptoms of PTSD. The PTSD scale used in the survey has higher reliability than other scales used to assess PTSD, as it was developed from the DSM and has been used by many researchers. However, the scale's validity is in question, as the DSM used has since been modified. The WEB scale the researcher will use has not been as frequently used as the PTSD scale to assess battered women. However, most common scales used to assess intimate partner violence use only nominal-level scaling, which makes the WEB scale more reliable than other scales.

The researcher hopes to obtain a sample size of fifty participants. The researcher intends to obtain half the sample from students at her university and half from residents of a domestic violence shelter. Each resident and student will have the option to take the survey to assess whether people who experience intimate partner violence have symptoms of PTSD.

Limitations

There are some threats to the reliability of this research study. The participants might feel that the questions about their intimate relationship violence were too personal to share. To reduce this limitation, the researcher will provide the participant with a confidentiality statement that ensures that information about the participant will not become known (see appendix). Furthermore, recalling incidents of past violence may trigger unpleasant memories. To help reduce this effect, the researcher will inform participants that they can stop the study at any time. If a participant at any time feels threatened or unsure about the research study, he or she can drop out without any repercussions.

Additional limitations include the small sample size and the fact that participants are limited to women's domestic violence shelters and students on the MSU campus. The sample size is based on convenience and includes women in domestic violence shelters and students attending MSU at the time of the study. The gender bias in the sample is mostly because domestic violence shelters are equipped to take in only female victims. Another limitation is that the age range of students in the comparison sample includes mostly traditional students, whereas women at the domestic violence shelter are older adults. An issue of reliability is that questions about their partners are sensitive topics, and respondents might be reluctant to answer such questions honestly.

Ethical Issues

The ethical issue the researcher faces is the dilemma of the benefits of the study outweighing its risk. The women in the domestic violence shelters have experienced a great deal of trauma and may even have symptoms of PTSD, which could in turn increase with recalling episodes of intimate partner violence. However, a benefit is that these women are in a safe setting that is providing support. For the benefits to outweigh the risk, the researcher aims for the outcome of the study to show that women who have experienced IPV should be assessed for more serious anxiety problems such as PTSD. This could be very important for social workers who assess victims of IPV, so that they understand the complicated and complex outcomes that are presented.

The victims might undergo more trauma while being assessed, and the social worker should become aware of the possible need to refer participants to a medical evaluation. Intimate partner violence is an issue that social workers will forever deal with. The outcomes are different for every individual, and once outcomes are identified, social workers can learn how to assist each person and his or her individual needs.

References

Barker-Collo, S. L. (2000). A cognitive-behavioral model of post-traumatic stress for sexually abused females. *Journal of Interpersonal Violence, 15*, 375–392. http://dx.doi.org/10.1177/088626000015004003

Bennice, J. A. (2003). The relative effects of intimate partner physical and sexual violence on post-traumatic stress disorder symptomatology. *Violence and Victims, 18*, 87–94. http://dx.doi.org/10.1891/vivi.2003.18.1.87

Browne, A., & Williams, K. (1993). Gender, intimacy, and lethal violence: Trends from 1976 through 1987. *Gender and Society, 7*, 78–98.

Carlson, B. E. (2008). Intimate partner violence. In *Encyclopedia of Social Work* [Web]. Oxford: Oxford University Press. http://dx.doi.org/10.4135/9781412963923.n248

Dutton, M. A. (2006). Intimate partner violence, PTSD, and adverse health outcomes. *Journal of Interpersonal Violence, 21*, 955–968. http://dx.doi.org/10.1177/0886260506289178

Laffaye, C., Kennedy, C., & Stein, M. B. (2003). Post-traumatic stress disorder and health-related quality of life in female victims of intimate partner violence. *Violence and Victims, 18*, 227–238.

Lang, A. J. Kennedy, C. M., & Stein, M. B. (2002). Anxiety sensitivity and PTSD among female victims of intimate partner violence. *Depression and Anxiety, 16*, 77–83.

National Center for PTSD. (2008). Retrieved November 13, 2008, from National Center for PTSD: http://www.mentalhealth.va.gov/MENTAL HEALTH/ptsd/fs_what_is_ptsdoddb.asp

Perez, S. (2008). PTSD compromises battered women's future safety. *Journal of Interpersonal Violence, 23*, 635–651. http://dx.doi.org/10.1177/0886 260507313528

Tjaden, P., & Thoennes, N. (2000). Extent, nature, and consequences of intimate partner violence (NCJ 181867). Washington, DC: Office of Justice Programs, U.S. Department of Justice. Retrieved from https://www.ncjrs.gov/pdffiles1/nij/181867.pdf

Wijma, K. (2000). Prevalence of post-traumatic stress disorder among gynecological patients with a history of sexual and physical abuse. *Journal of Interpersonal Violence, 15*, 944–958.

Woods, A. B. (2005). The mediation effect of posttraumatic stress disorder symptoms on the relationship of intimate partner violence and IFN-g levels. *American Journal of Community Psychology, 36*, 159–175. http://dx.doi.org/10.1007/s10464–005–6240–7

- -

Informed Consent

Name and Contact Information of Student Researcher
Jane Smith
Morehead State University
Morehead, KY 40351

Purpose of the Study: The purpose of this study is to research the adverse health effects of partner violence on a person. This research will further help social workers and health-care professionals understand the effects and in what ways they can assist those who have been battered in a improved manner.

Duration: My participation in this study will include the completion of this survey.

Procedures: I will be asked to complete this survey.

Potential Risks/Discomforts: There are no physical discomforts or risks.

Potential Benefits: Using the outcome of this study to improve the social work and health-care professions' understanding of the effects of intimate partner violence.

Confidentiality: All responses to this survey will be kept confidential. Your name or identity will not be linked in any way to the research data.

Right to Refuse or Withdraw: I understand that my participation is voluntary and I may refuse to participate or may discontinue participation at any time.

Individuals to Contact: If I have a question about my participation in this study, I can contact: Jane Smith (researcher)

I have read this entire form and I understand it completely. All of my questions regarding this form or this study have been answered to my complete satisfaction. I agree to participate in this research.

- -

Please read each question carefully and answer all questions fully and to the best of your ability.

What is your age? _____
What is your gender? Male _____   Female _____

What is your race?
a. Caucasian
b. African American
c. Asian, Pacific Islander
d. American Indian, Alaska Native
e. Hispanic
f. Other: (specify) _____

What is your education level?
a. Less than high school
b. High school graduate
c. Freshman in college
d. Sophomore in college
e. Junior in college
f. Senior in college
g. Graduate degree

What is your annual income?
a. Under $10,000
b. $10,000–$20,000
c. $20,000–$30,000
d. $30,000 and above

Do you currently have a partner or are in a relationship?
Yes ____   No ____

Have you experienced partner violence in the past 6 months?
Yes ____   No ____

- -

Put a mark in the box that best describes or described your relationship with your partner (in the past 6 months)

Description of how your partner makes you feel	Disagree strongly	Disagree somewhat	Disagree a little	Agree a little	Agree somewhat	Agree strongly
I feel unsafe even in my own home.						
I feel ashamed of the things he or she does to me.						
I try not to rock the boat because I am afraid of what he or she might do.						
I feel like I am programmed to react a certain way to him or her.						
I feel like he or she keeps me prisoner.						
He or she makes me feel like I have no control over my life, no power, no protection.						
I hide the truth from others because I am afraid not to.						
I feel owned and controlled by him or her.						
He or she can scare me without laying a hand on me.						
He or she has a look that goes straight through me and terrifies me.						

Directions: Below is a list of the problems that people sometimes have after experiencing partner violence.

Read each one carefully and fill in the number (0–3) that best describes how often that problem has bothered you in the **past 6 months**.

0 = Not at all or only one time

1 = Once per week or less, or once in a while

2 = 2 to 4 times per week, or half the time

3 = 5 or more times per week, or almost always

Items	0	1	2	3
1. Having upsetting thoughts or images about the traumatic event come into my head when I didn't want them to				
2. Having bad dreams or nightmares about the traumatic event				
2a. Having these bad dreams always center on being killed				
3. Reliving the traumatic event, or acting or feeling as if it were happening again				
3a. Reliving the traumatic event as if I were moving in a rewind motion				
4. Feeling emotionally upset when reminded of the traumatic event (e.g., feeling scared, angry, sad, guilty)				
5. Experiencing physical reactions (e.g., break out in a sweat, fast heart rate) when reminded of the traumatic event				
6. Trying not to think, talk, or have feelings about the traumatic event				
6a. Feeling dizzy when I try hard to not think about the traumatic event				
7. Trying to avoid activities, people, or places that remind me of the traumatic event				
8. Not being able to remember an important part of the traumatic event				
9. Having much less interest or participating much less often in important activities				

9a. Having much more interest in activities that are unimportant				
10. Feeling distant or cut off from people around me				
11. Feeling emotionally numb (e.g., being unable to cry or have loving feelings)				
11a. Feeling emotionally transparent (e.g., like people are unable to see you)				
12. Feeling as if my future plans or hopes will not come true (e.g., not have a career, marriage, children, long life)				
13. Having trouble falling or staying asleep				
14. Feeling irritable or having fits of anger				
15. Having trouble concentrating (e.g., drifting in and out of conversations, losing track of a story on television, forgetting what you read)				
16. Being overly alert (e.g., checking to see who is around you, being uncomfortable with having my back to the door)				
16a. Being overly aware of sensations or changes in my body				
17. Being jumpy or easily startled (e.g., when someone walks up behind you)				
17a. Being acutely aware of smells, especially body odor				

Example Research Report

We now examine the sample research proposal (presented in the previous section) as a completed research report. You will notice that the author has taken the future verb tense used mostly in the research proposal and changed it to past tense (e.g., "The researcher conducted" instead of "The researcher will conduct a study"). You will also notice that the author has added two additional sections: "Results" and "Discussion." In "Results" the author simply reports what he or she has found. "Discussion" allows authors to discuss their findings and possible reasons for what they have found. Here is the completed report.

- -

Symptoms of Posttraumatic Stress Disorder and the Effects of Intimate Partner Violence

Jane Smith

Morehead State University

The purpose of this article is to inform the reader about the researcher's findings on intimate partner violence in relation to posttraumatic stress disorder. The researcher's sample was from Morehead State University students and women in domestic violence shelters in eastern Kentucky. The purpose of the study was to find out whether those who have experienced intimate partner violence have symptoms of posttraumatic stress disorder, which can help health-care professionals properly evaluate those clients who have experienced IPV. The researcher found a strong, positive correlation between IPV and PTSD; however, they were statistically different.

Introduction

A wide array of symptoms have been associated with the experience of sexual and physical abuse, including depression, increased fears, sexual problems, anxiety, guilt, nightmares, sleep difficulties, nervousness, tendency toward revictimization, phobias, substance abuse, exaggerated startle response, and aggression. It has been suggested that posttraumatic stress disorder (PTSD) overlaps these common symptoms in victims. PTSD is characterized by reexperiencing of the trauma, numbing, avoidance of events associated with the trauma, and hyperalertness or exaggerated startle response (Wijma, 2000).

According to the National Center for PTSD (2008), PTSD is an anxiety disorder that can occur after one has been through a traumatic event, including sexual or physical abuse. PTSD symptoms can disappear over time, but about one in three people with PTSD may continue to experience some symptoms.

The purpose of this study is to examine the relative effects of intimate partner violence (IPV) and the outcome of PTSD. The findings of previous research show that there is a strong correlation of those who have experienced IPV with symptoms of PTSD. The hypothesis that PTSD symptoms are related to IPV was tested in this study using two scales, a ten-item scale that assesses battering and a seventeen-item scale that assesses symptoms of posttraumatic stress disorder. The purpose of this study is for mental health and social service professionals to obtain a better understanding of the adverse health outcomes that can occur for those who have experienced a traumatic event such as battering. This in turn will provide professionals with the knowledge and experience they need to assist their clients in linking them with the right resources.

Literature Review

A substantial body of research supports the notion that victims of intimate partner violence experience symptoms of posttraumatic stress disorder (Barker-Collo, 2000; Dutton, 2006; Laffaye, Kennedy, & Stein, 2003; Lang, Kennedy, & Stein, 2002; Perez, 2008; Wijma, 2000; Woods, 2005). Although few of these studies focus solely on posttraumatic stress disorder, PTSD is included among the outcomes resulting from intimate partner violence. Negative mental health outcomes are significantly evident in the research listed earlier, with a positive correlation between the outcome of intimate partner violence and mental health outcomes that adversely affect those who have participated in the research studies. Only on one occasion was posttraumatic stress disorder not related to physical violence, but a positive correlation was found between sexual violence and posttraumatic stress disorder (Bennice, 2003).

Most studies commonly define intimate partner violence as physical, sexual, and emotional or psychological abuse or violence perpetrated by intimate partners or acquaintances, including persons who are current or former spouses, cohabiting partners, boyfriends or girlfriends, and dating partners. It includes abuse in the context of same-sex as well as heterosexual intimate relationships (Carlson, 2008). However, studies show that women are more commonly victims of intimate partner violence, and according to the National Violence against Women Survey, women are most likely victimized by people whom they know (Browne & Williams, 1993; Tjaden & Thoennes, 2000).

Studies have also included sexual abuse, including rape, as intimate partner violence. Although all fifty states now recognize wife rape as a crime, some form of exemption still remains for husbands in more than half of the states, and as a consequence, married women may hesitate to question forced sex because they believe that they have no right to refuse sexual advances made by their husbands (Bennice, 2003).

The most common tool for assessing posttraumatic stress disorder is the PTSD Symptom Scale (PSS), a seventeen-item self-report scale based on the *Diagnostic and Statistical Manual*, 3rd edition, revised (DSM-III-R), PTSD criteria, including reexperiencing, avoidance, and arousal symptom clusters. According to Bennice (2003), the 0–3 response scale captures the frequency of each symptom over the previous two weeks. The PSS was found to have satisfactory internal consistency, high test-retest reliability, and good concurrent and convergent validity with rape victims (Bennice, 2003).

None of the literature has agreed on a scale to measure violence, although some used the Supplemented Conflict Tactics Scale, a nineteen-item measure that assesses ways of responding to conflict among couples. This scale, however, is also outdated in relation to the newest edition of the DSM. The scale is said to measure physical and sexual violence, but the variables are measured in nominal form, which makes them mutually exclusive, and so also creates a question of the methodological validity. Other literature focused mainly on sexual abuse, using the Sexual Experiences Survey, which assesses the type and severity of sexual victimization (Barker-Collo, 2000; Bennice, 2003; Wijma, 2000). Its internal consistencies are also questionable, as the variables are also nominal.

In summary, no scale has been consistently used in the literature to measure the amount of violence. Although many of the outcomes correlated PTSD with intimate partner violence—some including sexual violence in the definition of intimate partner violence—others focused on other mental health outcomes, including PTSD.

It is not as common for intimate partner violence to be perpetrated on males, although some literature exists on the subject (Browne & Williams, 1993; Tjaden & Thoennes, 2000). The literature focused mainly on female subjects, given the convenience of domestic violence shelters and gynecological physician's offices providing access to subjects who were willing to participate in the studies (Barker-Collo, 2000; Dutton, 2006; Laffaye et al., 2003; Lang et al., 2002; Perez, 2008; Wijma, 2000; Woods, 2005). Most studies also focused on a smaller sample size, most likely because of the use of convenience sampling (Barker-Collo, 2000; Bennice, 2003; Woods, 2005).

In conclusion, the literature that relates PTSD and intimate partner violence has consistently agreed that the symptoms of posttraumatic stress are in fact related to people who have experienced intimate partner physical violence, and more so in those who have experienced intimate partner sexual violence. The correlations between the two are significantly positive in relation to each other, although the variables in each slightly differ in studies. No research specifically stated that PTSD is in fact caused by intimate partner violence, and none directly focused on just intimate partner violence and posttraumatic stress disorder.

Methods

Women who have experienced IPV are more likely to have symptoms of PTSD than those who have not experienced IPV. The variables in this study are intimate partner violence and posttraumatic stress disorder, with IPV being the independent variable and PTSD being the dependent variable. These variables are measured using interval-level scales that other researchers have used (see appendix B). Demographic variables included in the study are participant gender, age, race, education level, and socioeconomic status.

The researcher used explanatory measures, based on existing research, for the research design. The results of the research varied, as the surveys were slightly altered and participants were different from those examined in the literature review.

Respondents

The researcher used voluntary participants from domestic violence shelters in Eastern Kentucky and a comparison group of Morehead State University (MSU) students. The sampling was a convenience sample, including individuals who have experienced intimate partner violence before going to a shelter. However, the issue of diversity arises, as the sample encompasses only a small portion of domestic violence victims, mainly women, with Morehead State University students as a comparison. The comparison sample is a convenience sample of students who attend Morehead State University. Each resident of the shelter and each student were invited to fill out a survey that encompasses the PTSD symptom scale along with the Women's Experience Battering Scale (WEB).

Instrumentation

The PTSD scale assesses whether there have been episodes of battering or partner violence, and the symptoms of PTSD. The PTSD scale used in the survey has higher reliability than other scales used to assess PTSD, as it was developed from the DSM and has been used by many researchers. However, the scale's validity is in question, as the DSM used has since been modified. The WEB scale the researcher used has not been as frequently used as the PTSD scale to assess battered women. However, most common scales used to assess intimate partner violence use only nominal-level scaling, which makes the WEB scale more reliable than other scales.

The total sampling was fifty-nine participants. Thirteen were from the domestic violence shelters and forty-six were students on the MSU campus. Each resident and student was given the option to take the survey to assess whether people who experience intimate partner violence have symptoms of PTSD.

Limitations

There were some threats to the reliability of the research study. The participants might have felt the questions about their intimate relationship violence were too personal to share. To reduce this limitation, the researcher provided participants with a confidentiality statement ensuring that information about the participant would not become known (see appendix). Furthermore, remembering the IPV might have brought up unpleasant memories. To help reduce this effect, the researcher informed participants that they could stop the study at any time. If participants at any time felt threatened or unsure about the research study, they could drop out without any repercussions.

Additional limitations include the small sample size and the fact that participants were limited to women's domestic violence shelters and students on the MSU campus. The sample size was based on convenience and included women in domestic violence shelters and students attending MSU at the time of the study. The gender bias in the sample was mostly because domestic violence shelters are equipped to take in only female victims. Another limitation was that the age range of students in the comparison sample included mostly traditional students, whereas women at the domestic violence shelter were older adults. An issue of reliability is that questions about their partners are sensitive topics and respondents might be reluctant to answer such questions honestly. It was also found that the researcher had limited access to a restricted population (e.g., domestic violence shelters and/ or victims), which yielded a smaller sample size than projected.

Data Collection Procedures

The researcher traveled to domestic violence shelters for women in the region, handing out anonymous surveys and then collecting them once the participants had completed them. Surveys were used to determine PTSD symptoms in women residing in domestic violence shelters in eastern Kentucky. There were no questions that could have identified any participant in the study. Previous studies, as discussed in the literature review, show that similar methods have been used to collect data related to PTSD symptoms from IPV victims. The scales implemented in this study were similar to those used in most of the previous studies (e.g., the PTSD scale), and the scales to detect PTSD symptoms and prevalence of IPV were both based on a ratio level, thus increasing validity. This gave the participants more options and better measurability and reliability of the outcome of results.

Ethical Issues

The ethical issue the researcher faced was the dilemma of the benefits of the study outweighing its risk. The women in the domestic violence shelters have experienced a great deal of trauma and may even have symptoms of PTSD, which could in turn increase with recalling episodes of intimate partner violence. However, a benefit is that these women are in a safe setting that is providing support. For the benefits to outweigh the risk, the researcher aims for the outcome of the study to show that women who have experienced IPV should be assessed for more serious anxiety problems such as PTSD. This could be very important for social workers who assess victims of IPV, to understand the complicated and complex outcomes that are presented. The victims might undergo more trauma while being assessed, and the social worker should become aware of the possible need to refer participants to a medical evaluation. Intimate partner violence is an issue that social workers will forever deal with. The outcomes are different for every individual, and once outcomes are identified, social workers can learn how to assist each person and his or her individual needs.

Usefulness to Social Work

Significant results showing that PTSD symptoms are relevant to IPV victims and the study can help future researchers to understand the complexities of the experience of IPV victims. This study builds on how to care for and treat people who have been in a violent relationship. It shows that victims not only are physically abused but also can have trauma disorders and require emotional and psychological care as well. This finding can greatly benefit social workers who work with victims of IPV, particularly in helping IPV victims get the care they need when being treated after having an abusive relationship.

Intimate partner violence is an issue that social workers will forever deal with. The outcomes are different for every individual, and once outcomes are identified, social workers can learn how to assist each person and their needs.

Results

The sample consisted of fifty-nine participants from Morehead State University and local domestic violence shelters. Demographics of the sample are listed in table 1. Participants averaged twenty-three years of age, and the most frequently occurring age was nineteen years. Of participants, 84.1 percent were Caucasian. The modal age was nineteen, and most participants had an education level of first year of college. Approximately 85.7 percent reported an income level of less than $10,000. Approximately 58.7 percent of participants were currently in a relationship.

[Insert Table 1 here]

Table 2 shows a relationship between the independent and dependent variable that is statistically significant at .000, with a correlative value of .855, thus showing a very strong, positive relationship.

[Insert Table 2 here]

The t-test between independent variables shows they are statistically different ($t = 4.317, p = .000$) (see table 3).

[Insert Table 3 here]

In table 4 IPV/PTSD is compared to having experienced partner violence in the past six months. The results were $r = .786$ and $p < .000$ for IPV compared to partner violence in the previous six months. Thus, the findings are significant and have a strong, positive relationship. Findings for PTSD compared to partner violence in the previous six months were also significant ($r = .738, p < .000$), also showing a strong, positive relationship.

[Insert Table 4 here]

Table 5 compares IPV and PTSD with gender. The findings for IPV and gender were $r = .345$ and $p < .012$, and for PTSD and gender they were $r = .302$ and $p < .029$. This shows that IPV and PTSD compared to gender are significant but have only a moderately positive relationship.

[Insert table 5 here]

Table 6 compares PTSD and income. The findings were significant (.002), with a moderate to strong positive relationship of .418.

[Insert Table 6 here]

Table 7 compares education level with PTSD. The correlation value was −.297. This is a weak inverse relationship but significant at .033.

[Insert Table 7 here]

Discussion

As discussed for tables 2 and 3, the independent variable IPV and the dependent variable PTSD have a strong correlation, but table 3 shows that they are significantly different. The tables do correlate, but correlation does not mean that IPV directly causes PTSD. This was a very important finding. The hypothesis stated that women who have experienced IPV are more likely to have symptoms of PTSD than women who have not experienced IPV.

In table 2, the bivariate analysis demonstrated a positive correlation between the two variables, IPV and PTSD. This means that as the age increased, so did the frequency of IPV and PTSD. Intimate partner violence compared to age was .728, which is a fairly strong relationship between these two variables. This shows that as age increased, so did IPV. The two variables, age and PTSD were also correlated ($r = .575$). These findings imply that risk of PTSD increases with age, which could be useful for social workers working with older adults.

The main variables of PTSD and IPV were statistically significant. PTSD and IPV had a very strong, positive relationship (.855) demonstrating a positive relationship between age and PTSD. This means that as the frequency of IPV increased, so did PTSD. And, the t-test in table 3 comparing IPV and PTSD demonstrated similar findings.

In table 4, the researcher examined the relationship between experiencing partner violence in the previous six months and the presence of PTSD. The comparison of PTSD and IPV in the previous six months showed that a relationship exists between experiencing partner violence and PTSD. Moreover, if a victim had experienced partner violence in the previous six months, then PTSD increased. This is an important finding, as it indicates that PTSD symptoms are likely to begin within six months of the abuse. Both findings were statistically significant, with a strong, positive relationship.

Table 5 shows that IPV compared to gender as well as PTSD compared to gender were significant, but the correlation was not strong. Both IPV and gender were correlated at .345, and PTSD at .302. The values of the relationships are moderate. This means that female respondents were more likely to experience IPV, which in turn correlates with PTSD. These results might affect the reliability of the research, as the WEB scale in clinical settings was targeted at women only.

Tables 6 and 7 compared PTSD with income and education. The findings for PTSD compared to income showed that as income increased, so did symptoms of PTSD; however, income did not correlate with IPV, which means that there may be confounding variables that the researcher did not assess, such as higher-paying jobs being more stressful and leading to PTSD. PTSD compared to education had an inverse relationship; as education level increased, the symptoms of PTSD decreased. The researcher deduced that women with higher education have more access to the job market and in turn may have more options to leave and feel less trapped in a relationship with IPV than do those who do not have the resources to leave their abusers.

One limitation that could have possibly affected the outcome of the findings was that the sample size of domestic violence respondents was relatively small compared to the comparison sample. The comparison sample also had males, who were not assessed in the WEB scale used for the survey. Also, the respondents might not have felt comfortable answering personal questions about their relationships, particularly males who might have experienced partner violence. The researcher took into consideration all of these limitations as possibly affecting the findings.

This research might benefit those working with intimate partner violence victims, but more larger-scale research needs to be conducted. Finding scales that address both sexes would also be beneficial to the study so that results have greater validity. Applying a comparison sample in this type of study is useful with known victims of IPV, as the test and retest methods may be useful in cases of ongoing abuse. If findings of future research continue to bear out these findings, then clinical and health-care settings could implement such policies and tools as training workers to identify symptoms of PTSD and IPV within six months of abuse, and use evidence-based interventions to help clients.

TABLE 1. DEMOGRAPHICS AND RELATIONSHIP OF SAMPLE ($N = 59$)

	FREQUENCY	PERCENTAGE	AVERAGE
Age			23
Gender			
Male	18	28.6	
Female	41	65.1	
Race			
Caucasian	53	84.1	
African American	2	3.2	
Asian, Pacific Islander	1	1.6	
American Indian, Alaska Native	1	1.6	
Hispanic	0	0	
Other	2	3.2	
Education			
Less than high school	5	7.9	
High school graduate	4	6.3	
Freshman in college	25	39.7	
Sophomore in college	15	23.8	
Junior in college	7	11.1	
Senior in college	2	3.2	
Graduate degree	1	1.6	
Income			
Less than $10,000	54	85.7	
$10,000–$20,000	4	6.3	
Currently in a relationship			
No	22	34.9	
Yes	37	58.7	

TABLE 2. IPV AND PTSD AND AGE

		IPVTOTAL	PTSDTOTAL	Age
IPVTOTAL	Pearson's r	1.000	.855*	.728*
	Sig. (2-tailed)		.000	.000
	N	52.000	49	52
PTSDTOTAL	Pearson's r	.855*	1.000	.575*
	Sig. (2-tailed)	.000		.000
	N	49	52.000	52
Age	Pearson's r	.728*	.575*	1.000
	Sig. (2-tailed)	.000	.000	
	N	52	52	59.000

*Correlation significant at the .01 level.

TABLE 3. PAIRED-SAMPLES TEST

	PAIRED DIFFERENCES							
			SE	95% CI OF THE DIFFERENCE				SIG.
	MEAN	SD	MEAN	LOWER	UPPER	t	DF	(2-TAILED)
Pair IPV TOTAL PTSD TOTAL	6.53061	10.58911	1.51273	3.48906	9.57216	4.317	48	.000

Note: SD = standard deviation; SE = standard error; df = degrees of freedom.

TABLE 4. IPV/PTSD COMPARED TO EXPERIENCING INTIMATE PARTNER VIOLENCE IN THE PREVIOUS SIX MONTHS

		IPVTOTAL	PTSDTOTAL
Have you experienced partner violence in the past 6 months?	Pearson's r	.786*	.738*
	Sig. (2-tailed)	.000	.000
	N	52	52

*Correlation significant at the .01 level.

TABLE 5. GENDER COMPARED TO PTSD

		IPVTOTAL	PTSDTOTAL
What is your gender?	Pearson's r Sig. (2-tailed) N	.345* .012 52	.302* .029 52

*Correlation significant at the .05 level.

TABLE 6. PTSD COMPARED TO INCOME

		What is your income?	PTSDTOTAL
What is your income?	Pearson's r Sig. (2-tailed) N	1.000 58.000	.418* .002 51

*Correlation significant at the .01 level.

TABLE 7. PTSD COMPARED TO EDUCATION

		PTSDTOTAL
What is your education level?	Pearson's r Sig. (2-tailed) N	− .297* .033 52

*Correlation significant at the .05 level.

References

Barker-Collo, S. L. (2000). A cognitive-behavioral model of post-traumatic stress for sexually abused females. *Journal of Interpersonal Violence, 15*, 375–392. http://dx.doi.org/10.1177/088626000015004003

Bennice, J. A. (2003). The relative effects of intimate partner physical and sexual violence on post-traumatic stress disorder symptomatology. *Violence and Victims, 18*, 87–94. http://dx.doi.org/10.1891/vivi.2003.18.1.87

Browne, A., & Williams, K. (1993). Gender, intimacy, and lethal violence: Trends from 1976 through 1987. *Gender and Society, 7*, 78–98.

Carlson, B. E. (2008). Intimate partner violence. In *Encyclopedia of Social*

Work [Web]. Oxford University Press. http://dx.doi.org/10.4135/
9781412963923.n248

Dutton, M. A. (2006). Intimate partner violence, PTSD, and adverse health
outcomes. *Journal of Interpersonal Violence, 21*, 955–968. http://dx.doi
.org/10.1177/0886260506289178

Laffaye, C., Kennedy, C., & Stein, M. B. (2003). Post-traumatic stress disorder
and health-related quality of life in female victims of intimate partner
violence. *Violence and Victims, 18*, 227–238.

Lang, A. J., Kennedy, C. M., & Stein, M. B. (2002). Anxiety sensitivity and
PTSD among female victims of intimate partner violence. *Depression
and Anxiety, 16*, 77–83.

National Center for PTSD. (2008). Retrieved November 13, 2008, from
National Center for PTSD: http://www.mentalhealth.va.gov/MENTAL
HEALTH/ptsd/fs_what_is_eptsdoddb.asp

Perez, S. (2008). PTSD compromises battered women's future safety. *Journal
of Interpersonal Violence, 23*, 635–651. http://dx.doi.org/10.1177/0886
260507313528

Tjaden, P., & Thoennes, N. (2000). Extent, nature, and consequences of intimate partner violence (NCJ 181867). Washington, DC: Office of Justice
Programs, U.S. Department of Justice. Retrieved from https://www.ncjrs
.gov/pdffiles1/nij/181867.pdf

Wijma, K. (2000). Prevalence of post-traumatic stress disorder among gynecological patients with a history of sexual and physical abuse. *Journal
of Interpersonal Violence, 15*, 944–958.

Woods, A. B. (2005).The mediation effect of posttraumatic stress disorder
symptoms on the relationship of intimate partner violence and IFN-g
levels. *American Journal of Community Psychology, 36*, 159–175. http://
dx.doi.org/10.1007/s10464-005-6240-7

- -

Informed Consent

Name and Contact Information of Student Researcher
Jane Smith
Morehead State University
Morehead, KY 40351

Purpose of the Study: The purpose of this study is to research the adverse
health effects of partner violence on a person. This research will further
help social workers and health-care professionals understand the effects
and in what ways they can assist those who have been battered in an
improved manner.

Duration: My participation in this study will include the completion of this survey.

Procedures: I will be asked to complete this survey.

Potential Risks/Discomforts: There are no physical discomforts or risks.

Potential Benefits: Using the outcome of this study to improve the social work and health-care professions' understanding of the effects of intimate partner violence.

Confidentiality: All responses to this survey will be kept confidential. Your name or identity will not be linked in any way to the research data.

Right to Refuse or Withdraw: I understand that my participation is voluntary and I may refuse to participate or may discontinue participation at any time.

Individuals to Contact: If I have a question about my participation in this study, I can contact: Jane Smith (researcher)

I have read this entire form and I understand it completely. All of my questions regarding this form or this study have been answered to my complete satisfaction. I agree to participate in this research.

- -

Please read each question carefully and answer all questions fully and to the best of your ability.

What is your age? _____
What is your gender?   Male _____   Female _____

What is your race?
a. Caucasian
b. African American
c. Asian, Pacific Islander
d. American Indian, Alaska Native
e. Hispanic
f. Other: (specify) _____

What is your education level?
a. Less than high school
b. High school graduate

c. Freshman in college
d. Sophomore in college
e. Junior in college
f. Senior in college
g. Graduate degree

What is your annual income?
a. Under $10,000
b. $10,000–$20,000
c. $20,000–$30,000
d. $30,000 and above

Do you currently have a partner or are in a relationship?
Yes _____ No _____

Have you experienced partner violence in the past 6 months?
Yes _____ No _____

- -

Put a mark in the box that best describes or described your relationship with your partner (in the past 6 months)

Description of how your partner makes you feel	Disagree strongly	Disagree somewhat	Disagree a little	Agree a little	Agree somewhat	Agree strongly
I feel unsafe even in my own home.						
I feel ashamed of the things he or she does to me.						
I try not to rock the boat because I am afraid of what he or she might do.						
I feel like I am programmed to react a certain way to him or her.						
I feel like he or she keeps me prisoner.						

He or she makes me feel like I have no control over my life, no power, no protection.							
I hide the truth from others because I am afraid not to.							
I feel owned and controlled by him or her.							
He or she can scare me without laying a hand on me.							
He or she has a look that goes straight through me and terrifies me.							

Directions: Below is a list of the problems that people sometimes have after experiencing partner violence.

Read each one carefully and fill in the number (0–3) that best describes how often that problem has bothered you in the **past 6 months**.

0 = Not at all or only one time

1 = Once per week or less

2 = 2 to 4 times per week, or half the time

3 = 5 or more times per week, or almost always

Items	0	1	2	3
1. Having upsetting thoughts or images about the traumatic event come into my head when I didn't want them to				
2. Having bad dreams or nightmares about the traumatic event				
2a. Having bad dreams that always center on being killed				
3. Reliving the traumatic event, or acting or feeling as if it were happening again				

3a. Reliving the traumatic event as if I were moving in a rewind motion				
4. Feeling emotionally upset when reminded of the traumatic event (e.g., feeling scared, angry, sad, guilty)				
5. Experiencing physical reactions (e.g., break out in a sweat, fast heart rate) when reminded of the traumatic event				
6. Trying not to think, talk, or have feelings about the traumatic event				
6a. Feeling dizzy when I try hard to not think about the traumatic event				
7. Trying to avoid activities, people, or places that remind me of the traumatic event				
8. Not being able to remember an important part of the traumatic event				
9. Having much less interest or participating much less often in important activities				
10. Feeling distant or cut off from people around me				
11. Feeling emotionally numb (e.g., being unable to cry or have loving feelings)				
12. Feeling as if my future plans or hopes will not come true (e.g., not have a career, marriage, children, long life)				
13. Having trouble falling or staying asleep				
14. Feeling irritable or having fits of anger				
15. Having trouble concentrating (e.g., drifting in and out of conversations, losing track of a story on television, forgetting what you read)				
16. Being overly alert (e.g., checking to see who is around you, being uncomfortable with having my back to the door)				
16a. Being overly aware of sensations or changes in my body				
17. Being jumpy or easily startled (e.g., when someone walks up behind you)				
17a. Being acutely aware of smells, especially body odor				

APPENDIX

Throughout this text, we have referred to portions of the National Association of Social Workers (NASW) Code of Ethics. The portions reprinted here are the sections we have referenced in the text. To review the code in its entirety, you may want to go to the NASW website (www.naswdc.org).

4.08 Acknowledging Credit
(a) Social workers should take responsibility and credit, including authorship credit, only for work they have actually performed and to which they have contributed.
(b) Social workers should honestly acknowledge the work of and the contributions made by others.

5. Social Workers' Ethical Responsibilities to the Social Work Profession

5.01 Integrity of the Profession
(a) Social workers should work toward the maintenance and promotion of high standards of practice.
(b) Social workers should uphold and advance the values, ethics, knowledge, and mission of the profession. Social workers should protect, enhance, and improve the integrity of the profession through appropriate study and research, active discussion, and responsible criticism of the profession.
(c) Social workers should contribute time and professional expertise to activities that promote respect for the value, integrity, and competence of the social work profession. These activities may include teaching, research, consultation, service, legislative testimony, presentations in the community, and participation in their professional organizations.
(d) Social workers should contribute to the knowledge base of social

work and share with colleagues their knowledge related to practice, research, and ethics. Social workers should seek to contribute to the profession's literature and to share their knowledge at professional meetings and conferences.

(e) Social workers should act to prevent the unauthorized and unqualified practice of social work.

5.02 EVALUATION AND RESEARCH

(a) Social workers should monitor and evaluate policies, the implementation of programs, and practice interventions.

(b) Social workers should promote and facilitate evaluation and research to contribute to the development of knowledge.

(c) Social workers should critically examine and keep current with emerging knowledge relevant to social work and fully use evaluation and research evidence in their professional practice.

(d) Social workers engaged in evaluation or research should carefully consider possible consequences and should follow guidelines developed for the protection of evaluation and research participants. Appropriate institutional review boards should be consulted.

(e) Social workers engaged in evaluation or research should obtain voluntary and written informed consent from participants, when appropriate, without any implied or actual deprivation or penalty for refusal to participate; without undue inducement to participate; and with due regard for participants' wellbeing, privacy, and dignity. Informed consent should include information about the nature, extent, and duration of the participation requested and disclosure of the risks and benefits of participation in the research.

(f) When evaluation or research participants are incapable of giving informed consent, social workers should provide an appropriate explanation to the participants, obtain the participants' assent to the extent they are able, and obtain written consent from an appropriate proxy.

(g) Social workers should never design or conduct evaluation or research that does not use consent procedures, such as certain forms of naturalistic observation and archival research, unless rigorous and responsible review of the research has found it to be justified because of its prospective scientific, educational, or applied value and unless equally effective alternative procedures that do not involve waiver of consent are not feasible.

(h) Social workers should inform participants of their right to withdraw from evaluation and research at any time without penalty.

(i) Social workers should take appropriate steps to ensure that participants in evaluation and research have access to appropriate supportive services.

(j) Social workers engaged in evaluation or research should protect participants from unwarranted physical or mental distress, harm, danger, or deprivation.

(k) Social workers engaged in the evaluation of services should discuss collected information only for professional purposes and only with people professionally concerned with this information.

(l) Social workers engaged in evaluation or research should ensure the anonymity or confidentiality of participants and of the data obtained from them. Social workers should inform participants of any limits of confidentiality, the measures that will be taken to ensure confidentiality, and when any records containing research data will be destroyed.

(m) Social workers who report evaluation and research results should protect participants' confidentiality by omitting identifying information unless proper consent has been obtained authorizing disclosure.

(n) Social workers should report evaluation and research findings accurately. They should not fabricate or falsify results and should take steps to correct any errors later found in published data using standard publication methods.

(o) Social workers engaged in evaluation or research should be alert to and avoid conflicts of interest and dual relationships with participants, should inform participants when a real or potential conflict of interest arises, and should take steps to resolve the issue in a manner that makes participants' interests primary.

(p) Social workers should educate themselves, their students, and their colleagues about responsible research practices.

Glossary

Abstract.   A brief summary of the research and its findings, usually no more than 250 words

Aggregate.   To compile data in a concise, manageable, and understandable manner so that they can be examined relatively quickly

Analysis of variance (ANOVA).   A statistical procedure that allows us to compare the mean scores of two or more groups simultaneously by computing a statistical average for one group as a whole and comparing it to another group or groups

Anonymity.   Assurance that the researcher will not collect any information that can identify the subject

Baseline.   A beginning point in research that establishes an initial sense of how a program, group, or individual is currently functioning and allows researchers to track progress over time

Bell-shaped curve.   The distribution of scores that are symmetrically shaped around the mean, where the majority of the scores are clustered around the mean and each side of the mean resembles the other

Beneficence.   The obligation in research to do no harm and maximize benefits while minimizing possible harm

Benefits.   Positive values related to health or well-being, which are expected, in research, to outweigh the risks

Bias.   The unknown or unacknowledged error created during the design of a study, in the choice of problem to be studied, over the course of the study itself, or during the interpretation of findings

Bivariate analysis.   An analysis that examines the relationship between one independent variable and one dependent variable (also known as simple regression)

Case study.   A detailed analysis of a single person or event (or sometimes a limited number of people or events)

Causal relationship.   A relationship in which three conditions must be met: (1) the independent variable must come before the dependent variable (known as temporal ordering), (2) the independent and dependent variables must be correlated, and (3) the correlation between the independent and dependent variables cannot be explained by the impact of another variable

Central tendency.   An estimate of the center of a distribution of values

Chi-square.   A nonparametric statistical procedure that is commonly used to determine whether there is truly a difference in groups when a researcher has a small sample size and a dependent variable that is nominal or ordinal

Citation.   Means of giving credit to authors for what is being reported, and is organized by last name then date

Cluster sampling.   A method for drawing a sample from a population in two or more stages through a process of listing naturally occurring clusters in the population and sampling the clusters (sometimes referred to as multistage sampling)

Coefficient.   The number by which a variable is multiplied

Conceptualizing a variable.   How we translate an idea or abstract theory into a variable that can be used to test a hypothesis or make sense of observations

Concurrent validity.   How well a measure correlates with some other measure of the same variable that is believed to be valid

Confidence interval.   An indication of the level of certainty we can have that our sample accurately depicts the real world; usually established at 95 percent (or .05) in statistical analysis

Confidentiality.   Assurance that a researcher provides to subjects that all information about them, and all answers they provide, will remain in the hands of the investigator and that no person outside the research process will have access to that information

Confounding variable.   A variable that obscures the effect of another variable

Construct.   The concept or characteristic that an instrument is designed to measure

Construct validity.   A form of validity related to the extent to which the items of an instrument accurately sample a construct

Content validity.   A form of validity related to how well the items in a measurement instrument represent the concept that is being measured

Control for.   A means of subtracting the effects of certain independent variables on the dependent variable by holding those variables constant

Control variable.   Any variable that researchers control for (i.e., hold constant)

Convenience sampling.   Reliance on available subjects; one of the most frequently used sampling techniques in social work research

Convergent validity.   How well the measures of a construct (e.g., depression, or alcoholism) that we expect to be related to each other are, indeed, found to correspond to each other (i.e., to measure the same construct). For example, we would expect that the concepts of loss of energy, loss of appetite, increase in sleeping would all be associated with depression.

Correlational relationship.   A relationship between two or more variables in which a change in one variable may be associated with some degree of change in the other variable

Criterion-related validity.   A form of validity related to a measure's ability to make accurate predictions (also called predictive validity)

Cross-sectional design.   A research design that looks at a cross-section or subset of a population at one point in time

Curvilinear correlation. A statistical relationship that starts off as either a positive relationship or a negative relationship and then begins to curve

Data abstraction. Using closed case records for obtaining information about a subject and/or data collection

Debriefing. The process of fully informing subjects of the nature of the research when some form of deception has been employed

Deductive research. The process of reasoning that moves from a general hypothesis or theory to specific results through the use of quantitative methods

Demographics. The physical characteristics of a population, such as age, sex, marital status, family size, education, geographic location, and occupation

Dependent variable. The variable that is changed or predicted by another variable or is said to depend on the other variable (the independent variable)

Descriptive design. A research design that uses descriptive language (e.g., how many, how much, what the statistical average is, how people view a topic) to describe a population or phenomenon

Descriptive inquiry. A strategy used in qualitative research to develop a greater understanding of issues by describing individual experiences

Descriptive statistics. Ways of organizing, describing, and presenting quantitative (numerical) data in a manner that is concise, manageable, and understandable

Dichotomous variable. A variable with only two responses to choose from, such as yes or no, or treatment group or nontreatment group

Discriminate validity. Measures of a construct that we would not expect to be related are indeed measuring different constructs

Distribution. A summary of the frequency of individual values or ranges of values for a variable

Elements. Individual members of a population or sample

Enumeration unit. A unit containing one or more units listed in the sampling frame

Equivalent form reliability. A measure of consistency between two versions of a measure

Ethnography. A type of qualitative research design that is centered on cultural behavior and that seeks to record the cultural aspects of a group

Evaluative design. A type of research design that can employ a qualitative, quantitative, or mixed-method approach using process evaluations and outcome evaluations to evaluate the effectiveness of a program or agency

Evidence-based practice. Practices whose efficacy is supported by evidence

Explanatory design. A type of research design that looks at the correlation between two or more variables and attempts to determine whether they are related, and if so, in what way and how strongly

Exploratory design. A type of research design that allows us to use our powers of observation, inquiry, and assessment to form tentative theories about what we are seeing and experiencing; generally used to explore understudied topics

External validity. The extent to which a study's findings are applicable or relevant to a group outside the study (also called generalizability)

Face validity. A form of validity related to whether a measure seems to make sense (be valid) at a glance

Faking data. Making up desired data or eliminating undesired data in research findings

Focus group. An open discussion in which individuals share their opinions about or emotional responses to a particular subject

Frequency. The number of times that a response occurs

Grand-tour questions. Large, overarching questions that identify the broad intent of a research study and are based on existing knowledge (e.g., experience, knowledge from others, tradition, prior research)

Grounded theory. A type of research design that utilizes a recursive form of question and analysis

Histogram. A vertical block graph used in statistics to visually present interval- or ratio-level data

Hypothesis. A research statement about relationships between variables that is testable and that can be accepted or rejected on the basis of the evidence

Independent-samples t-test. A type of t-test that is utilized when a researcher needs to compare two groups to see whether the independent variable has an effect on the dependent variable

Independent variable. A variable that the researcher controls or manipulates

Inductive research. The gathering of information based on observations and quotes that is organized into common themes

Inferential statistics. Statistical procedures that examine associations between variables and use significance tests and other measures to make inferences about the collected quantitative data

Informed consent. The process of educating potential research participants about the basic purpose of the study, informing them that their participation is voluntary, and obtaining their written permission to participate in the study

Institutional review board. A committee mandated by the federal government to oversee the protection of human and animal subjects in research

Internal consistency. The consistency among responses to the items in a measure; the extent to which responses to items measuring the same concept are associated with each other

Internal validity. A measure of how confident the researcher can be about the independent variable truly causing a change in the dependent variable (as opposed to outside influences)

Interobserver reliability. A measure of reliability that is used when two or more observers rate the same person, place, or event

Interval-level variables. Variables that are measured in such a way that there are equal gradations between each item, items are rank ordered, and each item is mutually exclusive and exhaustive

Intraobserver reliability. A measure of reliability that is used when one observer rates a person, place, or event two or more times

Justice. An ethical research principle regarding the fairness of distribution of benefits and risks among all individuals, which can be formulated in four ways: to each person an equal share, to each person according to individual need, to each person according to individual effort, and to each person according to merit

Keywords. Words that are found in the abstract of an article, and again as identifiers for the article, and that can be used as search terms in a database search

Laundering data. A way of statistically manipulating the data collected to reduce errors and make the findings more accurate

Leptokurtosis. The shape of a distribution of scores that is tall and narrow because the majority of scores closely resemble the mean

Likert scales. A method of asking respondents to rank their responses on a continuum (e.g., from strongly disagree to strongly agree)

Literature review. A search of the published research that allows us to synthesize what is known about the topic we are studying

Longitudinal design. A research study that follows one cohort over a period of time

Mean. The statistical average of a set of numbers

Measure. A tool or instrument that is used to gather data and has two parts: the item (stimulus) and the response

Measure of association. Any of several statistical procedures that allow you to measure the correlation between variables

Measure of dispersion. A statistical measure that shows how dissimilar or different the data are from each other; reported by the range of scores around the mean

Median. The midpoint of a set of numbers

Methodology. The research methods, procedures, and techniques used to collect and analyze information in research

Mixed-method design. A research design that uses both qualitative and quantitative methods

Mode. The most frequently occurring response for a variable

Multiple regression. A statistical procedure that measures the correlation between an independent variable and the dependent variable while holding other independent variables constant (also known as linear regression)

Negative correlation. A statistical relationship that occurs when one variable increases when the other decreases (also called an inverse relationship)

No correlation. The absence of a relationship between variables—one variable does not influence the other

Nominal-level variables. Variables that are measured in such a way that items are mutually exclusive and exhaustive

Nonparametric statistics. Statistics that are used when the data depart from the criteria established for parametric statistics, the most common of which is chi-square

Nonstandardized methods. Informal methods of collecting data, such as the use of broad and open-ended questions (recorded for accuracy) or a journal or field notes

Nonprobability sampling.   Techniques for selecting a sample in which every individual does not have a greater-than-zero chance of being selected

Normal distribution.   The symmetrical distribution of scores around the mean, with the most scores clustered around the mean and tapering off on both sides

Open-ended question.   An inquiry that is worded in a way that allows the respondent to answer in his or her own words as opposed to merely soliciting a yes-or-no response

Operationalizing.   How we define a concept so that it can be measured

Ordinal-level variables.   Variables that are measured in such a way that items must be mutually exclusive, exhaustive, and rank ordered

Outcome evaluation.   An external evaluation that measures the overall effectiveness of a program by looking at the goals and objectives established by the program to answer the question "Did this program accomplish what it set out to do?"

Outlier.   An anomaly or result that is far different from most of the results for the group and can skew the overall results (especially in a statistical average)

Paired samples t-test.   A test of significance of the differences between two different sets of scores for the same respondents (also known as dependent-samples *t*-test)

Parametric statistics.   A type of inferential statistics in which a certain set of assumptions or rules must be met: data must be normally distributed, the dependent variable must be measured at an interval or ratio level, and a sample size of at least fifty must be used

Pearson's r.   An analysis of correlation that seeks to determine whether a relationship exists between two variables (one independent variable and one dependent variable) and the direction of the relationship

Peer review.   Review of an article's content, accuracy, and methodological concerns by experts in the field that occurs before an article is accepted for publication

Phenomenology.   A type of research design that seeks to understand the lived experience (e.g., perceptions, thoughts, ideas, experiences) of the individuals who are being studied

Pilot test.   Submitting surveys or data collection tools to a small number of people so that the researcher can be sure that questions are measuring variables as intended

Plagiarism.   The act of taking credit for work that is not one's own, either in whole or in part

Platykurtosis.   The shape of a distribution of scores that is flat and wide because the majority of scores differ from the mean

Population.   A set of entities from which a sample can be drawn either to describe a subsection of that population or to generalize information to the larger population

Positive correlation.   A statistical relationship in which the independent variable increases as the dependent variable increases

Probability distribution theory. The theory that data are equally distributed on both sides of the mean in a normal bell-shaped curve and that 68.26 percent of the population will probably fall within one standard deviation, 95.44 percent will probably fall within two standard deviations, and 99.74 percent will fall probably within three standard deviations of the mean

Probability sampling. A sampling technique in which each and every member of the population has a nonzero chance of being included in the sample

Probability sampling theory. A theory that requires the researcher to select a set of elements from a population in such a way that those elements accurately portray the parameters of the total population

Probability value. A report of whether the strength of a relationship is statistically significant or whether it could have occurred by chance; generally set at .05 or lower

Problem statement. An open-ended statement that tells you what a study is intended to do but does not predict what the results might be

Process evaluation. An internal evaluation process that is initiated in the early stages of a program and has three main goals: to construct a program description, to monitor a program, and to assess the quality of services being provided

Program description. The delineation of the setup, routines, and consumer characteristics of a program

Program evaluation. A type of research design and analysis that evaluates specific characteristics of a program within an agency

Program monitoring. A program evaluation method that is used to examine what happens after people receive services from a program

Program objective. A measurable, objective, specific, and timelined goal that allows the effectiveness of a piece of a program goal to be evaluated

Purposive sampling. Selection of a sample on the basis of knowledge of a population or with some predetermined characteristics in mind

Qualitative research. A field of research that is largely exploratory but can also involve the use of descriptive methods; employed when little or nothing is known about a subject or phenomenon

Quality assurance. Means of determining the level of satisfaction of both services for consumers and programmatic issues for the staff

Quantitative data analysis. The process of analyzing data utilizing a variety of statistical procedures, including descriptive and inferential statistics

Quantitative research. A field of research that is used when a sufficient amount of information has been acquired that the researcher can develop hypotheses about what is being studied

Quota sampling. A means of selecting a stratified nonrandom sample in which a researcher divides a population into categories and selects a certain number (a quota) of subjects from each category

Random assignment. The selection and placement of individuals from the pool of all potential participants to either the experimental group or the control group, which increases internal validity and reduces the likelihood of bias

Random selection.   Means of selecting a sample from a larger population in which each member of the population has an equal chance of being selected for a study

Range.   The overall spread or variability of a variable that tells us the difference between the lowest (minimum) and highest (maximum) values (responses) for a variable

Ratio-level variables.   Variables that are measured in such a way that items are mutually exclusive and exhaustive: they are rank ordered, there are equal gradations between items, and there is an absolute zero

Reference list.   The alphabetical list of studies cited in a summary of a literature review or a research report

Reliability.   The stability and consistency of a measurement

Representativeness.   A condition that is met when characteristics of the sample are similar to those of the population from which the sample was drawn

Research.   The process of systematically gaining information; assimilating knowledge and gathering data in a logical manner to become informed about something

Respect for individuals.   An ethical research principle according to which the autonomy of an individual is acknowledged and those with diminished autonomy are protected

Risk.   The possibility that psychological, physical, legal, social, or economic harm may occur; sometimes expressed in levels, such as "no risk," "little risk," "moderate risk," and "high risk"

Rule of parsimony.   Reducing the number of items in a measure or survey to the absolute minimum requirements

Sample.   A group of subjects (elements) selected from a larger population

Sampling error.   An error that occurs because the research has contacted only part of the population

Sampling frame.   A list of all elements or other units containing the elements in a population

Sampling unit.   A population selected for inclusion in a sampling frame

Semistructured interview.   Prepared research questions that are used to start the interview process but also allow additional information to be solicited

Simple random sampling.   A method of sampling in which a sample is generated randomly from a population in which each person has been assigned a number

Single-subject design.   A method for evaluating an individual's progress over time that measures whether a relationship exists between an intervention and a specific outcome

Skewed distribution.   A distribution of scores that produces a nonsymmetrical curve because there are more responses on the left or right side of the mean

Snowball sampling.   A method of sampling in which the researcher starts by studying one or more members of a group to gain access to other members of the same group, through a referral system, for the purpose of building the sample

Speculative inquiry. A strategy used in qualitative research to generate a theory based on common experiences

Standard deviation. A measure of dispersion that is calculated by taking the square root of variance; the most commonly used measure of dispersion

Standardized measure. A measurement or instrument that has been given to enough people that we can compare one person's scores to those of other test takers

Statistical Package for Social Sciences (SPSS). A statistical program that social science researchers commonly use to analyze research data

Stratified random sampling. A method of sampling in which the population is divided into subgroups (strata) and a sample is drawn from each stratum

Structured interview. An interview that is limited to the research questions the researcher wants answered

Surveys. A research design in which a sample of subjects is drawn from a population and studied (usually interviewed) to make inferences about the population; surveys pose statements or questions to which subjects are asked to respond

Systematic random sampling. A method of sampling in which every nth number is selected at random (e.g., every third person, every tenth person)

Target outcome. The goal of the intervention

Test-retest reliability. A method of examining the consistency of your measure from one time to the next to establish reliability

Theory. A statement or set of statements designed to explain a phenomenon on the basis of observations and experiments; often agreed on by most experts in a particular field

Theoretical perspective. A model that makes assumptions about something, attempts to integrate various kinds of information, gives meaning to what we see and experience, focuses on relationships and connections between variables, and has inherent benefits and consequences

t-Test. A statistical procedure that compares the means of two groups to determine whether they are statistically different

Univariate analysis. A descriptive statistical method that involves the examination across cases of one variable at a time

Validity. How much a measurement tool measures what it is meant to measure

Variable. Any attribute or characteristic that changes or assumes different values

Variance. A statistical measure that is used to examine the spread of scores in a distribution

References

American Psychiatric Association. (2013). *Diagnostic and statistical manual of mental disorders: DSM-5* (5th ed.). Arlington, VA: Author.

Barton, B. (2006). *Stripped: Inside the lives of exotic dancers.* New York, NY: New York University Press.

Bryan, E. (1997). Services for families with multiple births: The United Kingdom model: Multiple pregnancy: New insights. *Journal of Reproductive Medicine, 42*(12), 790–792.

Ehrenreich, B. (2010). *Nickel and dimed: On (not) getting by in America.* New York, NY: Metropolitan Books.

Fischer, J., & Corcoran, K. (2007). *Measures for clinical practice: A sourcebook* (4th ed.). New York, NY: Oxford University Press.

Gorovitz, S. (1985). *Doctors' dilemmas: Moral conflict and medical care.* New York, NY: Oxford University Press.

Haney, C., Banks, C., & Zimbardo, P. (1973). Interpersonal dynamics in a simulated prison. *International Journal of Criminology and Penology, 1,* 69–97.

Haney, C., Banks, C., & Zimbardo, P. (2004). A study of prisoners and guards in a simulated prison. In Michael Balfour (ed.), *Theatre in Prison: Theory and Practice* (pp. 19–32). Bristol, UK: Intellect Books.

Ingelfinger, F. (1972). Informed (but uneducated) consent. *New England Journal of Medicine, 287,* 465–466.

Ingram, B., & Chung, R. (1997). Client satisfaction data and quality improvement in managed mental health care organizations. *Health Care Management Review, 22,* 40–52.

Jones, J. (1981). *Bad blood: The Tuskegee syphilis experiment.* New York, NY: Free Press.

Kiely, J. L., & Susser, M. (1992). Preterm birth, intrauterine growth retardation, and perinatal mortality. *American Journal of Public Health, 82*(3), 343–345.

Kogan, M. D., Alexander, G. R., Kotelchuck, M., MacDorman, M. F., Buekens, P., Martin, J. A., & Papiernik, E. (2000). Trends in twin birth outcomes and prenatal care utilization in the United States, 1981–1997. *JAMA, 284*(3), 335–341.

Malmstrom, P. M., & Biale, R. (1990). An agenda for meeting the special needs of multiple birth families. *Acta Geneticae Medicae et Gemellologiae, 39*(4), 507.

Milgram, S. (1963). Behavioral study of obedience. *Journal of Abnormal and Social Psychology, 67*, 371–378.

National Association of Social Workers. (2008). *Code of ethics of the National Association of Social Workers.* Washington, DC: Author.

National Commission for the Protection of Human Subjects of Biomedical and Behavioral Research. (1979). *The Belmont report: Ethical principles and guidelines for the protection of human subjects of research.* Washington, DC: U.S. Government Printing Office.

National Research Act (1974). Pub. L. No. 93–348.

Nuremberg Tribunals. (1949). Trials of War Criminals before the Nuremberg Military Tribunals under Control Council Law No. 10 (Vol. 2, pp. 181–182). Washington, DC: U.S. Government Printing Office.

Papiernik, E., Alexander, G. R., & Paneth, N. (1990). Racial differences in pregnancy duration and its implications for perinatal care. *Medical Hypotheses, 33*(3), 181–186.

Seltzer, M. L. (1971). The Michigan Alcoholism Screening Test: The quest for a new diagnostic instrument. *American Journal of Psychiatry, 127*, 89–94.

Sinetar, M. (1986). *Ordinary people as monks and mystics: Lifestyles for self-discovery.* New York, NY: Paulist Press.

Vincent, N. (2008). *Voluntary madness: My year lost and found in the loony bin.* New York, NY: Viking Press.

Walton, J., Collins, J., & Linney, J. (1994). Working together to meet the needs of multiple-birth families. *Health Visitor, 67*(10), 342.

Whyte, W. F. (1955). *Street corner society: The social structure of an Italian slum.* Chicago, IL: University of Chicago Press.

Index

About the Authors

SAMUEL S. FAULKNER is Professor of Social Work at Morehead State University in Kentucky. Professor Faulkner completed his PhD in social work at the University of Texas at Arlington in 2001 after receiving two master of science degrees: one in social work from the University of Texas at Arlington and the other in counseling education from Texas A&M University–Corpus Christi.

CYNTHIA A. FAULKNER is Professor of Social Work at Morehead State University in Kentucky. She received her BSSW from Kansas State University in 1984, an MSW from the University of Kansas in 1989, and her PhD from the University of Texas at Arlington in 2001. Professor Faulkner has practiced social work for more than twenty years in multiple settings and is a licensed clinical social worker.